Experiments

Lectures on Lawrence

John Worthen

Critical, Cultural and Communications Press

in association with the D. H. Lawrence Research Centre,
University of Nottingham

Nottingham
2012

Nottingham Lawrence Studies
General editors: Macdonald Daly, Sean Matthews and Andrew Harrison

Experiments: Lectures on Lawrence, by John Worthen.

First published in Great Britain by Critical, Cultural and Communications Press in association with the D. H. Lawrence Research Centre, University of Nottingham, 2012.

Critical, Cultural and Communications Press is an imprint of *Jet***stone** Publishers Ltd.

Cover design by Andrew Dawson.

ISBN 9781905510337

Reprinted with corrections 2018

'I know nothing that can be best taught by lectures, except where experiments are to be shewn. You may teach chymistry by lectures. – You might teach making of shoes by lectures!'

(Samuel Johnson, 1766)

About the author

John Worthen was born in London and educated at the Universities of Cambridge and Kent. He taught at Charlottesville and Swansea before writing *D. H. Lawrence: The Early Years 1885-1912* for Cambridge University Press and editing a number of Lawrence's works for the Cambridge Lawrence Edition. He became Professor of D. H. Lawrence Studies at the University of Nottingham in 1994 but took early retirement in order to write. He has published a composite biography (*The Gang: Coleridge, the Hutchinsons and the Wordsworths in 1802*, Yale University Press, 2001), as well as a commercial biography (*D. H. Lawrence: The Life of an Outsider*, Penguin Books, 2005) and the biography of a non-literary figure (*Robert Schumann: Life and Death of a Musician*, Yale University Press, 2007). In 2009, Haus Books published his new short life of T. S. Eliot. His *Introduction to S. T. Coleridge* for Cambridge University Press was published in October 2010.

About Nottingham Lawrence Studies

The D. H. Lawrence Research Centre at the University of Nottingham was founded in 1990 to provide a focus for research and teaching in Lawrence Studies, and to promote the Lawrence Collections. The Centre hosts conferences, symposia and lectures, as well as coordinating Lawrence-related classes and courses at undergraduate and postgraduate level. We also work closely with Lawrence Societies around the world, particularly the Eastwood D. H. Lawrence Society, and offer support for Visiting Scholars wishing to use the Lawrence Collections. Nottingham Lawrence Studies was established in 2008 to publish work in the field. We welcome submissions, and proposals, of work of interest to academics, students and general readers. These should be sent to:

The D. H. Lawrence Research Centre
School of English Studies
University of Nottingham
University Park
Nottingham
United Kingdom
NG7 2RD

Contents

Foreword

The first time someone asked me to introduce John Worthen was at a conference on Lawrence which took place in Bristol a long time ago. I can remember how staggered I then was when I looked over what were his ongoing, or recently completed, literary enterprises. As I said in my few words of introduction, the variety and number of these gave the impression that there must surely be at least two or three academics operating in the same field, under the same name, whereas I knew that, in fact, the man who was about to speak was the one and only John Worthen. Over the years, that description has come to seem to me increasingly appropriate for someone who has a combination of qualities which, if not absolutely unique, is nonetheless exceedingly rare. There cannot be many in the academic world who simultaneously display so much energy along with so much critical judgement; who have a passion for minutiae which in no way damages their respect for creative power (the talk reprinted here on annotating *Studies in Classic American Literature* is a case in point); or who have become deep scholars while retaining all the zest and freshness of the devoted amateur.

The phenomenon which is John Worthen might not have become so obvious to the world, or so quickly obvious, were it not for Mark Kinkead-Weekes. It was he who had been asked by Cambridge University Press to write a biography of Lawrence which could serve as a kind of companion piece to their edition of the letters and works. Accustomed as he was to working in collaboration with his colleagues at the University of Kent in Canterbury, but mindful also perhaps of just how much new material the Cambridge editions were unearthing, he took the innovative and generous decision to share the valuable commission he had received with two others. The question for him then was who those others should be. Whatever the quality of his judgement in general, his selection of John for the *Early Years* now looks inspired. In one sense it was an easy choice to make since, after graduating from Cambridge, and writing a Ph.D. on Lawrence at Kent, John had recently been editing *The Lost*

Girl for Cambridge, with its wealth of material about the Eastwood of Lawrence's childhood. Yet these facts themselves can hardly have prepared Mark for the extraordinary vitality his new collaborator began to display as he flung himself into the task of investigating Lawrence's social background, laying as he did so an unusually solid foundation for the Cambridge biography and establishing, in the process, criteria of accuracy and comprehensiveness which it would prove a stiff challenge to maintain.

What more precisely those criteria are will be clear from the previously unpublished pieces which are gathered together in this collection, as well of course from the very many more already in print. One characteristic many of them illustrate is John's understanding of the significance of locale in biographical writings. He is someone who always wants to know not only how and why but also precisely *where* a certain episode took place. Was it in the kitchen or sitting room, where exactly was the house concerned, and what would be the usual way of getting to that house? Finding answers to questions such as these has involved him in many different kinds of travel as well as a good deal of tramping the streets (in his case, the British Academy ought to have had available a special, discretionary grant for shoe leather). The persistence with which he can pursue details of this kind is astonishing and I often thought how uncomfortable I would feel if, having committed some crime, I suddenly learnt that he was on my case. One obvious reason that he is so dogged in his pursuit is that he is a fierce enemy of the more or less and wants to demarcate as neatly and crisply as he can the known from the unknown world; but another is that he realises how vagueness can militate against the effort to recreate certain happenings in the mind of his readers, to make the past come alive.

About ten years ago, there was a minor stir in the field of Shakespeare criticism when the tide of New Historicism gave the impression of going out and something called Material Culture appeared to be coming in. What this last term broadly meant was extending the notion of 'text' to material objects and then interrogating them for their historical significance. Yet in the field of biography, John Worthen had been doing that kind of thing from the beginning of his career, without any noticeable aid from Fernand Braudel or Walter Benjamin. No one shows greater excitement than John in the presence of a chair, a handbag or a picture which belonged to Lawrence, or to someone once associated with him, and no one is better able to coax biographical understanding from objects of this variety. An historian as well as a literary critic, he is always looking for the past in the present, and accepting the responsibility biography entails for making the meaningful connections. His ability to do that so successfully, combined with the intellectual rigour and sharpness which have made him such a formidable textual scholar, help to explain why he has come to occupy a dominant position in Lawrence studies over the years, and the man to whom broadcasters inevitably and naturally turn when they need someone to pronounce on any aspect of Lawrence.

John's writings on Lawrence, or on Frieda, have been so numerous and multifarious that it would be natural to assume that he has had time for nothing else. But that is very far from being the case. Before he came to Nottingham and was working in Swansea, he took a keen interest in modern drama, directing a number of plays (by dramatists such as Bond, for example), and nothing brings out his characteristic enthusiasm more than a discussion of Samuel Beckett. Fascinated by the theatre, he has, like all successful speakers, a broad vein of the theatrical in his own make-up. This was evident in the lecture which he gave when he was retiring from the post of Professor of D. H. Lawrence Studies at the University of Nottingham (one of the pieces printed here). Those who were present on that occasion will not easily forget the darkened stage, the engulfing music, the flash of light, and then the apparition of John confessing how he had often dreamed of suddenly appearing on stage as the Demon King. As he went on to deliver a stinging critique of the lack of provision certain of his university's authorities had made for replacing him, that is how many of them must have seen him. Even today, it still seems extraordinary that there could ever have been a time when a major university should have found itself with the best collection of Lawrence material in the country, and perhaps in the world, but no one to supervise students who wanted to come to Nottingham to work with it.

Modern drama is one of John's additional areas of expertise but so too is the first generation of English Romantics: he has written an important book on Wordsworth and Coleridge in 1802, and has just published an introduction to Coleridge for Cambridge. Yet anyone who has ever visited him in his home, and seen the rows of classical CDs lining many of its walls, will know how misleading it would be to limit the list of his extra-Lawrentian activities to literary matters. John is the kind of music lover who can talk authoritatively, and in detail, about the differences between one pianist's rendering of a particular Beethoven concerto and another's, or of why it is so much more satisfying to listen to a Schubert song cycle sung by singer A than singer B. Although not himself a trained musician, he demonstrates the unfairness of the way in which talents are distributed by being able to play almost any song he hears by ear. It is his love of music which has driven him to write a weighty and meticulously researched biography of Robert Schumann which was in most quarters very warmly received. How he has managed to do this, in addition to all his other achievements, is a mystery which does sometimes seem to belong to the realms of the demon king.

The interest which John takes in music is serious and profound but, for me, it has different, lighter associations and is indelibly associated with a talk I heard him give which is not collected here because it has already been published. The occasion was an anniversary of Lawrence's death and the audience, the members of the D. H. Lawrence society of Eastwood (which at that time still included two of Lawrence's nieces). Instead of the Eastwood public library, they had chosen for this special, commemorative address a large dining room in the Saracen's Head in Southwell, the inn which is the venue for that passionate encounter between Birkin and Ursula that literary critics have been arguing over for years. John has provided a convincing gloss on this much contested moment, as of course has Mark Kinkead-Weekes; but for his talk he avoided the subject and concentrated instead on what Lawrence was to term, looking back over his boyhood and youth, 'Hymns in a Man's Life'. All the pieces collected here are talks and give the substance of what he had to say on particular occasions, but they inevitably fail to register fully the excitement of listening to John lecture, the drama of the event as, like a dam bursting, the words come tumbling out, yet all of them clear and all of them controlled. His listeners at the Saracen's Head were certainly rapt as they were introduced, or in many cases re-introduced (the average age of the society's members was then quite high), to that whole world of non-conformist religion in which Lawrence had been brought up. They were already therefore more than satisfied with what they were hearing when the talk took a surprising turn. Standing against a side wall as he was, their speaker had been able to plug in a keyboard which then seemed suddenly to appear in front of him. In no time at all, he was playing on this instrument some of Lawrence's favourite hymns and inviting his audience to sing them with him. In one of his most famous poems, Lawrence describes how hearing the notes of a piano took him back over 'the vista of years' until he was back to 'the old Sunday evenings at home, with winter outside, / And hymns in the cosy parlour'. But it was not so much a cosy parlour which the sound of the keyboard then evoked. Rather it was, as the glistening eyes and open lungs of the singers made clear, that Congregational Chapel on the Nottingham Road, animated and presided over on this occasion, not by the Reverend Robert Reid, but their own John Worthen. It was a memorable moment which only his knowledge, talent and sense of occasion could have brought about, and which goes a long way to explain why so many of his admirers will be happy to discover here the texts of a number of talks which might otherwise have disappeared for ever.

David Ellis
University of Kent

Reference Abbreviations

Letters of Lawrence

1L *The Letters of D. H. Lawrence Volume I: September 1901–May 1913*. Ed. James T. Boulton. Cambridge: Cambridge UP, 1979.

2L *The Letters of D. H. Lawrence Volume II: June 1913–October 1916*. Ed. George J. Zytaruk and James T. Boulton. Cambridge: Cambridge UP, 1981.

3L *The Letters of D. H. Lawrence Volume III: October 1916–June 1921*. Ed. James T. Boulton and Andrew Robertson. Cambridge: Cambridge UP, 1984.

4L *The Letters of D. H. Lawrence Volume IV: June 1921–March 1924*. Ed. Warren Roberts, James T. Boulton and Elizabeth Mansfield. Cambridge: Cambridge UP, 1987.

5L *The Letters of D. H. Lawrence Volume V: March 1924–March 1927*. Ed. James T. Boulton and Lindeth Vasey. Cambridge: Cambridge UP, 1989.

6L *The Letters of D. H. Lawrence Volume VI: March 1927–November 1928*. Ed. James T. Boulton and Margaret H. Boulton with Gerald M. Lacy. Cambridge: Cambridge UP, 1991.

7L *The Letters of D. H. Lawrence Volume VII: November 1928–February 1930*. Ed. Keith Sagar and James T. Boulton. Cambridge: Cambridge UP, 1993.

8L *The Letters of D. H. Lawrence Volume VIII: Previously Uncollected Letters and General Index*. Ed. James T. Boulton. Cambridge: Cambridge UP, 2000.

Works of Lawrence

AR — *Aaron's Rod.* Ed. Mara Kalnins. Cambridge: Cambridge UP, 1988.

BB — *The Boy in the Bush.* With M. L. Skinner. Ed. Paul Eggert. Cambridge: Cambridge UP, 1990.

EmyE — *England, My England and Other Stories.* Ed. Bruce Steele. Cambridge: Cambridge UP, 1990.

FSLC — *The First and Second Lady Chatterley Novels.* Ed. Dieter Mehl and Christa Jansohn. Cambridge: Cambridge UP, 1999.

FWL — *The First 'Women in Love'.* Ed. John Worthen and Lindeth Vasey. Cambridge: Cambridge UP, 1998.

IR — *Introductions and Reviews.* Ed. N. H. Reeve and John Worthen. Cambridge: Cambridge UP, 2005.

LAH — *Love Among the Haystacks and Other Stories.* Ed. John Worthen. Cambridge: Cambridge UP, 1987.

LCL — *Lady Chatterley's Lover and A Propos of 'Lady Chatterley's Lover'.* Ed. Michael Squires. Cambridge: Cambridge UP, 1993.

LEA — *Late Essays and Articles.* Ed. James T. Boulton. Cambridge: Cambridge UP, 2004.

LG — *The Lost Girl.* Ed. John Worthen. Cambridge: Cambridge UP, 1981.

MM — *Mornings in Mexico and Other Essays.* Ed. Virginia Crosswhite Hyde. Cambridge: Cambridge UP, 2009.

MN	*Mr Noon.* Ed. Lindeth Vasey. Cambridge: Cambridge UP, 1984.
Plays	*The Plays.* Ed. Hans-Wilhelm Schwarze and John Worthen. Cambridge: Cambridge UP, 1999.
PO	*The Prussian Officer and Other Stories.* Ed. John Worthen. Cambridge: Cambridge UP, 1983.
Poems	*The Complete Poems of D. H. Lawrence.* Revised Edition. Ed. Vivian de Sola Pinto and Warren Roberts. Harmondsworth: Penguin Books, 1977.
R	*The Rainbow.* Ed. Mark Kinkead-Weekes. Cambridge: Cambridge UP, 1989.
RDP	*Reflections on the Death of a Porcupine and Other Essays.* Ed. Michael Herbert. Cambridge: Cambridge UP, 1988.
SCAL	*Studies in Classic American Literature.* Ed. Ezra Greenspan, Lindeth Vasey and John Worthen. Cambridge: Cambridge UP, 2003.
SL	*Sons and Lovers.* Ed. Helen Baron and Carl Baron. Cambridge: Cambridge UP, 1992.
St.M	*St. Mawr and Other Stories.* Ed. Brian Finney. Cambridge: Cambridge UP, 1983.
STH	*Study of Thomas Hardy and Other Essays.* Ed. Bruce Steele. Cambridge: Cambridge UP, 1985.
TI	*Twilight in Italy and Other Essays.* Ed. Paul Eggert. Cambridge: Cambridge UP, 1994.
WL	*Women in Love.* Ed. David Farmer, Lindeth Vasey

and John Worthen. Cambridge: Cambridge UP, 1987.

WP *The White Peacock*. Ed. Andrew Robertson. Cambridge: Cambridge UP, 1983.

Other works

E. T. E. T. [Jessie Chambers], *D. H. Lawrence: A Personal Record* (Jonathan Cape, 1935)

EY John Worthen, *D. H. Lawrence: The Early Years 1885-1912* (Cambridge: Cambridge UP, 1991)

Nehls *D. H. Lawrence: A Composite Biography*, ed. Edward Nehls, 3 vols. (Madison: University of Wisconsin Press, 1957-9)

Introduction

It's never much fun going over your own old work. Either it seems creaky, old-fashioned and unnecessary, or – much worse – it seems better than anything you've done recently. 'What genius I had then!' [1] is a phrase to haunt us.

In my case, revisiting the past has a peculiar nostalgia. In May 2003 I gave my retirement lecture in Nottingham as Professor of D. H. Lawrence Studies; that lecture is included in this collection. And since 2005, I have initiated no new work on Lawrence; my work since then is represented in this collection by couple of pieces about Frieda Lawrence. Most of the work I did between 1999 and 2005, however, was biographical in nature; I was working towards the single volume biography of Lawrence which Penguin Books published in 2005. So that although the pieces were written for locations scattered and occasions occasional, those from 1999 onwards have a common concern; they are things I started to find myself saying in the biography (and later, about Frieda Lawrence) in the 1990s and 2000s. Some of them actually reproduce drafts of the biography as I wrote it and tried it out on people; there are doubtless some overlaps with what actually got published in 2005.

Nearly all the pieces here are lectures. After I retired in 2003, I received quite a number of invitations to lecture, and especially between 2003 and 2005 I took those as opportunities to debate the Penguin biography with myself. However, rather than attempting to disguise the lecture format, now that the pieces are appearing into print, I have provided a brief note of the occasion of each talk, about why I gave it and to whom. I am thus attempting to preserve, in something very close to its original form, what was usually

1 Ascribed to Jonathan Swift, and quoted e.g. in Aldous Huxley, *Chrome Yellow* (1921), where the hero sees a copy of his own recently published poems lying on a table, and reads some lines: 'He put it down again, shook his head, and sighed. "What genius I had then!" he reflected, echoing the aged Swift' (p. 9).

written for a particular audience. I have, occasionally, added material in footnotes that dates from later.

I have not generally included lectures which subsequently appeared in print or as books. An obvious candidate for this collection was my 1994 inaugural lecture on the Weekleys and the von Richthofens, *Cold Hearts and Coronets*; but it was published as an occasional paper by the D. H. Lawrence Centre (as it then was) in 1995. My 1998 lecture 'Lawrence's Theatre of the South-West' appeared in the *D. H. Lawrence Journal* and also in *D. H. Lawrence: New Worlds*. And my announcement in Santa Fe that I would be henceforth be doing no new Lawrence work came in a 2005 lecture which has also appeared in print, in *Windows to the Sun*, in a slightly revised form.[2] I have however extensively revised my Naples lecture 'D. H. Lawrence: A Single Life', originally printed in the *D. H. Lawrence Journal*, and have included it. So it goes. The two lectures on Frieda at the end were both written when I imagined I would be writing her biography.

If I have learned one thing by going over this old work, it is why I became a biographer. What (to me) is above all fascinating about the biographical enterprise is its attempt to understand the past (and people in the past) not by extensive pursuit of any particular theory, but from struggling to understand the survival of the actual and objective things which come down to us out of people's lives (their notebooks, houses, family records, letters, bank-accounts, walking-sticks, clothes, wedding-rings). The surviving material – in every sense – provides a constant reminder to the biographer that everything has a context, and that it is the series of overlapping contexts infiltrating every life that the biographer needs to investigate. This is what links lectures on annotating Lawrence's *Studies in Classic American Literature* and

2 'Over some Frontiers', *Windows to the Sun: D. H. Lawrence's "Thought-Adventures"*, ed. Earl Ingersoll and Virginia Hyde (Madison, 2009), pp. 50-68.

research into the real-life origins of the novel *Lady Chatterley's Lover.* Though much is taken, much remains, from the past; but in every case we need to find the right questions to ask about it.

The real reason for this book's existence, however, is Sean Matthews's insistence that he wanted it. Every other publisher I have ever dealt with has had to be persuaded to print me. Sean asked insistently to be allowed to do so. How could I refuse him: he happy, I happy, both of us bubbling over with happiness.[3] I am very grateful to him; and I would like to dedicate this book to him, conscious as I am of what a gap in our lives he left when he, Meike, Janni and Klara went on to new challenges in the summer of 2010. I am very grateful to my friend Macdonald Daly for ensuring the book's publication and for taking such good care of it.

John Worthen
Oberhausen – Nottingham
January 2012

3 See Samuel Beckett, *Proust and Three Dialogues with Georges Duthuit* (1965), p. 123.

Lawrence in Shakespeare Street

Shakespeare Street, Nottingham, 24 August 1994

I gave this lecture at the headquarters of the School of Adult and Continuing Education in – of course – Shakespeare Street in Nottingham. It was my first public lecture in Nottingham City; Peter Preston had organised it for me. I had published D. H. Lawrence: The Early Years 1885-1912 *three years earlier and was still immersed in the world of that long, rich, amazingly researched, and (to me) now slightly unreal book. One can trace the same spirit of unhesitating acceptance of Lawrence in the lecture too: continuing evidence, perhaps, of an education at Downing College, Cambridge, in the 1960s. Lawrence is the man who gets more out of Nottingham than anyone else could have done.*

My title sounds a little like *Alice in Wonderland*; and though I didn't originally intend the parallel, it is a useful one. D. H. Lawrence at Nottingham University College in Shakespeare Street, Nottingham, between 1906 and 1908, *was* increasingly in a situation he found to be unbelievable. But quite *why* this was so is my topic.

First question: what was Lawrence doing in Shakespeare Street at all?

The foundation stone for Nottingham University College had been laid in 1877, with William Ewart Gladstone in attendance; and the College had opened here in 1881, with just two Departments: Arts and Science. There were originally three Professors in Science, and one Professor in Arts: J. E. Symes, who was Professor of Literature. He had three lecturers to assist him, and between them they taught Greek, Latin, Logic, French and German. Those were the days.

The College gradually expanded over the next twenty-five years. New buildings were erected, new departments started, and new chairs created: people moved upwards and onwards. Professor Symes, by 1904, found himself not just Professor of Literature (indeed responsible for almost all the College's literature teaching) but also the Principal of the College.

Modern Languages had acquired the 38-year-old Ernest Weekley as its Professor in 1898 (he would stay in post exactly 40 years); and, in 1905, the University College appointed its first Professor of Education, Amos Henderson. And it is *that* Department which most concerns us.

The major role of Henderson's Education Department in its early days was to offer Day Training Courses for those who wished to study (and sit the examinations) for their teachers' certificates. You didn't of course have to attend Nottingham University College to follow the course or to do the examination; many candidates worked as uncertificated teachers (for which you were paid £50 or £55 a year rather than the £80 or £90 you got as a certificated teacher) and did their studying in their spare time. Lawrence's great friend Jessie Chambers, for example, never went to College but studied and took her examinations externally; and passed well.

But early in 1905, when he was nineteen, it became startlingly clear that D. H. Lawrence was – academically – outstanding. During his time at Nottingham High School back in 1898-1901, in spite of his entrance scholarship and doing well in his first year, he had not shown much evidence of his ability: but in 1903, when he was 18 and working as a pupil-teacher in Eastwood, he passed the matriculation examination of London University, allowing him to go on to study for a degree, in theory. And, late in 1904, still as a pupil-teacher, he had sat the so-called King's Scholarship examination, which would be his means of gaining a training college or day training college place. In February 1905 he heard not only that he had passed, but that he had done so in Class I, division I. No fewer than 2603 male candidates from all England and Wales had sat the exam: 37 got into Class I division 1: and Lawrence was one of them. Lawrence's friend Gilbert Noon was in Class I, division 2: Jessie Chambers and Louie Burrows the following year would be in Class I, divisions 3 and 4 respectively.

That success and the promise (if he wanted it) of a college

place made a great deal of difference to Lawrence and to his family: I suspect an almost unimaginable difference. He remembered how he found himself 'suddenly figuring as a clever boy'.[1] But it actually meant a good deal more than that. It did a great deal, I suspect, for his confidence: he had at last proved that his elder brother Ernest – who had died so tragically back in 1900, and in whose shadow Bert Lawrence had always been – had not after all been the only clever one of the family. I myself don't think it can be a coincidence that it was that same spring, less than a couple of months after hearing his result, that Lawrence began to write: having read voraciously for years. In a piece he wrote about doing so well in the exam, he stated: 'I attribute my success in a great measure to a love of literature';[2] he would now embark on literature himself.

But, in purely practical terms, the King's Scholarship success confirmed that Bert Lawrence would indeed one day become a certificated teacher; and the fact that the local University College was opening its Education Department that same year, for students who wished to study for their teaching certificates, ensured that Lawrence would go to Nottingham University College as a student. He had, however, to put off going for a year, as he needed to earn and save; his College career would be yet another burden on the Lawrence household, with Arthur Lawrence having to fork out hard-earned money for his son to buy *Piers Plowman* and Spenser's *Faerie Queene.* So Lawrence worked as an uncertificated teacher in Eastwood during the academic year 1905-06, and did not go to College until September 1906.

1 *LEA* 36:35.
2 *EY* 117.

When he went to Shakespeare Street, he was not, however, simply like the other students doing the Day Training course. To judge by what he did when he arrived as a student – and by a recollection he wrote late in life – he actually came to Nottingham University College with the idea of following a degree course: in 1928 he called it the 'B.A. course'.[3] We know that his mother had long harboured the hope that he would not just study for his teachers' certificate but work for a degree; what has not generally been recognised is that, for one thing, Professor Amos Henderson personally and actively encouraged Lawrence to study for a degree. There were various ways of doing this. One would have been to transfer, while at College, to a degree course: and that option was on the cards for his first year, during which the teaching students were allowed to attend the classes designed for the degree students. The other and rather more likely way was for Lawrence to do his teacher's certificate work, but to go on availing himself of the chance of going to other classes too: so that, in the end, after a couple more years, he would be able to take his degree externally. For another two years at least, Lawrence himself went along with this idea, even after stopping going to all the elements of the B.A. course some time during his first year at Nottingham. He had already – back in 1903 – passed the matriculation examination of London University; and his best male friend at Nottingham University College, also following the teacher's course – Tom Smith, of Lincoln – would indeed first acquire his teacher's certificate in 1908, along with Lawrence, but then go on to take a degree, in Chemistry, externally in 1910. The fact that Lawrence dropped B.A. work during his first year in Nottingham did not actually matter, providing that he was prepared to go on studying and taking exams after he left. And three months after leaving Nottingham, in October 1908, Lawrence recorded in a letter the 'maternal advice' he

3 *LEA* 112:22.

was continuing to get, which was to 'get on – take your degree – then you can hope to leave the elementary teaching that you hate'.[4] A degree would qualify him to teach in a High School; consequently, when he went to Croydon in 1908 to start work as teacher, he was aware that he 'ought to continue to study for a degree': and for some months he tried to keep up his studies. 'I am making a vain attempt to study' he would tell Louie Burrows in October 1908, after going to Croydon; but 'Somehow I cannot bring my nose down to a good swot'.[5] A degree would certainly have offered him a way forward as a professional man; and Lydia Lawrence 'hoped her son, who was "clever", might one day be a professor or a clergyman or perhaps even a little Mr Gladstone'.[6]

The evidence for Lawrence's interest in degree work is, oddly enough, both thoroughly disguised and utterly clear. Lawrence hardly ever mentioned the matter when he wrote about these years: there are just those two references in letters to his feeling that he knew that he ought to be studying. Even Jessie Chambers, who knew him better than anyone, only knew that 'he dropped the degree course ... glad to be rid of the bother of working for a degree'.[7] I don't think that it was actually quite as simple as that; and not as simply dropped as an idea, either.

There is however no further reference in his correspond-dence to the idea after October 1908; it seems likely that the demands of the Croydon job, combined with the amount of time and effort he was now spending on his writing – and the useful distance from that 'maternal voice' in Eastwood which he had in Croydon – meant that he abandoned thought of a degree. But it is important to recognise that it *was* a real possibility, in these years. We are so used to knowing how

4 *1L* 85.
5 *1L* 84.
6 *LEA* 112:30-1.
7 E. T. 75-6.

Lawrence became a writer – and it seems so inevitable, as things do in retrospect – that we are in danger of ignoring the other possibilities of his life. We mustn't forget that Jessie Chambers' own brother David studied, got his degree, and eventually rose to the position of Professor of Economic History at Nottingham. Professor D. H. Lawrence is also by no means unimaginable.

The evidence of Lawrence's academic potential is actually everywhere you look in his writing, right down to his last work *Apocalypse* (for which he did some very heavy scholarly reading). We can follow just one strand of his learning if we look at his poetry notebooks, at references in *The White Peacock* and *Sons and Lovers* and his short stories, even at an inscribed wedding present he gave his friend Alan Chambers in October 1910. Lawrence was a regular user of – and quoter in – Latin. His first poetry notebook is actually headed 'D. H. Lawrence / Latin Notes', and commences with nine pages of notes on vocabulary (drawn from Horace's *Odes*); and at the back of the book are translations from Latin into English. He also quoted Horace (Odes books 1 and 3) in his letters: in April 1908, in June 1908, in January 1911.

Latin was not, of course, a subject necessary for someone doing the Training Course for the teachers' certificate: though it *was* required for someone studying for a degree. Lawrence's Latin is simply an indication of his scholarly potential. Both the Eastwood Minister the Reverend Robert Reid and Professor Henderson offered to help him with his Latin (though Henderson apparently let him down: another of the reasons why he gave up the idea of degree work at Nottingham). But he obviously worked his way through Horace's *Odes*, recording a mass of vocabulary and grammar in that college notebook: in such a way he was a quintessential 'good student'.

But his time at the University College in Shakespeare Street can also be summed up as a period of estrangement: from his past, from his mother's ambitions for him, and from a great many of the things he had up to then believed in. What went wrong, in Shakespeare Street?

First: Lawrence's teachers. His own response to the teaching he got was scornful:

> the prof's in coll. went on in such a miserable, jog-trot, earn-your-money manner that I was startled ... I came to feel that I might as well be taught by gramophones as by those men, for all the interest or sincerity they felt.[8]

Professor Amos Henderson was, he once remarked, a man he could himself teach 'with excellent advantage'; when he once used the word 'stallion' in an essay, one of his teachers – who may well have been Henderson, a 'well-meaning but timid and ineffectual man' – took him aside and told him 'My boy, stallion is a word we do not use'. And Edith Mary Becket, who taught him English, corrected – and at least once rejected – his essays in ways that humiliated him. 'Give me a *proper* essay this time' she told him.

> She told me some of my phrases are fine, but others ludicrous; that I was not entirely incapable of writing, but mixed up some sense with a great amount of absurdity ... I consent – I am merely a pupil, therefore I must work by rule.[9]

The University manuscripts department has some of the essays that were marked while Lawrence was a student. His essay on 'The character of Theseus' in *A Midsummer Night's*

8 *1L* 72.
9 *1L* 31.

Dream got 9 out of 10, but was also red-inked: Lawrence's elegant phrase 'the mind is master, and, happy mind, it commands' got cut down (probably by Edith Becket) to 'the mind is master and commands'.

In such ways, and for such reasons, his time at Nottingham was a constant journey into the loss of faith: in teachers, in authorities, in religion. Only two teachers really impressed him: one was the man who lectured to students about French literature. And that mainly because of his elegant manner.

> He's my favourite Prof ... . He really *is* a gentleman. He's quite elegant. He leans back in his chair and points to the blackboard, too elegant to get on his feet. And he addresses us as 'gentlemen'. He's sarcastic, of course.[10]

That was Professor Ernest Weekley.

The other one was even more significant. E. A. 'Botany' Smith was a lecturer in Botany: but he also worked in education (he actually led the way in adult education in Nottingham, and should be especially celebrated for that): a highly successful extra-mural lecturer in philosophy, sociology and ethics, as well as in botany, he started a new career as a Unitarian minister in 1917. I shall say more about him a little later. But Smith was the exception.

If it's not the academic work he did which distinguishes Lawrence in Shakespeare Street, what about his time outside the classroom? Think of Ursula walking through her college in *The Rainbow*: the notice board where she finds her letter from Skrebensky is at least as important to her as the teaching she gets. But we know very little indeed about Lawrence's activities outside the classroom at the University College. There are apocryphal stories of his missing lectures

[10] E. T. 76.

because of his affair with Professor Weekley's wife. But those are certainly not true: he didn't meet Frieda for another four to six years. He sent a poem to the student magazine *The Gong*: the magazine rejected it. Up to now that has been pretty well all we've known. Just one further scrap has recently come to light: both unexpected and predictable. Which student society do we know he joined – was indeed a founder member of? No: not the literary society. He was one of a group of 12 men and 6 woman who founded the 'Society for the Study of Social Questions' in 1908: the title ensures that it must have been a society for socialists. The year 1908 was when his interest in socialism was at its height: it was one of the phases he went through while at college. How often the society met (if they met), and what they talked about, we cannot tell; but 1908 was also the year when Lawrence gave his paper 'Art and the Individual' to the Eastwood Debating Society: the paper which began

> These Thursday night meetings are for discussing social problems with a view to advancing to a more perfect social state and to our fitting ourselves to be perfect citizens – communists – what not.[11]

That is the writing of a man helping to found that University society. Not only is Professor Lawrence, you see, one of his missed opportunities: so is Comrade Lawrence.

But most of his time in Shakespeare Street, of course, was spent on his teachers' training work. He was studying English Literature, Education, Mathematics, History with Geography, Botany and French: these were his examination subjects in the summer of 1908. He got distinctions in four of the six

11 *STH* 223:2-4.

subjects: those he missed out on were Education and English Literature. Jessie Chambers remarked that he was 'a little piqued' about his failure to get a distinction in English (in which she herself got a distinction). In addition, marks survive for Teaching, Reading, Drawing and Music – BAAB – the marks he got for his actual classroom work, internal marks kept by the Nottingham Department, together with a lengthy analysis of his performance as a teacher in the classroom. This extraordinary document I analysed carefully in *The Early Years*: [12] let me summarise what I said there. Lawrence is by no means the 'exceptionally good teacher' or 'one of the best teachers this year' which other students on the course got on their reports; nor could he – like others – be 'unreservedly recommended to any school authority'. Lawrence is presented as a quite exceptional case: 'emphatically a teacher of upper classes', 'quite unsuitable for a large class of boys in a rough district'; he 'has an obvious difficulty in finding words sufficiently simple': he is 'well-read, scholarly and refined', 'fastidious in taste'. He would 'easily tire amid the tedium and discouragement of the average classroom'. He is a problematic, talented but high-risk teacher: might do brilliantly, but couldn't be risked in most schools. It's a reference designed to put off head-teachers from employing him: and suggests perhaps how much he had got up the noses of those teaching him. It's rather surprising that he ever got a job, with such a reference. Shakespeare Street found him as weird and unlikely as he found Shakespeare Street, but for quite different reasons.

Perhaps our best way of thinking about what Lawrence went through here, however, is to consider the case of Ursula Brangwen, in *The Rainbow*, who also goes to College, in her

12 *EY* 187-9.

case to study for a degree. What Lawrence gives her, in her initial experience of College, is the first of three versions of an identical situation, two from a novel and one from a poem. In each case a student is looking down from a college window into the street, and thus on to the world outside. It is an image Lawrence returned to: it seemed to him to sum up, at different times and in different ways, the strangeness of the relationship he had as a College student with the world from which he came and to which he would return. What Ursula experiences in the first of the three examples, when she is new to the College, is this: she

> sat beside her window, rather far back. Looking down, she saw the lime-trees turning yellow, the tradesman's boy passing silent down the still, autumn-sunny street. There was the world, remote, remote.
>
> Here, within the great, whispering sea-shell, that whispered all the while with reminiscence of all the centuries, time faded away, and the echo of knowledge filled the timeless silence.
>
> She listened, she scribbled her notes with joy, almost with ecstasy, never for a moment criticising what she heard.[13]

Such a student finds the remoteness of the College world utterly appropriate for the new thing she is doing: attending to the timeless, placeless 'echo of knowledge'. That seems equivalent to the reverent attitude that Lawrence himself felt when he first went to Nottingham University College, but it also illustrates something else – the educational establishment as the modern monastery: hushed, with reminiscence of all the centuries.

13 *R* 399:28-37.

It was a fact unknown to me until the mid 1990s that a great deal of the University College as first built in the late 1870s and then extended (in science blocks) around 1892 is still visible. The four statues still in place on the Shakespeare Street frontage of the old University College, for example, make up an 1881 pantheon: a real (and unreal) wonderland of intellectual history. Two predictable writers (Shakespeare and John Milton) and one predictable scientist (Isaac Newton): one scientist as strange as *Alice* (Francis Bacon).

You can in fact follow a great deal of Ursula's progress around that building, to this day. To Ursula in 1902, when she goes to college, 'Its architecture was foolish, she knew from her father'. [14] But little has changed in ninety years: 'Its rather pretty, plaything, Gothic form was almost a style, in the dirty industrial town.' It's even more 'almost a style' today. When Ursula goes in, she sees 'the hall, with its big stone chimney piece'. [15] The chimney-piece is today exactly as Lawrence describes it and Ursula sees it in *The Rainbow*: 'of cardboard-like carved stone, with its armorial decoration'. [16] That's to your left as you go in: if you look right you can see, again, what Ursula sees, the 'Gothic arches supporting the balcony above'. But she also sees how 'the chimney piece ... looked silly just opposite the bicycle stand and the radiator, whilst the great notice-board with its fluttering papers seemed to slam away all sense of retreat and mystery from the far wall.'[17] These days, there is no bicycle stand, and the notice-board is reduced, but you can see the radiator rather better.

What in particular struck me, going round the Shakespeare Street building, was how extensively the Gothic exterior corresponded still to a Gothic interior: so that Ursula's feelings about her College having in it 'a remin-

14 *R* 398:40–399:1.
15 *R* 399:2-4.
16 *R* 399:6-7.
17 *R* 399:4-5, 6-10.

iscence of the wondrous, cloistral origin of education' [18] seem nothing but the clear and obvious truth of the matter. The building still resembles nothing so much as a monastery or church: it even has cloisters, of a kind. In 1906, the main Chemistry Laboratory was a medieval Hall with a hammer beam roof, like that in Nottingham's Wollaton Hall. It is not surprising that we find how Ursula's 'soul flew straight back to the mediæval times, when the monks of God held the learning of men and imparted it within the shadow of religion'.[19] That is exactly what the 1881 University College building encouraged; and in some ways the 1892 science section extension took the case even further. They built, in effect, a cathedral, with the three traditional storeys: main body, triforium (with stunted gothic windows), clerestory. The ground floor was a laboratory, but if you go up to the top of the building you find that the room with the rose window is actually one of a set of teaching rooms. Another room in the middle section, with short stunted Gothic windows, was designed as a raked lecture theatre. Today, the windows are of opaque glass, but in 1902 Ursula can sit

> beside her window, rather far back. Looking down, she saw the lime-trees turning yellow, the tradesman's boy passing silent down the still, autumn-sunny street. There was the world, remote, remote.[20]

Gradually, however, Ursula's feelings about College change. It is Botany that turns out to interest her most: 'Then came the lovely, peaceful afternoons in the Botany laboratory':[21]

18 *R* 399:10-11.
19 *R* 399:11-14
20 *R* 399:28-31.
21 *R* 400:23-4.

> They were few students. How she loved to sit on her high stool before the bench, with her pith and her razor and her material, carefully mounting her slides, carefully bringing her microscope into focus, then turning with joy to record her observation, drawing joyfully in her book, if the slide were good.[22]

A number of such drawings still survive in one of Lawrence's poetry notebooks. But this is before a kind of disillusion sets in, in Ursula (and in Lawrence), with the whole business, but also with their teachers. I now want to move on to what finally went wrong for Lawrence in Shakespeare Street, and why it became that Alice in Wonderland experience for him.

Lawrence wrote a poem about looking down from the College window: wrote it, in this form, sometime in the late summer of 1908, and copied it into the same notebook as contained his Latin notes. It was a symbolic casting out of one kind of material to be replaced by another. The second half of the poem runs:

> Beyond the limes that overhang the street
> Along the clean flagged pavement gleaming white
> Passes the world with shadows at their feet
> And there a scarlet sunshade flutters bright
> And there a beggar slouches through the heat
> And all remote from me in my high window seat.
>
> Remote though I hear the beggar's cough
> And see the lady's rose-lit fingers hold him a coin:
> These are fragments of an incoherent play, and we scoff
> As we read, we onlookers, and say in our souls we will

22 R 400:24-8.

never join
This ill-played drama, we, like gods in the window-seat
Uplifted in wisdom, half-amused by the play in the
street.

The role the narrator gives himself is a very strange one. It makes the student obviously ridiculous, sitting up there saying he will never join the masses below. A degree student might not. But those about to enter the arena of Standard VI in a tough school salute you: elementary school teachers of Lawrence's generation and type felt they were thrown to the wild beasts when they entered the classroom. The student as god is absurd: a tin-pot little god he makes.

The poem also says that the student, looking down, will never understand what happens below: 'fragments of an incoherent play' are all they can observe. It is a poem angry with students, with study, with college.

And yet it also co-operates with the very distance it shows to be humanly idiotic. As it makes those beautiful little pictures of street, of woman with parasol, of beggar, it adopts the same kinds of distance which it criticises. It is a poem that hates its own aesthetic distancing. It is extraordinarily incoherent. It is what Lawrence could write in 1908: he was still too close to the experience.

I've already quoted to you Ursula's initial wondering awe at the cloister of study she feels she has entered: just like Lawrence going to College so hopefully in 1906, in what Jessie Chambers called 'a mood of wistful anticipation. He felt it might be a step into a fuller life'. Then we can see a new development in the college student: the way in which her looking down makes the world absurd. Remains the third passage: Ursula looking down yet again, around 1904-05, like Lawrence at the end of his course, and working with some of the same materials: the shadows, the street, the woman. But now those things are transformed.

> At the Anglo-Saxon lecture, in the afternoon, she sat looking down, out of the window, hearing no word of Beowulf or of anything else. Down below, in the street, the sunny grey pavement went beside the palisade. A woman in a pink frock, with a scarlet sunshade, crossed the road, a little white dog running like a fleck of light about her. The woman with the scarlet sunshade came over the road, a lilt in her walk, a little shadow attending her. Ursula watched spell-bound. The woman with the scarlet sunshade and the flickering terrier was gone – and whither? Whither?
>
> In what world of reality was the woman in the pink dress walking? To what warehouse of dead unreality was she herself confined?[23]

This time, the view from the college window reminds the student of what she lacks in her education: of a 'world of reality' which does indeed exist, but outside – not inside – the establishment; down below. There is no self hatred, no irony, no contempt: but a revelation of the real world, not as a play, but as something itself infinitely fascinating, something that draws the imagination to sympathise and to question. The unreality is specifically the warehouse to which she is confined: she really is in Alice's Wonderland, in College.

It took Lawrence seven years to work out that account of Shakespeare Street. But the further he got from it, the more disillusioning college became. Disillusion, when it comes, comes like a flood.

It was not simply something within himself which was the problem. One of the things I have only recently discovered about Nottingham University College was that, in the period

[23] *R* 403:32–404:2.

1903-1910, it was actually at a very low point in its history; it was a period which culminated in the great scandal of 1910, when both the Principal, Professor Symes, and the Bursar resigned. It had been felt for some years that the Principal had been carrying too many responsibilities – how on earth could he be simultaneously Principal and the main teacher of Literature? And it was felt that he was not (anyway) an ideal choice either as Principal or as Professor. We should not forget Lawrence's comment to Jessie Chambers when the latter was about to go in to Nottingham one Saturday morning to hear Symes lecture, 'warning me that the lecturer mumbled so, I probably shouldn't be able to make out a word he said. "But they'll put him in the smallest room, so perhaps it will be all right ..."' There had been too many questions asked about academic standards at the College for comfort, during Symes' period of office. The time it took the University College to acquire full University status (not until 1928) was a reflection of the anxiety felt in many quarters about the education it was offering in this period. And then, in 1910, an error led to the College returning wrong statistics, claiming more money from central funding than it was entitled to; and then the mistake was noticed. There doesn't seem to have been any criminal intention; but it *was* a scandal, and the Principal and the Bursar had to go. And the College's case for full University status received a huge set-back.

What then did Lawrence get from Shakespeare Street? Given the low standards prevailing at the College at the time, Lawrence was perhaps more justified in his criticism of his teachers than you might have expected. But Botany Smith was the man from whom, in a very practical way, Lawrence learned to explore the new universe opening up to him as his Christian faith shrivelled and new realms of science and thought came into focus, down his microscope, like that Marsh Marigold stem. Smith was a kind of mentor as Lawrence went on a whistle-stop tour of philosophical positions: he recalled how Smith showed him 'a way out of Monism, past Pragmatism, into a sort of crude but appeasing

Pluralism ...' Ursula has her most important College experiences, significantly, not only looking out of the College window but looking down her microscope at the unicellular creature on the slide, and having a revelation of self:

> She could not understand what it all was. She only knew that it was not limited mechanical energy, nor mere purpose of self-preservation and self-assertion. It was a consummation, a being infinite. Self was a oneness with the infinite. To be oneself was a supreme, gleaming triumph of infinity.[24]

Lawrence too seems to have realised that the Haeckelian cellular universe which he had started to think was all in all was, in fact, only a little of what he was seeing, when he looked through that microscope. He too seems to have had both a revelation of the nature of selfhood, of being a self, which stayed with him for the rest of his life. He also realised that the inner circle of light and consciousness in which he lived and moved as a student, and which he saw on his slide, was actually surrounded by considerable darkness and threat. He once remarked of his socialist friends in Eastwood, Sally and Willie Hopkin, that 'you two led me over some frontiers'.[25] Smith helped him do the same, at a time when no one else at College seemed able to take him seriously.

For what he had started to learn at Nottingham was the unreality of so much that passed for serious study and knowledge. As an elementary schoolteacher in training, he was in a very good position – a much better position than his teachers, in fact – to know exactly how empty the rhetoric of idealism could be, when up against the reality of people on the street. In 1908 he quoted one of the dicta he was doubtless supplied with by his teachers: 'The ultimate goal of

24 *R* 409:2-6.
25 *4L* 327.

Education is to produce an individual of high moral character'.[26] In his long essay *Education of the People* years later he would remember what he had learned as a teacher and insist that teaching simply cannot do that. It has to relate to the kind of society in which its pupils are going to live, and cannot exist in some ideal moral universe of its own. So that, for example, teaching self-expression was useless: and teaching moral character was useless. 'It's no good feeding our young with a sticky ideal education till they are fourteen years old, then pitching them out, pap-fed, into the whirling industrial machine and the warren of back streets'.[27]

His Nottingham teachers were – Smith apart – tempted to dismiss him as sensitive, scholarly, intellectual and impractical: a kind of self-created aesthete, fastidious and refined. That was indeed one of his own versions of himself: the Cyril Beardsall, we might say, narrating *The White Peacock* through a haze of self-pity and poetic language. It confined him to the role of the student at the window looking languidly down at a world he could not face.

But they were deceived by his pose. In a way that reminds me of T. S. Eliot's remark that Shakespeare got more essential history out of Plutarch than most people would get out of the whole British Museum[28] – Lawrence seems to have learned more by looking out of his college window, and down his microscope, than anyone might have expected. He saw the significance of seeing a real world enriched by symbols, and the importance of making others see it too: as he remarked in 1913, 'I do write because I want folk – English folk – to alter, and have more sense'.[29] The seeds of that determination were sowed in Shakespeare Street.

And (anyway) it was he who would have the last word:

26 *STH* 135:35–136:1.

27 *RDP* 106:19-22.

28 T. S. Eliot, 'Tradition and the Individual Talent', *Selected Essays* (1951), p. 17.

29 *1L* 544.

writers tend to. 'Nottingham! Cursed, cursed Nottingham, gutsless, spineless, brainless Nottingham, how I hate thee!' [30] It was he who was real and who could assert and make his own reality: and assert that reality was not Nottingham, not Shakespeare Street; it lay instead wherever he chose to find it ... in Italy, or Germany, or New Mexico, or Australia, or Mexico, or France. But here in Nottinghamshire too; closer home than he often cared to admit.

[30] *3L* 509-10.

Clearing Melville's Overcrowded Deck

School of English, Nottingham, winter 1998

I was out of academic life and away from Nottingham for two years, 1997-1999, first on study-leave but then taking unpaid absence. I was grim and depressed, living most of the time in Budapest, writing my composite biography The Gang *and working on the annotation for* Studies in Classic American Literature. *During the second year of exile I came back to Nottingham a couple of times and gave this talk to the D. H. Lawrence Centre one dark, damp winter evening in the School of English's old seminar room A64. I was still very shaky; a student with a camera who suddenly flash-photographed me in mid-sentence put me off my stride completely.*

I am in the middle of a piece of work, and have briefly come to the surface for air. Some of what I am going to say is questionable, and I very much hope that you *will* question it.

I am one of a team of three editing Lawrence's *Studies in Classic American Literature* for the Cambridge edition: the others are the Americans Ezra Greenspan and Lindeth Vasey. I am doing the annotation. Let me start polemically: let me spend ten minutes telling you what is wrong with scholarly annotation.[1] Notes are evils, necessary evils: we all know that. But have you really become aware of how little there is to be said in favour of them?

Why impose yourself on an author, in the first place? Editors can never hope to match, imitate or emulate the particular range of reading, allusion and context which any individual text demonstrates. Well-intentioned partial annotation (as all annotation is) may well direct attention to

1 My annotation of DHL over the years includes (for Penguin) *The Rainbow* and (for CUP) the *Prussian Officer* stories; the *Love Among the Haystacks* stories: *The Lost Girl*; *Women in Love*; *Lady Chatterley's Lover* (for Michael Squires); *The First Women in Love*; half of DHL's *Plays*; and (with N. H. Reeve) *Introductions and Reviews*.

the trivial (which the editor happens to know about) and ignore the significant (of which the editor is ignorant): and so effectively appropriate the text for the editor's or publisher's own purposes. It is also perfectly obvious that even if we sat down together, we should never agree about what needed annotation, and the extent of what was necessary, either. If we attempt to justify annotation as an attempt to recover (or at least allude to) an historical context, then we must also conclude that annotation is probably not the right way to go about such a task, although – I agree – this function is more defensible than most.

I have however hardly ever read an annotated book where I have not come across something which (obviously) needed some kind of historical annotation, which the editor had ignored: usually, I am sure, because they had no idea how to find the answer to the problem. (Gowlands lotion in *Persuasion* is a good example.) [2]

Who is one annotating for? The notes that I need are not

[2] Reading *Persuasion* this spring, I came across the reference to Sir Walter Elliott complimenting Anne on her looks and assuming that it was "Merely Gowland" (Volume II, chap. IV) she had been using. My Penguin edition tells me that Mrs Vincent Gowland's Lotion was "an established treatment by then" (p. xxx). Very useful, I must say. A new edition (Broadview Literary Texts, ed. Linda Bree, 1998) however reproduces an 1814 advertisement for Gowlands "as the most pleasant and effectual remedy for all complaints to which the Face and Skin are liable... ". Gowlands was thus supposed to treat things that were *wrong* with the skin; Sir Walter thinks it may help with Mrs Clay's freckles, as well as improving Anne's wrinkles and faded colour (suggesting either something pretty drastic in the way of cream or ointment, or – alternatively – a heavy kind of make-up; or possibly both). But should we or should we not be gaining the impression that Sir Walter knows what he is talking about? Is he *pretending* knowledge in an area where he imagines he is especially knowledgeable? Or does he really know? That is, ideally, what a note would tell us.

the notes that even (e.g.) Peter Preston needs. He will not need William Morris annotating: I will. To put the argument in its simplest terms: do I need to annotate Charles Dickens for the readers of a Cambridge Lawrence edition – that is, give his dates, and say that he was an English novelist? If that's not necessary, and not many people would think it was, then do I annotate Wilkie Collins? or Charles Reade? or William Black?[3] But every decision of this kind means that an odd kind of imbalance is created, if Wilkie Collins *is* being annotated, and Dickens is not.

The real point, of course, is that there is no homogeneous reading public to which the traditional idea of the 'note' was meant to appeal: the educated middle-class reading-public, who would certainly know *this* but who would probably not know *that.* I suspect that such a reading-public was always a fantasy: I know it is, today. But it is so easy to find out information about writers like Dickens and Collins. Shouldn't I simply direct all enquiries to the Microsoft Encarta Encyclopaedia on CD ROM,[4] or – for the less advantaged – to Collins English dictionary, which includes miniature biographical entries (including entries on Dickens, Wilkie Collins and Charles Reade, but not William Black)? There is no 'reader' in the old or ideal sense; but there are at least, today, some de facto standard reference works. The only thing which is certain is that there *is* no point at which perceived ignorance sets in.

3 William Wilkie Collins (1824-89): e.g. *The Woman in White* (1860); Charles Reade (1814-84): e.g. *The Cloister and the Hearth* (1861); William Black (1841-98): e.g. *The Strange Adventures of a Phaeton* (1872).

4 A period touch: the internet as the main source of encyclopaedic information did not exist in 1998, and CDs seemed the way forward for reliable electronic information in bulk.

Should I – to come at the problem from a different direction – ignore words found in a normal largish dictionary – say Collins? In which case, I should probably *not* annotate (a real example from my work on the *Studies in Classic American Literature*) the odd word 'Homoiousian', nor distinguish it from the equally interesting word 'Homoousian'.[5]

But it seems to me that I should, nevertheless, certainly annotate Homoiousian: the sheer breadth of knowledge contained within the reference should be annotated, even if it is not necessary to explain the word. But the choices I shall make will always be questionable, and will necessarily be wrong for individual readers: while one cannot even hope to start matching the range of reference of the author one is annotating. At times, the annotator rightly feels like a flea annotating an elephant upon which he or she has briefly hopped.

For although notes are a nuisance, for both editor and the reader (both when notes exist, and when they do *not*), they serve a function beyond that of simply providing selective information; and this perhaps is their best defence of all. Looking up Homoiousian, and discovering to my astonishment that Lawrence knew all about the crucial decisions of the Council of Nicea of 325 AD, while stuck down in Cornwall with hardly a book in the house in 1917, was illuminating, to say the least ... The fact that the reference is so interesting is – in that case – really rather more important than what the word means (which anyone can find by looking it up in a dictionary). The annotation allows one to do a genuine service by pointing out Lawrence's range of knowledge in an unexpected area.

The same happens in a note on Lawrence's knowledge of

5 Homoiusians believed Christ was of like but not identical substance with God the Father; Homoousians believed that Christ was of the same substance with the Father. The disagreement culminated in crucial debate at the Council of Nicea, which the Homoousians won.

Spanish and North African early writers in Latin and Greek, provoked by a sentence at the start of *Studies*, and the very extraordinary possibility that he had come across the crazy theory of a German classicist in the 1890s that Lucretius was born in Spain. How he could have come across this, I have no idea; and my nephew Jeremy Worthen (who is an authority) has no idea either. But not to record the weird possibility would be silly. Again: there really is no need to annotate St Francis of Assisi: it is very easy to look him up (and does it really matter to the reader whether he was born in 1181 or 1182?) I have, however, included him in the notes for *Studies*, because Lawrence refers to his preaching to the birds: and Lawrence has some interesting things to say about that elsewhere. My note currently runs as follows:

> St Francis of Assisi (?1181-1226), founder of the Franciscan Order, and traditionally remembered for his love for brother animals and sister birds – see *The Little Flowers of St. Francis*, tr. W. Heywood (1906), p. 26: 'and he went into the field and began to preach to the birds ... on this wise: "My sisters the birds"'. Cf. DHL: 'I have never been to Assisi – but I feel that I must consult the birds before I claim sistership with them – they might object to my lack of feathers' (*3L* 712).

Annotation, I think – both doing it, and reading it – should mean a good deal more than just the provision – and the acquisition – of information. One makes more than local discoveries by annotating, or reading annotation: Lawrence's ironical distancing of himself from St Francis is the point of my note, not the information about St Francis. The very need to annotate may sometimes make one read more carefully. I noticed, for example, last December, while reading proofs for the *First Women in Love*, that the word *counterfoil* used as a verb both in that novel and in its successor *Women in Love* was so unusual as to need some investigation – and explanation –

and *that* was a text I had known for 30 years, and thought I knew very well.[6]

But – what would *you* want, in a note on St Francis? Tell me at the end, if you feel like it. Is Lawrence's comment about the birds impertinent, unnecessary, silly? I think that if forced to justify the writing of notes, I would fall back on an appeal to scholarly self-indulgence: the annotator's *and* the reader's. *I* get closer to the author this way; the reader may too. It may be that explaining things is only one – even a secondary – function of notes.

Critics have been arguing over the merits of Lawrence's *Studies in Classic American Literature* ever since its first appearance in 1923; it has found itself discussed in a number of unexpected places (for example, history after history of American literature, written from the 1950s onwards). Reference to Lawrence's book often speculates about why Lawrence should have written such virulent essays about some of his chosen authors.

But what very few people, to the best of my knowledge, have ever tried to do is to answer some very simple and obvious questions. How did Lawrence choose his classic American authors? In what texts did he read them? How did

6 The passage runs:

> ... her pity for him was as cold as stone, its deepest motive was fear of him, fear of his power over her, which she must always counterfoil. (*FWL* 409:8-10)

There is no precedent for "counterfoil" being used as a verb, or in this sense: it's a kind of portmanteau word, which implies response to aggression both in the "counter" part, and also in the "foil" part: and so is different from anything implied by the normal use of the word counterfoil. It *is* now annotated in *The First Women in Love,* though not in *Women in Love*, where it should have been (*WL* 443:6-8)

he subsequently treat their texts, as he went on writing and revising the essays – did he re-read the texts too? Until we are equipped to answer such questions, we can hardly say what kind of a critic he was.

I find it surprising that so few people seem to have researched at all deeply into why or how he chose the authors and texts he did. As an annotator, I decided fairly early on that one of my jobs would be not only to track down the quotations Lawrence was using, from his classic American authors, and (of course) to check them, but also to spot all the references he made to parts of the text he was not actually quoting, as well as to note the occasions when he simply paraphrased the texts he was using.

To do this I discovered, fairly early on, I had to find out exactly what texts of his authors Lawrence had in his hands. At least four of the books he was concerned with – the Franklin *Autobiography,* the Melville *Typee,* the Whitman *Leaves of Grass* and the Dana *Two Years Before the Mast* – existed, in the period when Lawrence was working, in two different versions (the first three censored or bowdlerised in one way or another, the last having an extra chapter added). So far as I could discover, no one had ever tried to find out about this either.

Partly as a result, the first and perhaps initially the most surprising thing which I came upon was the fact that Lawrence's original selection of authors and texts was primarily influenced by two things. The first, of course, was what he already knew of American writing. He had, for example, known Whitman's poetry since 1906, and it was inconceivable – if he were to contemplate writing a series of essays on American literature – that he would, or could, have left Whitman out. Whitman, from the start, seems to have occupied the position of final, and most modern, writer in the series of writers and works he would examine. Lawrence had also known the work of Fenimore Cooper for years, and Cooper was also part of the conception of the book from the start.

He had also read a number of American books during 1916: unsystematically, I suspect, but in a way that probably suggested to him that he might have a subject for a new non-fictional book at a significant moment. With *The Rainbow* banned, his fiction had potentially no chance at all; his travel book *Twilight in Italy* had come out in June 1916, and there was nothing else in the locker. He had, however, re-read Dana's *Two Years Before the Mast* early in June 1916 and a few weeks earlier had read *Moby Dick*. (You will, incidentally, find in the new *First 'Women in Love'* Birkin asking Ursula if she has ever read *Moby Dick*, and going on to say why American classic literature is so fascinating:[7] this bit of the novel was probably written in May 1916.) Lawrence had also borrowed a copy of Crèvecoeur's *Letters from an American Farmer* sometime before the end of August 1916; while in June he had asked a friend if she happened to own a copy of Melville's *Typee,* and by the end of the year had read that as well. This reading probably began without any thought about where it might lead, but by June 1916 he may well have started to focus on the idea of doing a book of American essays. A very important additional reason was his desire to write essays – and a book – which might be published *in* America. After the disaster of *The Rainbow*, and the effective drying up of publishers' interest in his work in England, he very badly needed to develop his market in America.

However, to an extent I found most surprising, Lawrence was also deeply influenced in his choice of authors, topics, and background reading by what actually existed in print in 1916 in the series Everyman's Library, run by J. M. Dent and edited by Ernest Rhys. This series had been in existence since 1906, and was the first series of serious and relatively cheap hardback reprints of the classics on which any publisher had ventured. When Ford Madox Hueffer had taken Lawrence – as a very young and unknown author whom he, Hueffer, had

[7] *FWL* 135:14-25.

recently 'discovered' – to see Ernest Rhys up in Hampstead, one Sunday evening in the middle of November 1909, it was as 'Dents Everyman's'[8] that Lawrence described him to his friend Louie Burrows. Over the years Lawrence had regularly used and read volumes in the series which, by 1916, numbered over 400 books. They normally cost 1/- each, as opposed to the selling price of a new novel of 7/6; they were thus not as cheap (for example) as Nelson's Classics (at 6d, only half the price of an Everyman); but they were *relatively* cheap, they were substantial volumes, often surprisingly scholarly, and in general presented the classics in good and comprehensive texts, well bound and on good quality paper. In June 1916, not surprisingly for a man stuck down in Cornwall, a long way from libraries, we find Lawrence asking Barbara Low if she could 'Send me an Everyman *list* one day, will you? I should be grateful'.[9]

I had however always been puzzled by the entry in Lawrence's letter to Robert Mountsier of 4 January 1917[10] which sent his American friend (just returned to London) a list of books which clearly represents his first developed thinking about essays on American writing. (Mountsier and his girl friend Esther Andrews had spent Christmas and New Year down in Cornwall; and Lawrence had obviously taken his chance of discussing the project with them both.) However, he mentioned in his letter of 4 January not only authors who did not subsequently figure in the series of essays, but books which not one English person in a thousand would have known about: their very existence in print in England was rather surprising. Lawrence already knew about Crèvecoeur (Middleton Murry had put him on to the book, and Lawrence had sent his copy back to him in the

8 *1L* 144.
9 *2L* 614.
10 *3L* 65-6.

late summer of 1916)[11] but now he needed his own copy, and only one edition of the book was currently available in Britain: of course, in Everyman's Library. I am less surprised by the presence on his Mountsier list of *Émile*, by Jean-Jacques Rousseau – which anyone planning to write about the late eighteenth century might have wanted – than by the presence of two genuine oddities. Why did he think he might need a volume of speeches by Abraham Lincoln? I would be seriously interested in any suggestions you might have. And how on earth did he come up with *The Federalist,* a book by the eighteenth century diplomat Alexander Hamilton? Both were among the books he asked Mountsier for on 4 January. And what exactly was he asking for in his request for volumes of essays by Ralph Waldo Emerson? Emerson would never figure in any of the versions of the book which Lawrence worked on; but he sent Mountsier a request which runs:

> Emerson – Essays, 3 vols.
> – Society and Solitude,
> – Nature,
> – Conduct of Life.[12]

But is that a request for three books: or four: or six?

These mysteries are all explained if we look at the List of Everyman books for the period, which give the titles in short form followed by the number of the volume in the series.

> Emerson's Essays, 12
> " Representative Men, 279
> " Nature, Conduct of Life, etc., 322
> " Society and Solitude, etc., 567

Either Barbara Low had sent him the list, or one of the

[11] John Middleton Murry, *Son of Woman* (1931), p. 226.
[12] *3L* 66.

Everyman books he had acquired had a copy included at the back (some volumes did, to make up for a short number of pages). It is clear from the Everyman list exactly which volumes of books by Emerson he was asking Mountsier to send. He wanted the Everyman volume of Emerson simply called *Essays*; he wanted the volume called (in the list) *Nature, Conduct of Life*, even though the volume was actually called (on its spine) *The Conduct of Life*; he wanted the volume called *Society and Solitude and Other Essays.* He did not want *Representative Men.*

And Everyman, of course, had in print (its only English publication) that most unlikely book 'Hamilton's The Federalist, 519' too. In the Everyman list, too, of course, Lawrence could also find 'Rousseau's Emile, 518' and the other real oddity, 'Lincoln's Speeches, etc., 206'; he could find the three volumes of Fenimore Cooper he asked for, and the two volumes of Melville, and of course 'Crèvecoeur's Letters from an American Farmer, 640' and Whitman's *Leaves of Grass* (in the particular edition he used and quoted from: which contained no poems after *Memories of President Lincoln*). Everyman also had all three Hawthorne volumes he asked for, and they had a volume by Poe: it was in fact where he had to find the Poe, because the particular volume he asked for – *Tales of Mystery and Imagination* – was the title of the Everyman selection.

The first selection of reading for the American essays would thus seem to have been done in consultation with Mountsier over Christmas 1916, working from the Everyman List. Mountsier would perhaps have known about Hamilton, and may also have recommended the Lincoln speeches; though why, I don't know.[13]

[13] Hamilton's book is a collection of essays written in 1787 and 1788 about the problems of a federal republic; it was crucial in the development of the American federal constitution. Ernest Rhys (1859-1946) included the book in the Everyman series because (a) he was interested in the subject and (b) because he

Lawrence very rarely discussed in his correspondence the actual texts he was using, but in February 1918 he confirmed the identity of one of them. Thrown out of Cornwall in October 1917, living in Berkshire, and needing to go back to the Poe essay he had first drafted in Cornwall, he wrote to his friend Koteliansky in London asking for a copy of the Everyman Poe edition, as he could no longer lay his hands on his own (it was probably still down in Cornwall). The Everyman edition of course contained the exact selection of Tales which Lawrence was using, in the order to which he referred to them; we can observe that when he writes a phrase such as '*Eleanora*, the next story ... '[14] And in July 1985, Sotheby's sold an Everyman's Library copy of Hawthorne's *Scarlet Letter*, with autograph notes by Lawrence: the actual copy he worked from, inscribed 'D. H. Lawrence, Zennor, St Ives, Cornwall, Jan. 1917': the one which Mountsier sent him. Another document only recently discovered is a five page entry in a 1917 notebook containing comments about and quotations from the *Scarlet Letter* with page numbers – and the latter, too, refer to the Everyman text.[15]

Not every book Lawrence acquired was an Everyman Library text, however. He was almost certainly using the Nelson Classics edition of Dana's *Two Years Before the Mast*, which he had read in July 1916, some months before the essay project started. The books he did *not* ask Mountsier for, but went on to use, are revealing. They suggest texts which he either already had in his possession, or texts which he knew so well that he felt he did not need a copy of them. Everyman had a Dana in print, but he did not ask for it; so we can be

---

recognised that Ireland would shortly be breaking away from the UK, and he wanted to assist discussion of the kind of constitution it should have.

14 *Studies* 235:33.

15 See *Studies* 371-7.

fairly sure that he still had his Nelson Classics copy.[16] He did not ask Mountsier to send a copy of Cooper's *The Last of the Mohicans*, either, so it is possible that he already had one; but the fact that the character he referred to throughout his essay as Natty or Leatherstocking is called Hawkeye throughout *The Last of the Mohicans*, and the fact that Lawrence refers to Cora's sister throughout as Lily (her name is actually Alice) suggests to me that he was relying entirely on memory when writing this particular essay.

My textual researches have not yet revealed exactly which editions he had in his hands for *all* the texts he was using; but Everyman texts of the Franklin, the Crèvecoeur, the Melville, the Poe, the Cooper, the Hawthorne and the Whitman are certain. The Franklin he had, for example, was the full text, not the usual cheaply reprinted censored text, which significantly missed out Franklin's instruction to himself 'Rarely use venery' – which however the excellent Everyman text included, and which Lawrence would comment on so memorably: 'I always thought books of Venery were about hunting deer ... Never "use" venery at all'. [17] If he had been using the Nelson Classics version of Franklin he would not have found the instruction at all.

16 He did not ask Mountsier for an Everyman copy of Melville's *Typee* either, although he had wanted one back in June 1916; but in his correspondence with Mountsier he made a number of references to it: he must have had a copy by December 1916. The old Rananim idea had been re-named 'Typee' in a letter Frieda wrote to Mountsier on 4 January 1917; while in his own letter DHL mentioned 'the Marquesas Islands, Nukuheva' (*3L* 65). Although the CUP Letters edition rightly gives the geographical location of Nukuheva, the important thing is that it is the setting of the start of Melville's *Typee*. DHL must have had a copy of the book, and have been soaked in it to an extent that made passing references to it to Mountsier perfectly comprehensible.

17 *Studies* 24: 22-3, 28:15.

Having established what books, at least in some cases, Lawrence actually had in his hands, the question follows: how did he use what he had? Here let me concentrate on the essays on Crèvecoeur and Whitman. Lawrence's methods were characteristic. The reader of the Crèvecoeur essay will discover how

> The Farmer had an Amiable Spouse and an Infant son, his progeny. He took the Infant Son – who enjoys no other name than this – ... to the fields with him, and seated the same I.S. on the shafts of the plough whilst he, the American Farmer, ploughed the potato patch. He also, the A.F., helped his Neighbours, whom no doubt he loved as himself, to build a barn ... .[18]

It may come as a surprise to you to learn that Crèvecoeur never uses the words Amiable or Spouse in the whole of his book, never uses the phrase Infant son, never ploughs a potato patch, and never helps his neighbours build a barn.

This is not just what I first thought it might be, either – the result of Lawrence's five years spent in revision of the essays, so that over the years errors crept in. This did happen in some cases, and I shall give you examples in a moment. But the first surviving version of the Crèvecoeur essay, written in the second half of 1918 and published in January 1919, contains the following phrases:

> ... the *Letters from an American Farmer* ... tell of Crêvecoeur's struggles to establish his farm in the wilderness, of the beneficent help of his 'amiable spouse', the joy of seating his infant son on the shafts of the plough, the happiness of helping a neighbour build a barn ...[19]

18 *Studies* 33:19-27.

19 *Studies* 195:1-5.

The infant son here is a description, not the reference which it subsequently became: the 'amiable spouse' is a way-of-speaking set out in inverted commas which in later versions became an actual – or apparent – quotation. The non-existent barn is still there (and is the faulty memory of the account of a group of neighbours getting together to build Andrew the Hebridean a house); the potato patch, as you might have guessed, was simply a later fantasy. But even in the early version of the essay there are other, new errors which simply got left out – not corrected – in later revisions. Lawrence – knowing that Crèvecoeur went to America and did indeed struggle to build up his farm – completely ignores the narrative of the actual book, which pretends that the author (named James) inherits the farm from his father, and so has no wilderness to struggle with. The struggles are those of others, like the almost certainly fictional Andrew the Hebridean.

Such oddities make it to me fairly clear that Lawrence almost certainly did not re-read Crèvecoeur after first writing about him, or – at least – did not check back; so that errors made in early drafts of the essay were always likely to survive, and in some cases to grow even more striking, in subsequent drafts. It appears, too, almost certain that no new quotations of the actual texts used anywhere in *Studies in Classic American Literature* (or in the intermediate versions of the essays) were introduced into later drafts. The later versions of the essays simply reproduce (or sometime cut down) the original quotations, even though at times they do very different things with them. It is as if the first writing, and the arrival of the quotations, set the pattern for all subsequent versions of the essays. Only in one case have I found evidence to suggest that Lawrence may actually have re-read a book or added to its quotations, subsequent to the first surviving version. However, as he always hand-copied his quotations into the next draft (or at times hand-copied them from intermediate typescripts), those quotations also acquired a steadily increasing patina of errors as time went by.

On the other hand, it is also clear from the notes Lawrence made, and the passages he listed while reading *The Scarlet Letter*, that – after that initial period of reading and note-taking – he *did* subsequently read the whole book again, when he actually wrote his own essay. All kinds of things from the book get into the essay which were never there in the initial notes. It's only when the essay had been written that the quotations seemed, as it were, to stabilise, and no longer get added to; and that, of course, was when errors started to accumulate.

In some cases, things went wrong for other reasons. The number of times Lawrence copied and re-copied led, I think, to a number of oddities. In the Whitman essay, for example, you find a remark about the 'poems, Democracy, En Masse, One Identity'[20] – and you will look in vain for such poems in Whitman. What happened? a list of leading ideas was subsequently converted into a list of underlined words, and in the next draft seems to have got transmuted into supposed poem titles. Again, early in the essay Lawrence uses the phrase 'ENDLESS LOVERS'[21] as if it were a quotation from Whitman, but it isn't: it's a synthesis of his poetic language. Let me just quote four lines from different parts of 'Song of Myself': 'Endless unfolding of words of ages!' (l. 477): 'And that all the men ever born are also my brothers, and the women my sisters and lovers' (l. 86): 'Every room of the house do I fill with an arm'd force, / Lovers of me, bafflers of graves' (ll. 1012-13): 'My lovers suffocate me! / Crowding my lips, thick in the pores of my skin' (ll. 1169-70). In the final version of the essay, Lawrence makes great play with Whitman's remark 'I reject nothing', but Whitman never actually writes that anywhere. However, what he *does* write is 'They pass, I also pass, any thing passes, none can be interdicted, / None but are accepted, none but shall be dear

20 *Studies* 151:29.

21 *Studies* 148:13.

to me' ('Song of the Open Road', ll. 23-4) and – even more pithily – 'I love all – I do not condemn anything' ('City of Ships', l. 14): very close to the Lawrence, but not actually the same. Lawrence also offers us the quotation 'Athletic mothers of these States –', but – again – this is not Whitman: it is, however, an intensely Whitmanesque creation. Whitman wrote about 'America, her athletic Democracy' ('To Foreign Lands', l. 2); 'The athletic America matron speaking to ... the individuality of the States' ('Our Old Feuillage', ll. 61-2); he also wrote 'Have you vivified yourself from the maternity of these States?' ('By Blue Ontario's Shore', l. 191). Lawrence transmuted these into a good Whitmanesque line.

Not many of these errors are especially important – they don't at any point destroy the arguments Lawrence is mounting – though I was happily struck by the error which gave me my title. In the essay on *Moby Dick* Lawrence quotes the phrase 'I ascended to the over-crowded deck'. [22] But this comes in a passage which he had rewritten at least three times, and in one of its rewritings it got changed. In Melville, the narrator actually goes up on deck on a cloudy day, and tells how he 'ascended to the over-clouded deck'. I think I prefer 'the over-crowded deck' for its suggestion of these *wretched* sailors milling about everywhere.

But, of course, words get missed out of the quotations on many occasions in the *Studies*; punctuation goes awry, paragraph breaks are inserted and omitted, things are sometimes mangled; so that a description of Stubb in *Moby Dick*, 'brave as fearless fire', emerges in Lawrence's text as a quotation 'Fearless as fire'.[23] And I am glad to say that at times Lawrence could not read his own handwriting either, at exactly the place where textual editors also have problems – where the multiple upright loops of a word like 'any' (with the 'a' indistinguishable from any other upward stroke) mean

22 *Studies* Textual apparatus 138:19.

23 *Studies* 137:11.

that it could be 'any' or 'my'. It turned into 'my' in one of Lawrence's own hand-written copies, so that Melville's already puzzling 'any meditative Magian rover' became the even odder 'my meditative Magian rover'[24] in the final version of the essay.

So is the story simply one of carelessness, accident, error? Not only. Whatever else is true, we are not simply confronted by errors in the way in which Lawrence handles his authors. The fake Whitman quotations are all remarkably accurate to the kind of writing Whitman does. To use a word I've employed elsewhere, they 'mimic' Whitman. They don't reproduce him, but nor do they distort him; they are the product of a period of extraordinary immersion in the text so that – like 'Pierre Menard, Author of the Quixote', in the story of that title by Borges – Lawrence can actually *write* Whitman. And although the words 'Amiable Spouse' never actually appear in the text of *Letters from a American Farmer*, they seem to me to be wholly accurate as a way of describing the tone of Crèvecoeur's references to his wife. It *is* true that he never gives his wife her name; nor does he ever name his children; and his Rousseauesque reverence towards them perfectly justifies Lawrence's ironical phrase, the 'Infant son'. Lawrence's account of such things as Crèvecoeur's relationships with his wife and child makes the book sound thoroughly unreal and – at times – fictional; and that is exactly how it reads.

On the other hand, the fact that – after first reading, making notes, and writing the essay's first draft – he does not seem to have revisited his original texts, or have checked his quotations, meant that Lawrence occasionally totally rewrote what his authors were saying. I can offer you a particular

24 *Studies* 143:28.

blatant example of this from a passage in Crèvecoeur describing the trouble he had with some nesting boxes he had put round his porch. Lawrence wrote as follows in the first surviving version of the essay:

> The wrens took a fancy to the nest of the swallows, and determined to occupy it. They pugnaciously attacked the larger, swift birds, attacked them and drove them from the nest. The swallows returned upon opportunity. But the wrens, coming home, violently drove them forth again. Which continued until the swallows patiently set about to build another nest, whilst the wrens installed themselves in triumph.
>
> This event Crèvecoeur watches with full delight. He takes no sides and feels no pangs ...[25]

By the time of the 1923 version of the essays, this had developed a little further, into the following:

> They pugnaciously (I like the word pugnaciously, it is so American) attacked the harbingers of spring, and drove them away from their nice adobe nest. The swallows returned upon opportunity. But the wrens, coming home, violently drove them forth again. Which continued until the gentle swallows patiently set about to build another nest, while the wrens sat in triumph, in the usurped home. The American Farmer watched this contest with delight, and no doubt loudly applauded those little rascals of wrens. For in the Land of the Free, the greatest delight of every man is in getting the better of the other man.[26]

Lawrence's commentary in both cases is, however, riddled

25 *Studies* 197:40–198:8.
26 *Studies* 35:37–36:5.

with errors. Crèvecoeur only mentions one swallow and one wren but Lawrence makes it sound as if there were numerous birds (or two of each, at least). The swallow's nest was not (of course) made of adobe (a very south-western concept: he would not, I think, have written that phrase before going to America in September 1922); and there were not, as both accounts say, *two* campaigns at all, with the swallows returning in the middle, and the wrens finally winning, but just one, when a single wren successfully drove off a single swallow. Nor did the swallow build another nest; it did not need to. The wren did not take over the site of the swallow's nest at all: it removed the nesting material and took it to the nesting box which Crèvecoeur had provided for it. The swallow simply re-acquired nesting material, and moved back to where it had been. And far from taking 'no sides', or approving, Crèvecoeur describes the wren's behaviour as 'a remarkable instance of selfishness', and calls it both 'plunder' and 'injustice'. The word 'pugnaciously', finally, is not used in the Crèvecoeur text; and 'pugnacious' is, anyway, not an American word at all, but a word used in England since the seventeenth century, even if the adverbial form *did* first appear in Noah Webster's 1847 dictionary, published in New York.

At times like these, however, rather than feeling my chest swelling with pride as I set Lawrence right, I actually feel rather absurd: a small-minded pedant making tiny, accurate but ultimately foolish and unnecessary points, and starkly revealed for what I am by the creative writer. Yet I also believe that it *should* be recorded that, in order to make his individual points clear, Lawrence at times distorted his American authors, Crèvecoeur and Whitman; or, in what is probably a more accurate way of putting it, having made up his very intelligent mind what Crèvecoeur and Whitman were like as writers and thinkers, Lawrence was not in the least interested in re-reading them or bothered about checking to see what they actually wrote. In you or me, this would be a silly mistake. But because Lawrence is a creative writer, who works at times by mimicking his author, and writing out of that mimicry, and is also a highly intelligent and intuitive thinker, his grasp and understanding of Crèvecoeur and Whitman can be both powerful and extraordinary in spite of the manifest errors. My scholarly points simply bounce off Lawrence's essays, almost insignificantly. Does it matter how many swallows or wrens there were? Or how athletic the American matrons were? Lawrence is seeing into Crèvecoeur, and deeply into his attitude to the world around him, and even to represent the episode as showing Crèvecoeur cheering on the wrens is not silly. It would have been more characteristic of Crèvecoeur than the actual – very brief – moral criticism of the wren which he *does* offer; but the rather superior and detached moral criticism is also characteristic. Lawrence, misremembering but creating, tells at least as much of the truth as the accurate reader and careful scholar would do. He works by altering his author; but such alteration may at times tell more of the truth than the original text does.

I think that Lawrence's Franklin, and Lawrence's Crèvecoeur, and Lawrence's Whitman, stand as creations in their own right who reflect light back on their originals. The fact that there are numerous errors in the versions of the authors which Lawrence presents is, in a way, interesting; but it should also help us see how Lawrence created the subjects of his essays, not simply (or even mainly) how slack or unscholarly he was.

The annotator is in a unique position, getting as close to his author as this. I can, if I feel like it, rap my author over the knuckles for getting things wrong, but what is actually far more interesting is to help the reader see how Lawrence builds up his subject by making his narrative say what he wants it to say. As annotator of the passages from Crèvecoeur and the poems by Whitman, however, as opposed to the fascinated critic, I clearly have a problem. We are not going to correct Lawrence's quotations in the CUP volume; we are going to treat *Studies* as a Lawrence book in which misquotations stand (but are annotated), rather than as a book about American literature (where we would normally do our best to get the quotations accurate). This is consistent with the whole of the Lawrence edition, where several volumes have acquired this peculiar status as published texts complete with errors, where (normally) one's job as part of a publishing team is to get rid of errors. Most notably, the Cambridge *Movements in European History* reproduces error after error, because either Lawrence or one of his authorities made the errors (they are of course all corrected in the notes). We do *not* think it likely that anyone will use *Movements* to teach (or study) history.

I have, furthermore, decided that – in the case of *Studies* – I can't simply refer the reader of (say) the swallow-and-wren passage in the Crèvecoeur essay to the appropriate corresponding page of the Everyman edition, as if everything there corresponded to what Lawrence described. I shall give the Everyman page reference; but I shall also list Lawrence's divergences from what appeared on it, as succinctly as I can. That seems to me to be part of my duty as an annotator; though I would welcome your comments on that, and whether you would expect a scholarly or critical edition to tell you when a paraphrase in a text was not accurate, and how. I remain, however, surprised that no one seems ever to have noticed these distortions. Perhaps no one has ever read the passages in Whitman and Crèvecoeur carefully before.

Something strange also happened in Lawrence's essay on Melville's novel *Typee*; and here we are lucky in knowing that he was using the Everyman text. The book was first published by John Murray in London in March 1846, but in August 1846 a 'Revised Edition' was published in New York. This was a censored edition, though Melville himself was responsible for the censorship; it was subjected to extensive cuts. The passages most profoundly affected were those where Melville had attacked missionaries for their injustice and their folly; these passages were removed wholesale from the revised New York edition.

During the period 1846 to 1916, editions published in England followed the uncut text; those published in America were cut.[27] When Ernest Rhys included the volume in Everyman in 1911, however, he unfortunately chose to use the American text, which was thus printed for the first time in Britain. He was probably misled by the fact that it claimed itself to be the Revised Edition. But this became the text which Lawrence used and read, and the fact that he did so influenced his essay to a considerable extent. Most readers of the essay who know the full-length *Typee* will probably have been surprised that Lawrence declares that Melville was 'horrified' by what he saw of cannibalism. On the contrary; the book is extraordinarily and refreshingly enlightened about it. The narrator points out that 'those who indulge in it are in other respects humane and virtuous'; he pointedly asks whether cannibalism is actually any worse than the European practice of hanging, drawing and quartering traitors, or than what he memorably calls the 'remorseless cruelty' of the white; and he points out that cannibalism is, anyway, only used against enemies killed in battle. He comments: 'so far as the relative wickedness of the parties is concerned, four or five Marquesan islanders sent to the United States as Missionaries might be quite as useful as an equal number of Americans dispatched to the Islands in a similar capacity'. It looks as if Lawrence – insisting on Melville's horror – is being extremely unfair. But the fact is that not a single one of

[27] That however issued by the Christian Knowledge Society in London in 1903 naturally used the American text, with its censorship of the attacks on the missionaries.

the enlightened comments I have quoted appears in the Everyman edition which Lawrence was using; and to that extent Melville apparently justified Lawrence's scorn. At some later stage he *does* seem to have had access to another copy of *Typee* (or at least to parts of it); it may have been in the critical book on Melville which he consulted late in 1922.[28]

I have only recently started this work and am still in the middle of it. But we shall publish both what Lawrence actually wrote, and quoted, and explanations of what he had actually read, as opposed to what he seemed to have read. We'll clear the overcrowded deck in the notes (though not in the text). In the text, the crowds will continue to gather. In the annotation, the clouds will return, the crowds will disperse.

28 It was: see *Studies* Explanatory note on 126:15.

Lawrence's Versions of America

Norwich, Spring 2003

In the spring of 2003, in spite of my protests that I was not an Americanist, I was pressed to attend an American Studies symposium at the University of East Anglia. It turned out to be a very lively and cheerful occasion (Andrew Harrison and Sean Matthews were both there), and I took the chance of presenting some of the material which Ezra Greenspan, Lindeth Vasey and I had been gathering for the edition of Studies in Classic American Literature *which we had finally brought out.*

So what is D. H. Lawrence doing offering versions of America to this symposium of yours? Not even born in the USA: not arriving in the Americas until his thirty-seventh birthday: leaving just after his fortieth: spending just twenty-four months in the country, on four separate visits.

But when he first arrived in the USA in September 1922, he brought with him *Studies in Classic American Literature.* He re-wrote the book completely during his first winter in New Mexico, revised it again in Mexico in the spring, and it was published in New York in August 1923. This is what I want to talk about; the Cambridge edition is just published.

During 1916, down in Cornwall, Lawrence read *Moby Dick*, Dana's *Two Years Before the Mast* and Crèvecoeur's *Letters From an American Farmer*; with no intention of doing anything with them, I think, except enjoy them (the last he had simply been given by a friend). But by the end of the year, with the war continuing, and America still not engaged in it, he grew certain

> a. That I want to go away from England for ever.
> b. That I want ultimately to go to a country of which I have hope, in which I feel the new unknown.
> In short, I want, immediately or at length, to transfer all my life to America.[1]

1 *3L* 25.

His belief in America had been shaped in part by what he had been reading, partly by a couple of young Americans he got to know at Christmas and New Year 1916-17, and – almost immediately – by the idea of a set of essays which would be publishable in America, at a time when he found it almost impossible to get his work published in England: 'a set of essays for America, in the hopes that they may get published by the ninnies and blockheads of the public world'.[2]

A book about American writing would, in a very practical way, give him an American public, crucial if he were really going to go there. As a teenager he had read Fenimore Cooper and Melville and Hawthorne; later on, Franklin and Poe and Whitman; he had read Emerson and Thoreau, Henry James and William James. And out of that – and what he had read in 1916 – he developed a series of essays on what he called, from the start, Classic American Literature.

This was a distinctly odd book for an Englishman to write: but it would also have been an odd book for an American author of that date to have written. Ezra Greenspan has pointed out to me that an 'American Classic' was a 'term so new in the second decade of the twentieth century that it was still an oxymoron to many of Lawrence's contemporaries in the United States, no less than in Britain':[3]

2 *3L* 201.

3 DHL seems to have used the word 'classic' for American literature first in the earliest draft of *Women in Love*, sometime before September 1916: e.g. 'It surprises me how much older, over-ripe and withering into abstraction, this American classic literature is, than English literature of the same time' (*FWL* 135:21-3). See too his remark from August 1916 about 'your classic American Literature' (*2L* 645). He first used it about his own project ('I have got in my head a set of essays, or lectures, on Classic American literature') on 9 January 1917 (*3L* 73).

> the field of American literature was not yet part of the curriculum in most American universities, while the first professorship in American letters was not established until 1919. Similarly, the founding of the American Literature Group of the Modern Language Association did not take place until 1921, and its journal, American Literature, began publication only in 1929.[4]

Henry Irving Brock, assistant editor of the *New York Times Book Review*, reviewing *Studies in Classic American Literature* in 1923, would raise an eyebrow at 'what [Lawrence] calls classic American literature', while another reviewer, Kurt L. Daniels, would describe the phrase as 'new to most of us'.[5]

If the title of the book was striking; so was its final selection of Classics: Franklin, Crèvecoeur, Cooper, Poe, Hawthorne, Dana, Melville, Whitman. But Lawrence was attuned to the mood of the times; even authors who, when Lawrence began the project, would not have been regarded by his contemporaries as especially significant – even seen as children's authors – were acquiring a new status. Fenimore Cooper, for example, would be dignified by the publication of the first ever edition of his correspondence, two volumes of it, in 1922, the year Lawrence actually arrived in the USA, while Raymond Weaver's influential book on Melville (partly

4 For a discussion of these developments, see Kermit Vanderbilt, *American Literature and the Academy: The Roots, Growth, and Maturity of a Profession* (Philadelphia, 1986), chaps. 13-15 passim. There had been a Professor of English Literature and History at King's College in the University of London as early as June 1840.

5 'D. H. Lawrence Strings Some American Literary Pearls', *New York Times Book Review*, 16 September 1923, p. 9; 'Mr. Lawrence on American Literature', *New Republic*, xxxvi (24 October 1923), 236.

biographical, partly critical) came out in 1921.[6]

And Lawrence would be greeted in the USA by Stuart Sherman's book *Americans*, with its essays on Franklin, Hawthorne and Whitman overlapping, of course, with the essays in Lawrence's own book. (Lawrence would review Sherman: Sherman would review Lawrence.)

Lawrence survived the war in England; his attempt to get passports for America in 1917 came to nothing. Eight of the *Studies* essays appeared in the *English Review*. When the war ended, he moved swiftly to leave England (and ended up in Sicily), but going to America no longer seemed so urgent, though he was sure that he would go one day. By 1922 he had compelling professional reasons to make the trip. With many of his works now circulating in the USA, because of the determination of his American publisher, Thomas Seltzer, and his reputation rising, he believed that he needed to be in closer touch with what had become the primary market for his work. This was what his American agent Robert Mountsier had told him in 1921 – 'Your chief publishing field is here, and the nearer you are to it the better.'[7]

6 *Correspondence of James Fenimore-Cooper*, ed. James Fenimore Cooper, 2 vols. (New Haven, 1922). DHL would be anxious to secure a copy when he arrived from Australia in September 1922 (it would influence his own essays on Cooper quite considerably in their American re-writing). We don't know how DHL acquired it (or access to it), but see *Studies*, Explanatory note on 52:29. Seltzer supplied DHL with Weaver's book, *Herman Melville, Mariner and Mystic* (New York, 1921); see *Studies*, Explanatory notes on 126:15, 128:16, 129:5, 131:3, 131:8, 131:23.

7 *3L* 685 n. 1. Adele Szold Seltzer, the sister of the pioneering Zionist Henrietta Szold, was as much an enthusiast for DHL as was her husband: see DHL, *Letters to Thomas and Adele Seltzer*, ed.

In February 1922, the Lawrences left Sicily; they had been offered a house in New Mexico by the arts devotee Mabel Dodge Luhan.

Lawrence had last worked on the essays in Sicily in 1920. The most striking thing to happen to Lawrence's book in its whole period of composition was the revision he gave it in America. He took far longer over the job than might have been expected for a man who regularly wrote a novel in six weeks, but he was totally re-writing the essays; he described what he was doing as 'Americanising them'. And he was pleased that this made them 'much shorter', 'much sharper, quicker'.[8]

After a month's work, however, he was starting to express doubts to Mountsier: 'you may think them too violent, now, to print. Anyhow they are the first reaction on me of America itself.' A fortnight later, he went further: 'They'll no doubt horrify you.'[9]

He marked his completion of the essays, in December 1922, with a celebratory 'LOBO, NEW MEXICO' at the bottom of the final page of manuscript;[10] he had finished it up at the Del Monte ranch on Lobo mountain. It was the first time he had ever put the place of writing at the end of a prose work; he was staking a kind of claim.

When he said that the essays were now, perhaps, too violent to print, he cannot yet have got to the revision of the Whitman essay; but he had finished work on it when he said that Mountsier would be horrified. I shall concentrate during the rest of this paper on what is, I think, the primary example of a process that Lawrence simultaneously conceived of as 'Americanising' and making 'violent'.

Gerald M. Lacy (Santa Barbara, 1976), p. 220.

8 *4L* 338, 342.

9 *4L* 343, 358-9.

10 *Studies* Explanatory note on 161:32.

Lawrence had intended to include a Whitman essay from the very start of the project, and probably wrote a draft in 1918. But the essay is the only one of which nothing at all survives from the very first stage. We can only pick up the progress of the essay from a 1919 version, which has been published in full for the first time this year, in the Cambridge *Studies*. It is extremely respectful of Whitman; it starts by calling him 'the last and greatest of the Americans', and although critical of various things in his poetry (Lawrence hates the way it sometimes dumps down 'cartloads of material, cartload after cartload. All is shovelled out uninspired') the essay ends by saluting Whitman 'before any other man, because I owe the last strides into freedom to you. And in saluting you, I salute your great America.'[11]

That was 1919.

Lawrence did very little or no re-reading of source material between writing the versions of his essays; he re-used the same quotations time after time, often making strikingly different points as he did so. In the 1919 Whitman, he had used a poem from the 'Children of Adam' section of *Leaves of Grass*:

> I am he that aches with amorous love;
> Does the earth gravitate? does not all matter, aching,
>   attract all matter?
> So the body of me to all I meet or know. [12]

Lawrence had commented 'This is Whitman. It is his accession into wholeness, his knowledge in full. Now he is

[11] *Studies* 358:4, 369:10-11, 13-15.

[12] *Leaves of Grass (I) & Democratic Vistas* (1912), p. 93: the edition of Whitman which DHL apparently used in 1917-18. See *Studies* Explanatory note on 148:2.

unified with everything, *consciously*. Now, consciously, he embraces all things into a oneness with himself ... By vivid, imaginative sympathy, or love, Whitman is identified with whatever and whoever he sees, or even thinks of.'[13]

And though Lawrence had seen love as a kind of 'merging' (Whitman's own word) he had also insisted that, in Whitman's version of 'manly love', what the poetry did was set up poles of opposition, and kept them firmly distinct – so that Whitman's kind of love was 'not truly a *merging*'.[14]

When revising the essay in Sicily in 1920, Lawrence had used the same quotation and said similar things about it: but he was still clearer about the merging which he believed natural to heterosexual love. This time, however, he removed his theorising about 'manly love' not being a merging; he stressed instead the tender love of male-male sexuality, the beauty of ultimate comradeship. And he continued to insist 'What a great poet Whitman is.'[15]

In New Mexico in 1922, his revision transformed the essay. I shall quote from what he actually wrote at this point – not what was published, toned down, the following August. The first reference to the Amorous Love quotation comes only half a page after the start and is put in capital letters, so that they leap off the page:

I AM HE THAT ACHES WITH AMOROUS LOVE.

The next line reads 'You bet!'[16] He then turns to another matter for a moment – quotes the capitalised bit again – and asks

13 *Studies* 359:22-24, 35-37.

14 *Studies* 366:21.

15 *Studies* 414:18.

16 *Studies* 421:16-17.

> What do you make of that? I AM HE THAT ACHES. First generalisation. First uncomfortable universalisation. WITH AMOROUS LOVE! Oh god! Better a belly-ache. A belly-ache is at least specific. But the ACHE of AMOROUS LOVE!
>
> Think of having that under your skin. All that!
>
> I AM HE THAT ACHES WITH AMOROUS LOVE.
>
> Walter, leave off. You are not HE. You are just a limited Walter. And your ache doesn't include all Amorous Love, by any means. If you ache you only ache with a small bit of amorous love, and there's so much more stays outside the cover of your ache, that you might be a bit milder about it.[17]

And Lawrence concludes that the statement 'Reminds one of a steam-engine. A locomotive. They're the only things that seem to me to ache with amorous love. All that steam inside them. Forty million foot-pounds pressure. The ache of AMOROUS LOVE. Steam pressure. CHUFF!'[18]

He does the same kind of thing over and over again. He quotes 'And of these one and all I weave the song of myself' and comments:

> Do you, my boy? Well then it just shows you haven't got any self. It's a mush, not a woven thing. A hotch potch, not a tissue. Your Self.
>
> Oh Walter Walter, what have you done with it? What have you done with yourself? With your own individual self? For it sounds as if it had all leaked out of you when you made water, leaked into the universe when you peed. Oh Walter, you're a leaky vessel.[19]

17 *Studies* 421:31–422:2.

18 *Studies* 422:6-9.

19 *Studies* 423:8-13.

This was too much for Seltzer, who either persuaded Lawrence to tone it down, or toned it down himself, and cut the bits about peeing and leaking – and half a page later cut the comment on 'I reject nothing': 'If that is so, Walter, you must be a pipe open at both ends, so everything runs through.'[20]

What Americanising here means is not just ridiculing, but refusing to let the great cultural American icon be an icon. The Whitman essay, as written in Taos, told stories (again, not in the version finally published) about how Whitman used to walk naked in his own back garden in Camden: 'stark naked and fat and excited with his own nudity and his grey beard'; and how 'he used to stop the little girls coming home from school, with senile amorousness'.[21] The essay no longer honours the great poet: it assassinates the image. Again, Seltzer had all this removed.

In a rather thin literature of comments on this final version of the essays, it has on the one hand been claimed that all Lawrence was doing was using 'a popular, flippant style', a 'lighter humorous mode'.[22]

On the other hand, it has been said that the 'hysterical tone' of the essays was the result of his 'violent hate against Mabel Dodge and Toni Luhan ... a state of extreme nervous tension resulting in almost insane outbreaks against his wife, his friends, his animals, against America as a whole'.[23]

Such commentators not only underestimate the violent destruction of the icons, they miss the massive attack upon idealism which seems to be Lawrence's primary point in 'Americanising' these essays. He writes ('F — — K it!!'[24]) in a

20 *Studies* 423:30-1.

21 *Studies* 423:19-20, 21-2.

22 David Cavitch, *D. H. Lawrence and the New World* (New York, 1969), p. 142; Michael Herbert, 'Introduction' to *D. H. Lawrence: Selected Critical Writings* (Oxford, 1998), p. xiv.

23 Armin Arnold, ed., *The Symbolic Meaning* (Arundel, 1962), p. 6.

24 *Studies* 425:18.

more popular style than one would have thought possible, given his subject: partly, doubtless, in an effort to capture an audience with his first book of the Americas, but mostly to refuse the kind of willed seriousness he had already perceived as dogging American intellectuals: 'everything is taken so damn seriously that nothing remains serious'.[25]

The role he has chosen is that of the enfant terrible, who will shout aloud that emperor Whitman has no clothes. The Americanising in which Lawrence engages is the construction of a style both popular and direct, at times American ('you bet!') but mostly a way of attacking self-conscious idealism, love as bullying power over another, and 'the screwed up human will'.[26] These were the qualities he had discovered in Whitman:

> As soon as Walt knew a thing, he assumed a One Identity with it. If he knew that an Esquimo sat in a kyak, immediately there was Walt being little and yellow and greasy, sitting in a kyak.[27]

There is not a single reference to a kayak in Whitman's poetry. There are simply lines like these from 'Salut Au Monde':

> I see the regions of snow and ice ...
> I see the seal-seeker in his boat poising his lance.[28]

25 'Indians and an Englishman', *MM* 114:1-2.

26 *4L* 311.

27 *Studies* 424:10-12.

28 'Salut Au Monde!', ll. 124-6; *Leaves of Grass* 119. Cf. 'At home on Kanadian snow-shoes or up in the bush, or with fishermen off Newfoundland, / At home in the fleet of ice-boats, sailing with the rest and tacking' ('Song of Myself', ll. 339-40; *Leaves of Grass* 38). Cf. too: 'Seal-fishers, whalers, arctic seamen breaking passages through the ice' ('Song of the Broad-Axe', l. 206; *Leaves of Grass* 163).

That does not deter Lawrence. He continues to harangue Whitman – and gets an answer.

> Now my dear Walter, will you tell me exactly what a kyak is?
>
> Who is he that demands petty definition? Let him behold me sitting in a kyak.
>
> I behold no such thing, Walter. I behold a rather fat old man full of a rather senile, self-conscious sensuality. Animality on the brain.
>
> DEMOCRACY. EN MASSE. ONE IDENTITY...
>
> He reaches the state of ALLNESS.
>
> In a nasty little back-yard, with the neighbours pulling down their back blinds to shut the view out.
>
> Of course I am being personal, I intend to be.
>
> Whitman was never really an esquimo. Never even saw one. It was all just prize conceit.
>
> Whitman being everything! Just think of it! The cheek! Had never even been out of America. Impudent provincial.[29]

This seems to me to be an extraordinary mix of unfairness and insight, into the characteristics of the poetry and into how Whitman has been constructed as a universal icon of love and sympathy and democracy and equality. It takes, you will observe, a Nottingham boy to call the great American poet provincial. In the end, to 'Americanise' is to find a way of getting out from under the dead weight of the past, and its ideals, and to become a lonely, individual voice.

> Equality is superseded, when you get deep enough. And love is superseded. You find something else.
>
> You find your own stark isolation.[30]

[29] *Studies* 424:10-33.
[30] *Studies* 429:31-3.

Although 'Whitman's essential message was the Open Road' – 'The leaving of the soul free unto herself, the leaving of his fate to her and to the loom of the open road. Which is the bravest doctrine man has ever proposed to himself' – yet, 'Alas, [Whitman] didn't quite carry it out. He couldn't quite break the old maddening bond of the love-compulsion, he couldn't quite get out of the rut of the charity habit. For Love and Charity have degenerated now into habit: a bad habit.' But even satire, Lawrence once wrote, is a form of sympathy. It certainly is here.

How did American readers of the *Studies* view this treatment of American writers? The reviews, predictably, were hostile: a study in 'egotism' said one review, another thought the book 'a criticism of a life of which Lawrence knows nothing'. Even those who liked the book regarded it as 'eccentric' and wildly generalising (which is obviously fair); and those who didn't like it found plenty to attack. Raymond Weaver asserted that Lawrence's 'ignorance of American literature is comprehensive and profound'. Henry Irving Brock commented: 'If upon the subject properly in hand he writes like a man of insight and a clever workman with the edged tools of language, the next sentence might often be composed by a gum-chewing Main Street soda-fountain cut-up or a blear-eyed, bar-room bum.' That would have pleased Lawrence: he was a good mimic, and he would have liked to hear that he was able to undermine one kind of American icon with another kind of American speech. Newton Arvin, however, thought the style 'tedious' and overwrought.[31]

And Stuart Sherman ticked Lawrence off for actually being old fashioned. 'I suspect that our younger literati will tell him that this coal-heaver style was quite the thing ten

[31] *Studies* lxi-ii.

years ago, but it is now regarded as rather out of date.'[32]

I think that misses the point. It's not Lawrence trying to be contemporary, but Lawrence imitating a range of cultivated and uncultivated speech in order to undermine the very seriousness with which the subject (and Whitman's defenders) normally take themselves. In the *Studies* he wants to get round the back of conventional criticism; to offer a new kind of writing; to flesh out a reading of America itself, conducted through its iconic writers; and to locate the national fixation with power and death. That all sounds very contemporary ...

I'm terribly conscious of only scratching the surface of this area of work. It would be good to know a good deal more about how Lawrence was perceived as a writer in America in 1923; the first materials were gathered by Ezra Greenspan, and there are reviews quoted in a number of other volumes in the Cambridge Lawrence edition, but tracking down reviews and newspapers in American libraries is very difficult. And I know practically nothing about response to the work after that initial bout of reviewing. I would also like to know more about the coal-heaver style.

I am also fairly sure that there is more work that could usefully be done on Lawrence's penetration of the American literary market. My perception is that Lawrence existed almost entirely on the surface of American literary life and was never seen as anything more than a rather quaint European; the fact that his first publisher was a total enthusiast, Thomas Seltzer, who went bust in 1925, leaving Lawrence's work to be published and rather unenthusiastically distributed by a number of others – Knopf, Boni, Cape and Smith – none of them with much financial success – means, I suspect, that his star waned pretty quickly, after the strenuous efforts Seltzer had made between 1921 and 1923. But this also needs work.

32 Arnold, *Symbolic Meaning*, p. 7.

Lawrence also got to know relatively few American writers; he met Willa Cather briefly, but nothing came of the contact; he quarrelled on and off with Witter Bynner; he didn't like Mary Austin; and his most interesting reviews of American writing (of Anderson, Dos Passos and Hemingway) were all done after he had returned to Europe. There's work to be done here too. This, however, is the point at which to hand over to you, the audience ...

Lawrence and Film

Nottingham, Broadway Cinema,
D. H. Lawrence Festival, 1999

In the spring of 1999, the Broadway Cinema in Nottingham staged a season of Lawrence films (the most wonderful pieces were dug out of the archive, including one of the original ITV short films for television of Lawrence stories – 'The White Stocking'). They also asked me if I could do a Saturday morning lecture to accompany the films. I have in this case expanded the brief original text by adding some of the material I used in a talk entitled 'The Same Old Show' given at the Eastwood Lawrence Festival some years later.

When Constance Chatterley is driven the length of the main street of the mining village of Tevershall, half way through Lawrence's novel *Lady Chatterley's Lover,* she has a kind of composite vision. She sees a sharply imagined, invented place called Tevershall, and – simultaneously – a powerfully recollected recreation of Eastwood, the Midlands township where Lawrence had himself been born in 1885, and towards which he had such ambivalent thoughts. Place after place which Constance sees, along the route of her drive, turns out to have some real life original in Lawrence's own memories of Eastwood, though the added-on details are sometimes invented. But Lawrence was one of those people gifted with a quite extraordinary memory: for places, people, feelings. And though his writing career shows him moving spectacularly far away from Eastwood (he died in the south of France; his ashes are in the USA; he wrote a novel about Australia while there in 1922 and another one about Mexico in 1925: and he wrote *Lady Chatterley's Lover* in the neighbourhood of a villa in the countryside of northern Italy) – yet in one sense he never really left Eastwood, or Nottinghamshire. The old place was always there in his recollection and imagination; a kind of perpetual presence. Not always pleasantly, either: sitting outdoors in a late, long, warm and sunny Italian autumn, writing the final version of *Lady Chatterley's Lover*, he recreated the Midlands in a typical wet and muddy winter:

> The car ploughed uphill through the long squalid straggle of Tevershall, the blackened brick dwellings, the black slate roofs glistening their sharp edges, the mud black with coal-dust, the pavements wet and black.[1]

Constance sees 'The Congregational chapel, which thought itself superior' and which is (appropriately) built not just of brick or of normal stone but of 'rusticated sandstone'; Lawrence includes a characteristic touch, the deflating detail: the chapel 'had a steeple, but not a very high one.' Lawrence knew that chapel and its steeple terribly well; he had attended it, once, twice or three times every Sunday, throughout his childhood and adolescence in Eastwood. Not just for the normal services: he had gone to Sunday school there, as a child; when he went to the morning service there, or the evening, he sat with his mother; it was to the chapel that he had gone with his first girl-friend, Jessie Chambers; and when he started life as a teacher, it was in the school attached to the chapel, just ten yards down Albert Street. Now Constance sees that self-same chapel – and observes the difference (which we know Lawrence saw too) between the Congregational Chapel and the other Eastwood Chapels: the Wesleyan, and also 'the new big Primitive Methodist chapel', which Constance sees as 'primitive enough in its stark brick and big panes of greenish and raspberry glass in the windows'. Like the desperately unappealing-sounding glass, the shops in Tevershall are also horribly unattractive:

> The stacks of soap in the grocers' shops, the rhubarb and lemons in the greengrocers', the awful hats in the milliners', all went by ugly, ugly, ugly.

In one way, Constance is on a long, continuous, tracking shot

1 *LCL* 152:7-10.

of the place, Tevershall/Eastwood, taken from the travelling car; the camera (or narrative voice) never stops, but films the place in a particular way that makes things as normally inoffensive as hats and soap and rhubarb and lemons (putting those two together, of course, makes them especially sour tasting) sound quite appalling.

But, very appropriately, as the camera follows this long tracking shot through Tevershall, around the middle point of the shot comes another building which Lawrence certainly knew. It had actually been built in 1913, just after he had left; but he would have seen in it the summer of 1913, when he was back in Eastwood, and again in 1915, and again in 1918 and 1919; and then again in the summer of 1925 and in the late summer of 1926. It was Eastwood's first purpose-built cinema, 'run-up' by the builder and decorator (and speculator) George W. Stubbs, who when young had been 'an obscure and illiterate nobody', but who after his cinema enterprise 'had a motor car' and though 'rather stout, frail in health' was still 'silent and insuperable'. [2] The old Empire, so famous in its time, is actually still there (at least the shell of it); next time you go through Eastwood, watch out for the building that was (until recently) Woolworth's, and you will see a building quite unlike a normal shop: a great barn of a place, with a front which is half a classical temple and half a building which does not know what to do with itself.

But what *should* a cinema look like? By the 1930s, as we all know, the answer was simple: it should look Art Deco. In 1913, no one knew what a cinema looked like. Why the pitched roof and classical portico? Why the circular window in the front? The building is only sensible when it stops trying to be something else, and becomes what in essence it is (as you can see if you walk round the side): a long, brick building, entirely functional – and also, in Lawrence's terms, 'ugly, ugly, ugly'.

[2] *LG* 85-6.

But in the 1920s it was rather different (I should add that the date in the fiction for Constance's journey is May 1924). The Empire was booming: in a 1919 story, Lawrence had referred to 'the cinema ... just going in, and the queues ... tailing down the road to the corner'.[3] And that's what she sees next. After the ugly milliners and the awful shops with their awful soap and rhubarb and lemons and hats, on Constance's journey, comes the 'plaster-and-gilt horror of the cinema with its wet picture announcements ...'[4] Today, the gilt has all gone, along with the announcements, though some of the plaster is still there: but in Eastwood, this spectacular building (the longest in town bar the Parish Church) was the Empire Picture House, the first and only permanent cinema in town. In *Lady Chatterley*, it is unnamed, identified only by the name of the film it is supposed to be showing: 'A Woman's Love'. That name, at least, is thoroughly fictional; there is no record of a film with exactly that title ever having existed, though it sounds entirely authentic for the middle 1920s (and is a parody of sentimentality, too, as well as of Lawrence's own novel *Women in Love*).

But it was by no means the first time that cinema and film had got into Lawrence's novels. Back in 1912, he had shown Paul and his new girl-friend Clara using the cinema in Nottingham in a way that was entirely typical of the period. You didn't gear yourself up to go to A Film, you went in as into an amusement arcade, or as (in my childhood) people would still go into a news (or 'newsreel' – the word dates from 1916) cinema (or theatre), just for half an hour, to kill time. As children in the early 1950s, my brother and I were regularly dropped off in a newsreel cinema in London, while my mother went shopping. The idea of the news cinema seems to have started in 1910, when

3 *EmyE* 155:15-16.
4 *LCL* 152:17-18.

> Messrs. Pathé ... conceived the idea of showing the news of the week on films at the cinematograph theatres.[5]

This may well be what Paul and Clara are going to see in *Sons and Lovers*, when they pop into the cinema for a few minutes while he is waiting for his train:

> As they sat, he saw her hand lying near him. For some moments he dared not touch it. The pictures danced and dithered. Then he took her hand in his. It was large and firm, it filled his grasp. He held it fast. She neither moved nor made any sign. When they came out his train was due.[6]

What is on the screen is obviously the last thing on Paul's mind. And that was perfectly normal; you'd not have gone in *just* to watch the news, or whatever it was: you were filling in time – and in the case of Paul, you were going in with your girl-friend, into a darkish auditorium. In the 1970s you could still go into the Castle Cinema in Swansea and sit in one of the little upholstered sofas for two at the back of the main auditorium, designed specifically for couples: I once went to a film there with a woman friend who was visiting, and felt most embarrassed at being put into one of the 'love seats', as they were called, when both of us had other partners.

But note how, with most of his attention being on Clara, and on the utter *firmness*, the solidity of her hand, out of the corner of one eye Paul sees the total contrast of the screen 'dithering'. Now that is a word Lawrence uses more than once in his work, and not just about the cinema, either. 'Dithering' doesn't have the modern meaning of not being able to make your mind up, but the old meaning of quivering

5 *Punch* (15 June 1910), 433/1.
6 *SL* 347.

and trembling, with a good mixture of the *other* old meaning: 'to confuse, perplex, make nervous'. The officer in Lawrence's story 'The Prussian Officer', when tormenting his orderly, displays a 'dithering smile' [7] as he torments and tortures the boy; thoroughly unsettling. In the same way, the cinema screen jumps around, and so leaves you feeling confused and unhappy as you watch it. And by contrast, as Paul sits there, Clara's hand feels *so* solid and firm, while the screen quivers.

There were reasons for the film 'dithering', of course. The cinema, at that date, would certainly have had a hand-cranked projector: the projectionist having the job of making sure that the film was wound through the projector and into and past the gate at the right speed. It may surprise you to hear that there was no official standard film speed before 1917, when there was an attempt to make 16 frames a second the world standard rate: but this was widely ignored (not until the coming of sound was a new rate of 24 frames a second accepted as standard). The advantage of a projectionist hand-cranking a projector was, of course, that he could adjust his rate of projection to the demands of the film he was showing: he wasn't condemned to project the film too fast or too slow because the gearing of the projector dictated it. Part of the projectionist's skill was to get the speed right, to suit the film he was projecting, and to keep up the same steady pace throughout: but it was an extraordinarily difficult job, and the film would certainly 'dance and dither' as a result if he were *not* a skilled operator (you can imagine the results if the operator sneezed). Again, although the principle of the projector had been worked out back in 1895 – the film moved intermittently, 'with periods of rest and illumination far in excess of the periods of movement' – not until advanced projectors were introduced, with two gate openings per frame, was it possible to keep the projection steady.

7 *PO* 7:37.

Otherwise (especially before the First World War) the film would inevitably dance and dither, no matter how good the projectionist. And the projectionist couldn't afford to go too slow and steady, either: because if the celluloid film stayed too close to the projector's hot electric lamp for too long, it might very well catch fire, being highly inflammable (one cinema fire in the early 1900s killed 140 people, and actually led to the 1909 Cinematograph Act, requiring cinemas to be licensed by local authority, and empowering local authorities to censor).

Anyway, 'dither' was one of Lawrence's favourite words for the experience of film, to describe its worrying, confusing, unsettling quality. I suggest, however, that this was not simply a visual phenomenon, but also a more general reaction to the experience of film. He used the word in 1912; and in particular he used it twice in his novel *The Lost Girl* in 1920: 'the dithering eye-ache of a film',[8] 'the dither on the screen'. [9] *The Lost Girl* (Lawrence declared its very title to be 'such a film title')[10] is unique in his writing in that it concerns a small-town entrepreneur who decides (after a number of failed ventures) that the future is to be found in a combination of film and music-hall; and so, in 1913, he sets up an old portable wooden theatre structure to be the third source of cinema entertainment for the small town of Woodhouse (you can probably hear 'Eastwood' hidden in that name). From 1913, Eastwood had of course George Stubbs's purpose-built 'Empire Picture House' and also a still older temporary structure in the Cattle Market area ('Parker's Picture Pavilion'). In real life, a man called George Henry Cullen set up a third cinema, 'Cullen's Picture Palace', down in Langley Mill: and this is the one Lawrence recreates in *The Lost Girl.* It's a shoe-string organisation; the recreation of Cullen, James

8 *LG* 86:26.

9 *LG* 110:18-19.

10 *3L* 528.

Houghton, for example gets some second-hand seating from a chapel that is being rebuilt, so that the cinema audience actually sit in pews. The building, too, is wooden and distinctly second-hand, and the films James hires sound pretty awful, and obviously very old and cheap.

> 'The Human Bird,' which turned out to be a ski-ing film from Norway, purely descriptive; 'The Pancake,' a humorous film: and then his Grand Serial: 'The Silent Grip.'[11]

The serial, of course, will show an episode every week, encouraging the audience to come back on the same day next week. But James's new manager, Mr May, has to learn how to project films (he explains how 'I spend every evening with the operator at Marsh's in Knarborough'[12] – probably Moss's Empire Theatre of Varieties in Nottingham). But he ends up not very good, all the same. This is how the film entertainment at James Houghton's little cinema starts: the title gives it away.

> The lamps go out: gurglings and kissings – and then the dither on the screen: 'The Human Bird,' in awful shivery letters. It's not a very good machine and Mr May is not a very good operator. Audience distinctly critical.[13]

Even James's daughter Alvina admits that 'our pictures aren't good enough ... We should have to get a new machine, and pay for the expensive films. – Our pictures do shake, and our films are rather ragged'.[14] They don't make enough money, however, to be able to invest in the 'new machine and finer

11 *LG* 107:4-6.
12 *LG* 101:12-13.
13 *LG* 110:18-21.
14 *LG* 117:6-8.

lenses'[15] which James knows they need; they just struggle along.

As you'll have realised, Lawrence is often pretty savage about the experience of going to films. When you see old films projected with modern technology in modern cinemas, or on TV, you really get no idea of how different (and usually how very much worse) the experience would have been in the first three decades of cinema in the twentieth century. In *The Lost Girl*, on the one hand the narrator goes on comparing the 'dither' and 'dithering eye-ache' of film with the actual capacity of live entertainers *really* to entertain an audience ... but on the other hand, he is fascinated by the whole enterprise of silent film, and recreates it in loving detail; the building, the film, the audience, the live music at the piano – for Alvina Houghton is obliged by her father to use her rather superior piano playing skills to bash out popular favourites to accompany the action of the silent film. One tune which Lawrence mentions is 'the seductive "Dream Waltz"', [16] and we also hear of her 'banging off the *Merry Widow Waltz*, and, in tender moments, *The Rosary*. Time after time, *The Rosary*'.[17]

But James Houghton has got it wrong, even in 1913. Lawrence knows which way the future lies; the music-hall entertainments which at 'Houghton's Pleasure Palace' are still scheduled between the films have, in other cinemas, been replaced by entire evenings of films: 'it's much cheaper to run'. There's a bit of Lawrence, for sure, in the manager's comment 'I can't believe they want nothing but pictures. I can't believe they want everything in the flat'.[18] And yet he knew very well that cinema was here to stay, and would replace music-hall.

[15] *LG* 115:1-2.
[16] *LG* 110:32-3.
[17] *LG* 99:33-4.
[18] *LG* 115:22, 24-5.

Accordingly, there are regular references to cinema-going in Lawrence's work and in his biography; often critical of the experience, but by no means always. The worst occasion seems to have been his experience in September 1928 of the silent, two-year old *Ben Hur* (the *Gladiator* of its day); he and his friends the Brewsters were changing trains in Strasbourg and had time to kill. They went into the Cathedral, but that time of year it was bitterly cold and Lawrence was a very sick man with advanced (and advancing) TB: he would be dead within 18 months.

> Lawrence decided to keep warm with *Ben Hur* at the cinema until train time. Half an hour we watched doves fluttering around baby-faced blonde dolls, brutal Romans accursed with hearts of stone, galleys of inhuman slaves, galloping horses whizzing perilous chariots. There was no human touch, nothing resembling a reality of any phase of life we knew or could imagine. Lawrence gasped out that he was going; if we did not take him out immediately he would be violently sick; such falsity nauseated him; he could not bear to see other people there open-mouthed, swallowing it, believing it to be true.[19]

This is often quoted to reveal how much Lawrence hated film. But that is not quite what it shows. It certainly shows that he hated pretentious epic film; but it shows that he was most of all concerned not with the film as such, but with how the audience watched it. We can see exactly the same in his satirical painting 'Close-Up (Kiss)', which shows a grotesque naked man just about to kiss a grotesque naked woman in a grotesque kiss: the tight positioning of the characters within the frame confirming his oppressive version of a cinema screen. The man is rapacious, the women entirely passive: something which Lawrence elsewhere complained about, in

[19] Nehls, iii. 248.

cinema. He saw how both convention and censorship demanded that 'a film heroine shall be neuter, a sexless thing of washed-out purity', whereas 'real sex-feeling shall only be shown by the villain or villainess'.[20] His painting is obviously a parody of film, and of how film was watched; it asks the question 'how ever could you take this disgusting parody of feeling seriously, or believe that it might be in some way sexual, or tender, or arousing, or in any way like life?'

But that was only one experience. In Mexico City back in April 1923, for example – Lawrence and his companions had gone down to Mexico from the south west of the USA, and had decided to stay there for Holy (Easter) Week, to see what a thoroughly religious country was like at such a time – what did he and they do but go to see an old French silent film called *The Life and Passion of Christ*, dating from 1902 (pretty ragged and dithering, I would guess, after more than twenty years of being hand-cranked across two continents). This is what they saw:

> We watched Jesus loom forward with a lamb on His shoulder, nearer and larger into the hearts of His audience …

There was music in the cinema, of course, but – as it was Mexico – not a piano: 'marimbas played a gaily swinging tune to welcome Him'. It got a good deal stranger: 'during the Crucifixion the tune was "Three O'Clock in the Morning"'. But Lawrence was once again interested not so much by the film as by the audience's mixed response: 'One moment ... you would think they were agonised by the old tragedy. The next moment they're gadding in the streets, full of gaiety and pulque...'.[21] Such a response was not, at any rate, a passive

20 *LEA* 242:12-13.

21 Witter Bynner, *Journey with Genius* (1953), p. 46. Pulque is a Mexican alcoholic drink.

experience, either to church religion or to film. It was passivity and stupid acceptance which Lawrence would, in a picture like 'Close-Up (Kiss)', later satirise in the film audience.

Later in 1923, we find Lawrence back from America in dank and dark London in winter, but again voluntarily in a cinema, this time to see the brand new cowboy Western *The Covered Wagon*, directed and produced by James Cruze. He's gone because he is intensely nostalgic for the American south west, where he has himself lived for six months in and near Taos the previous year; where for example he learned to ride, and lived the life of a rancher; where he had been to Taos Indian pueblo and to various Indian ceremonies; and now he wants to recapture some of it if he can. He insists on a group of friends coming, and one of them (Dorothy Brett) provides the account, though rather weirdly she calls Lawrence 'you' throughout. It is, I think, the only account which exists of Lawrence actually watching a film and commentating on it as he watches it. It tells us a little of what he was looking for, in a film. But before the film started, as was common at that date, some supposedly genuine characters appeared on the stage: a cowboy and some Indians.

> I am sitting next you in that long, dark movie house [in the Strand, in London]. You are tense with excitement, and we are all infected by your love for the West. You snort at the smart cowboy, in his white shirt, white pants, black cowboy boots and big white Stetson. He irritates you, and you feel sure he has never sat on a horse. The house darkens again, and then a spotlight falls onto the stage; seven real Red Indians are supposed to walk on before the movie begins.
>
> 'Will they be real?' I ask you. And you say,
>
> 'Wait. I'll know when they walk; they move differently from us.'
>
> A man, wrapped in a blanket, with his hair in a knob at the back of his head, walks on. I look at you

> quickly. 'Yes,' you whisper, 'he is real,' and you suddenly sigh, heavily, as if the sight of him makes you homesick for New Mexico. You seem to be greeting old friends, far off across that long, dark movie house.
>
> The light fades down and the Covered Wagon begins. You are watching it, as if you were part of it yourself. 'How like it is, how like it is,' you keep on saying; and you hum very softly to me the song that is the keynote to the story: 'Oh, oh Susanna, don't you sigh for me, for I'm waiting here in Oregon with my banjo on my knee.'[22]

Lawrence had no time for pretend cowboys: he had met another Hollywood actor out in California a few months earlier, in September 1923, and had been both amazed and disgusted by the experience:

> Lawrence described a 'tea' in Hollywood, at which an appalling pint of whiskey and soda was thrust into his hand by the host, an actor wearing white riding breeches and carrying a riding crop, while the shrinking, refined wife drooped in a corner and a small son marched about dressed up exactly like his father and swinging his little whip.[23]

And in his short novel *St. Mawr*, he would be scathing about 'the noble cowboy of the films ... self-conscious film-heroes ... flat shapes, exactly like men, but without any substance of reality, rapidly rattling away with talk, emotions, activity, all in the flat, nothing behind it'.[24]

I think we can see a kind of pattern in this mixture in

[22] Dorothy Brett, *Lawrence and Brett* (Philadelphia, 1933), pp. 26-7. The music, of course, was added 'live' in the cinema: it was a silent film.

[23] Nehls, iii. 289.

[24] *St.M* 131:29, 32-3, 11-13.

Lawrence of distaste and fascination with film. On the one hand, there is a sharp moral and critical mind eager to say that the cinema trades in the second-rate, the commercial, the unreal, and that it gives such feelings to its audience while trying to lull them into the belief that it *is* real (when there is, both literally and figuratively. 'nothing behind it'). He wrote brilliantly of the 'luscious filmy imagination' of film: like an oil film on water, the thing is genuinely 'filmy': superficial, brilliant, insubstantial, deceitful. On the other hand, he also found some cinema intensely *real* and powerful, and responded to the magic of the free creation of another world in it, and to the way in which film encourages its audience to live freely (if briefly) in that created world. In this way, the magic of film is akin to the magic made by the creative writer: eternally fascinating, as it makes you another world which you don't just encounter but in which you actually live, while it is going on. Lawrence's regular anger with film was precisely because of its power to take people over; he wasn't just being a cheap moralist, like Mrs Bolton in *Lady Chatterley's Lover*, blaming moral decline in the twenties on the cinema:

> I'm sure it's awful, the way the old ones go on! Why, they're a *lot* worse than the young, and a sight more disgusting. I lay it down to the pictures [a word first used around 1913], myself. But you can't keep them away. I was always saying: Go to a good instructive film, but do for goodness sake keep away from these melodramas and love films.[25]

There is no record of Lawrence ever going to an 'instructive' film; and he obviously finds Mrs Bolton absurd.

We can, however, see another example of just that same pattern of ambivalent responses to film in Lawrence's only known extended encounter with genuine movie actresses and actors and technicians. This happened not in Hollywood

[25] *LCL* 102:26-30.

(where he lived only briefly in 1923, staying with painter friends who were painting film sets and backdrops) but on board ship, when the Lawrences were sailing from Australia to San Francisco in August 1922. The ship called, of course, at various islands on the way across the Pacific; and at Tahiti, a 'Crowd of cinema people' came aboard for the onward journey to San Francisco. They had been making a film melodrama to be released in February 1923, its working title *Captain Blackbird* but to be released as *Lost and Found on a South Sea Island* (a naval captain loses his daughter to warring natives, and after many adventures gets her back). Lawrence wrote to a rather snooty English friend about his first encounter with the 'cinema people': 'They are rather like successful shop-girls, and the men like any sort of men at the sea-side. Utterly undistinguished. That's how it all is – so undistinguished, so common' [26] – which sounds utterly contemptuous, not to say snobbish. To his hostess in Taos when he got to America however, Mabel Luhan, he went a good deal further, and showed that his further acquaintance with the 'cinema people' had changed his opinion completely. He also said something else very significant as well:

> Their unrestraint and their wild, care-free love making amazed and at the same time infuriated him. He became acquainted with some of them. They were like a new species of creature he had never seen before. He watched and registered every move ... [he] made us *see* that ship; the long, slow passage through the blue sea, the reckless, sensational crowd on board ...[27]

That certainly changes things: he was obviously as much fascinated as repelled. And from an unpublished letter written by his wife, Frieda, on board the boat, it is clear that he spent

26 *4L* 287.

27 Mabel Dodge Luhan, *Lorenzo in Taos* (New York, 1932), p. 47.

a lot of time with the film crowd: she describes how this 'wild company of "filmstars"' came aboard

> who had worked with 800 natives in Tahiti, it costs millions ... Lawrence looks very good, better than ever. He doesn't work, people amuse him ...

He always worked on such voyages, so this laziness was obviously special. And a couple of days later she added to that letter:

> People play, people dance, people stuff themselves and flirt excessively – a new kind of people these. Or perhaps there have always been people like this – the mayflies – but they are all the same something else again ...[28]

It's clear that Frieda too was fascinated, and by no means repelled. When on shore in San Francisco, too, Lawrence went on seeing his 'shipboard friends' and reported that they were 'still a friendly company';[29] and he showed how little he was repelled by this experience of movie people by the fact that, within two days, he was again in a cinema. I would guess that this was almost certainly in the company of some of those movie experts, who would have known exactly where to take him in San Francisco to experience the latest cinematic developments:

> I went to a cinema and with jazz orchestra and a huge and voluminous organ. Either it is all crazy or I am going.[30]

[28] Frieda to Anna von Richthofen, 25 August – 1 September 1922 (HRC).
[29] *4L* 289.
[30] *4L* 290.

A very long way from Alvina bashing out her piano tunes in the tin-roofed cinema in Lumley, near Woodhouse; or, for that matter, from a moralistic artist deciding that film was wicked.

And it was, I think, with just that complexity of feelings as he had on that journey to San Francisco that Lawrence viewed cinema; as a repellent, utterly commercial and immoral industry, unreal to the core, trading off people's gullibility and having no standards of any kind – but also of being eternally fascinating, powerful and capable of incredible realism; detached from the normal restraints of morality, and at times drawing its audience into experiences that were haunting and unforgettable. He wrote a strange little poem in 1929 about film, which probably harks back to *Ben Hur*: but says something else too; it's called 'When I went to the film'.

> When I went to the film, and saw all the black-and-
>   white feelings that nobody felt,
> and heard the audience sighing and sobbing with all
>   the emotions they none of them felt,
> and saw them cuddling with rising passions they
>   none of them for a moment felt,
> and caught them moaning from close-up kisses,
>   black-and-white kisses that could not be felt,
> It was like being in heaven, which I am sure has a
>   white atmosphere upon which shadows of people,
>   pure personalities
> are cast in black and white, and move
> in flat ecstasy, supremely unfelt,
> and heavenly.[31]

It wasn't just film, to Lawrence, which made people like this; he is not attacking film so much as a whole kind of acted-up emotional self-conscious inauthenticity about *feelings* which he

[31] *Poems*, i. 443-4.

writes about because he *knows* it is part of his period's way of talking; and he is actually very funny about it and its unreality. Another very similar poem from the same period, and *not* about film, is called 'To Women, so far as I am Concerned':

> The feelings I don't have, I don't have.
> The feelings I don't have, I won't say I have.
> The feelings you say you have, you don't have.
> The feelings you would like us both to have, we neither of
> us have.
> The feelings people ought to have, they never have.
> If people say they've got feelings, you may be pretty sure
> they haven't got them.
> So if you want either of us to feel anything at all
> you'd better abandon all ideas of feelings altogether.[32]

Film, you see, seemed to Lawrence an arena where people (film-stars and audience alike) very often *did* pretend to have feelings when they didn't have them. And earlier he had of course painted his 'Close-up (Kiss)', which is all about the pretence of showing feelings which you most certainly don't have. We might add that it takes an artist in creating fiction (which he was) to be so fascinated with those whose fictional creations were fake as well as fictional.

So was he unredeemably against film? No. Think of him humming along in that cinema in the Strand in 1923, watching the film as if he were part of it, and saying 'over and over' '"How like it is, how like it is"': totally immersed. Think of him going to the cinema over and over again. Think of him praising John Dos Passos's novel *Manhattan Transfer* in 1927 for being 'a very complex film', for the way in which

32 *Poems*, i. 501.

> It is like a movie picture with an intricacy of different stories and no close-ups and no writing in between ...[33]

If a film was doing either something real or something complex, then he could admire it and love it and lose himself in it. It was when the film seemed palpably unreal, pretentious, pretending thrills and trading in unreal emotions, that he hated it or laughed at it.

It is also arguable that his own work shows the influence of film. Over and over again it is possible to see how his use of p.o.v. in his fiction is incredibly carefully controlled, exactly as in film. If for instance we ask the simple question 'who is speaking?' about the narrative passages between the characters' speeches, then it turns out that the narrator (and narrative) of his fiction is hardly ever neutral. The narrative constantly occupies the position of, and takes on the language of, the characters: it is just like the camera position constantly shifting so that we see X as Y sees him: we hardly ever *just* see the characters neutrally. And this way of narrating is intensely like film in its kind of control; though I suspect Lawrence would have denied the fact.

But even so, he would have agreed that there were things which film could do which writing could not do, for a professional writer. He responded happily to a telegram of 11 January 1924 from his American publisher which had run 'Had five thousand dollar offer cinema Women Love Shall I accept Cable'. At that date, $5000 was a very good lump sum: about £500, when he could live for a year on a little more than one hundred. Did he resent the prostitution of his work to the cinema? No. He answered the telegram with a telegram of his own, the shortest extant Lawrence letter: 'ALL RIGHT ACCEPT LAWRENCE'.[34] It could, of course, have been two words, not four: 'ALL RIGHT' is his concession to

33 *IR* 310:12-14.

34 *8L* 87.

cynicism, an admission that he is falling in with another man's scheme, not one he would probably have initiated. But he would write to Seltzer a few days later: 'I had your cable last week, and answered Accept – the $5000 for film rights of *Women in Love*'.[35] That film was (sadly) never made (none of Lawrence's works was filmed before the 1949 *Rocking Horse Winner*): but, long after his death, in 1954, Frieda (now Americanised) also wrote most cheerfully to her son Monty after a similar deal: 'I am having a wonderful time here ... We sold *Sons and Lovers* to the movie'.[36] That led to the Jack Cardiff film: and whatever you think of that film, I think Lawrence would totally have approved of Frieda's cheerful reaction on selling it 'to the movie'.

There is no recording of Lawrence's voice, no film of him. When Compton Mackenzie suggested taking a boat to the south Pacific, with Lawrence and others on board, to make 'a film record and a film novel all at once', Lawrence was not even tempted: 'though I like Mackenzie, I couldn't bear to be ravelled up [that is, entangled] in a film'.[37] People still seem to think that Lawrence was like Alan Bates playing that weird mixture of Lawrence and Birkin in the Russell film of *Women in Love*, being outrageously shocking in public at the garden table, reciting his poem 'Fig'. That kind of thing was in reality as far from Lawrence's public behaviour as one could imagine.

But his dramatic skill found its way into his novels and poems; the sense of a multitude of voices talking in his fictions is one that is hugely underestimated. People tend to imagine that it is Lawrence himself banging on and on, all the time, in his own voice. Just the opposite. One of his break-

35 *4L* 558.

36 Frieda Lawrence, *Memoirs and Correspondence* (1961), p. 349.

37 *3L* 504.

throughs as a writer was to perfect an immensely subtle sequence of narrative voices, which interweave with each other: pure external narrative in Lawrence's fiction is actually rather rare. Let me draw tonight to an end with an especially interesting account of Lawrence as performer, from one of those who saw him at his happiest, David Garnett in 1912.

> ... the person whom Lawrence most constantly made fun of was himself. He mimicked himself ruthlessly and continually and, as he told a story, acted ridiculous versions of a shy and gawky Lawrence being patronised by literary lions, of a winsome Lawrence charming his landlady ... of a bad-tempered whining Lawrence picking a quarrel with Frieda over nothing. There was more than a little of Charlie Chaplin in his acting: but bitterer, less sentimental.[38]

It would be Chaplin[39] whom Lawrence would single out in his *Studies in Classic American Literature* as one of the most characteristically *real* things in North America,[40] and whom, in 1928, he would again single out, after complaining that people thought Rudolf Valentino the epitome of the handsome:

> To stick to the film – there is a greater essential beauty in Charlie Chaplin's odd face, than ever there was in Valentino's. There is a bit of true beauty in Chaplin's brows and eyes, a gleam of something pure. But our sense of beauty is so bruised and clumsy, we don't see it, and don't know it when we do see it.[41]

38 Nehls, i. 177.

39 Charles Chaplin (1889-1977) had been enormously successful as a British film-maker, actor and comedian working in Hollywood; for DHL in 1923, he had most recently directed *The Kid* (1920).

40 *Studies* 11:24-5.

41 *LEA* 146:7-12.

I very much like that pairing of English dramatic genius: Charlie and Bert – with Lawrence the bitterer one.

D. H. Lawrence: A Single Life

Naples, 16 June 2001

I was only able to attend the very last day of the 2001 International Conference in Naples (on the Friday I was external examining in Swansea, and had to get to Gatwick for a late flight to Naples, in order to give my conference paper on the Saturday afternoon). I had planned the lecture as a complete surprise for its audience: a wholly fictional account of Lawrence's life, which I thought would only be interesting if people imagined I would be talking about the forthcoming Penguin biography (a 'Single' life as opposed to the CUP three-volume life). I was distressed to discover, when I joined the conference on the Saturday morning, that my brief synopsis (which gave the game away) had been printed in the conference programme. But it was too late to change anything. It's perhaps worth recording that the 'Elfriede' whom Lawrence meets in Heidelberg, in this account, is my wife's grandmother, whom I knew slightly (I never asked her about Lawrence, though). I have revised this piece extensively.

This is at present the conclusion of Chapter Three in my *Single Life* – my single-volume life – of Lawrence, which Penguin Books have commissioned for publication in 2005.

> On the morning of Sunday 3rd March Lawrence took the train into Nottingham, almost certainly getting off at the Carrington station he would have known from his last two years at the High School, and then walking up the Mansfield Road, into the airy, middle-class, north-eastern suburbs. The day was sunny, spring-like and warm; the walk would have taken him fifteen minutes or so. He may have arrived early, or Weekley may have been delayed in coming home; either way, his host was not there. Lawrence was shown into the drawing room, with its big windows looking out over the garden where children were playing, to be greeted

> by Weekley's wife. And the next half-an-hour changed his life.[1]

No. Let me redraft those last two sentences:

> Lawrence was shown into the drawing room, with its big windows looking out over the garden where children were playing. Frieda Weekley was indisposed and did not come down for lunch. Weekley arrived late to give Lawrence advice, but the latter left the house without having met the woman whose reputation for beauty and whose later, uninhibited behaviour became legendary in University circles.

So similar, so different ... biographical narrative easily makes the known the inevitable. But in our own lives we constantly reminisce about what might have happened if, when the road forked, we had taken the other way: not just because, as Robert Frost says in 'The Road not Taken', it might have 'made all the difference',[2] but because in the 'growing, dizzying web of divergent, convergent and parallel times' in which arguably we exist, and which necessarily contain '*all* possibilities' – 'Time forks, perpetually, into countless futures'[3] – Lawrence only met Frieda in one such future. I'm quoting Borges' story 'The Garden of Forking Paths'. And if Lawrence had not met Frieda this time ... then he would have walked back down the Mansfield Road, and Frieda Weekley

1 This became my *D. H. Lawrence: The Life of an Outsider* (2005), p. 107.

2 Robert Frost, 'The Road Not Taken', *Mountain Interval* (New York, 1916), p. 8.

3 Jose Luis Borges, *Collected Fictions*, tr. Andrew Hurley (1999), p. 127.

would have remained merely a name to him. So what might have happened down *this* particular fork, into *this* alternative future?

He walked back down the Mansfield Road ... and of course went to Germany, as planned, in May 1912, to stay with his cousins the Krenkows in Waldbröl, in the Rhineland. He took with him the almost-finished manuscript of his novel *Paul Morel*, knowing that he wanted to revise it. He believed he would stay abroad 'probably a year'.[4] Jessie Chambers had given him some excellent advice about the novel; and so had Edward Garnett. Lawrence reckoned he could probably finish the job in a month. He also intended to write essays for the *Westminster Gazette*; his acquaintance with Walter de la Mare had given him an opening that he hoped to be able to exploit.

Lawrence's weeks with his mother's relations in Waldbröl were profoundly uneventful; he worked on his novel, flirted with his cousin Johanna, and visited Bonn and the Drachenfels with the Krenkow family. He also wrote a sketch for the *Westminster Gazette* describing a day when overpowering heat broke up a burgeoning *tendresse* with a woman very like Johanna; but Waldbröl was not a good place to write publishable journalism (nothing ever seemed to happen: the passage of a pair of oxen down the main street was an event). By the end of May he had completed his revision of *Paul Morel* and had proudly sent it off to its potential publisher Heinemann; and, taking a break from his work, he followed the advice of the Krenkows and went to visit Dresden, staying in a small pension they knew of near the centre of the city. Here he was at least able to write some more German sketches, about the fashionable people he saw

4 E. T. 196.

walking on the Brühler Terrasse, about the ordinary people staying in his pension, about the tourists he saw visiting the city's churches and art galleries. To these he added a recreation of sleepy Waldbröl, written with some distance and irony; he had every reason to be proud of what he was accomplishing, on holiday from the novel. He posted his sketches to the *Westminster*, and headed back to Waldbröl.

It was a nine-hour train journey, with two changes: and what he found waiting for him was a letter from William Heinemann turning down *Paul Morel* flat, because it was immoral, and asking where the manuscript should be sent. [5] All Lawrence could do was write helplessly to Edward Garnett about what had been done to him, and send him *Paul Morel*; and Garnett came to the rescue, as with *The Trespasser*, and sent Lawrence a list of the things he would have to do, if Duckworth were going to accept the book. Lawrence gratefully agreed to do everything Garnett suggested. What he really needed now was to spend a couple of months rewriting the book.

But above all he had to decide whether to stay on in Germany. He could have continued to live with the Krenkows, but his letters suggest that he was no longer entirely happy there: in July he referred to Johanna's husband – with whom he had occasionally gone drinking – as 'a bit tipsy and a big fool'.[6] Above all, Waldbröl was extremely dull; he did not want to base his entire writing experience of Germany on eight weeks spent in rural Rhineland and ten days in Dresden. He wanted to travel; and a suggestion from Walter de la Mare proved helpful. The *Westminster Gazette* was not likely to print more than a couple of sketches of German life of the kind he had written so far, but de la Mare had friends in Heidelberg: and he suggested that Lawrence should offer the *Westminster* a monthly 'Letter from Heidelberg'

5 *1L* 421 n. 4.
6 *1L* 406.

describing his experiences. De la Mare thought that his friends could help Lawrence get pupils for English lessons, and they could also introduce him to student life. A monthly essay would not tax Lawrence too much; he would be able to work at *Paul Morel*; and he could also earn some money.

Lawrence set off to Heidelberg on 15 July 1912, and with the help of de la Mare's friends the Meyers (and a small loan from them) he found lodgings in Turner Straße near the South Cemetery. With the Meyers' assistance he acquired his first pupil, and settled into a routine of writing in the morning, teaching after lunch, and socialising with friends in the evening. The *Westminster* had agreed to pay him £7 each for six 'Letters from Heidelberg' (the first of which would appear on 21 September 1912); and best of all, Garnett had persuaded Duckworth to pay him his fifty pounds owing for *The Trespasser*. On 1 September, six weeks after arriving in Heidelberg, Lawrence was able to repay the Meyers what he had borrowed and felt secure for the rewriting of the novel.

It was in Heidelberg, too, that he found the first woman to attract him (as opposed to the first woman who would flirt with him) since leaving England. The fair-haired married sister of one of his pupils regularly came to collect her younger brother at the end of his lesson, and one sultry afternoon arrived to tell Lawrence that her brother was ill and could not come. All that we know about what happened next comes from information in three letters that Lawrence wrote to Edward Garnett. On the first occasion they met, Elfriede (we only know her first name) and Lawrence apparently went for a walk through the south cemetery (refreshing, green and shady on an afternoon in early August); they sat on a bench shielded by a bush from the main path, and kissed; and they agreed to meet there again the following afternoon. When they did, Lawrence persuaded Elfriede to come back with him to Turner Straße. What happened then we have no idea: but the letters to Garnett suggest an affair. They probably met a number of times during the autumn (there is another reference to Elfriede in a letter Lawrence wrote to McLeod in

November). It seems very probable that Paul Morel's relationship with the married Clara in the re-written *Paul Morel* owed something to Lawrence's meeting and relationship with this almost unknown, fair-haired married German woman.

For, all the time that he was living in Heidelberg, Lawrence was hard at work on the novel. Garnett had thought it formless, without a central and controlling theme; he had also believed the opening too detailed, and the ending too weak. Jessie, too, in letters she was now starting to write to Lawrence, seems to have been arguing that Paul's relationship with Miriam should *not* be a sexual one. Lawrence could not afford to resist Garnett's desire to help him, but he also thought that the opening would not need cutting if the theme of the son's love for his mother were brought out more strongly. By the middle of December he has finished this final version of *Paul Morel*, and wrote Garnett a letter designed to show that he had done everything Garnett wanted; he also wrote to Jessie admitting that Paul's relationship with Miriam had indeed become sexual: 'I'm sorry it turned out as it has. You'll have to go on forgiving me.'[7]

With the novel finished, but with no prospect of further money apart from the monthly £7 from the *Westminster* (and it had been made clear that there could be no extension of his six-month contract), and with his family urging him to come back to England – Lawrence decided to bring his life in Heidelberg to an end. He finished his last 'Letter from Heidelberg' in mid-January, using material from a snowy excursion up the Neckar valley – 'we drink with the mountain peasants in the Gasthaus, and dance a little' he wrote to Garnett;[8] whether he was accompanied by Elfriede or not we have no way of knowing, but a character called 'Thusnelda'

7 *1L* 408.
8 *1L* 441.

appears in the last 'Letter' as the narrator's companion – and with whom would he otherwise be drinking and dancing? He finished his teaching, packed up around 20 February 1913, and took the train back to Calais and the boat to Dover. So far as we know, he never saw Elfriede again.

He had, however, attempted to persuade her to accompany him to England. She had told him how unhappy she was in her marriage. Lawrence told Garnett: 'She is ripping – you must above all things meet her'.[9] But Garnett never saw her. We have to conclude that – like Clara Dawes in *Paul Morel* – she refused to leave her husband or to accompany Lawrence abroad.

On his way back to the Midlands he naturally called in at the Cearne to see Garnett, to find the latter in the process of making a few small cuts to the novel. Lawrence was grateful for his friend's efforts, but retained his opinion of the book's merits without them. Nevertheless, he badly needed another novel in print. On 1 May 1913, *Paul Morel* was finally published – and seems to have fallen almost dead from the press. It apparently sold only 400 copies in its first six months; many reviewers were actively hostile. The *Evening News* mourned the fact that the fine writer of *The Trespasser* should have bogged himself down in a tedious family chronicle; the *Morning Post* complained that immorality in the Midlands is really just tedious; and – aggravatingly – an anonymous piece in the *English Review* complained that the book's central theme (the son's love for his mother) was not only sentimental but problematic, given what recent psychoanalytic theory had suggested: the reviewer implied that Lawrence knew nothing about Freud, and that it would have helped him if he had. Nearly all the reviews, however,

9 *1L* 384.

complained that the book contained a great deal of unnecessary sexuality. There was, as a result, no library demand for the book, and Duckworth lost money on it; it would be the last Lawrence book he would publish. Lawrence was left distressed and angry: 'my cursed, rotten-boned, pappy-hearted countrymen', he commented.[10] Whilst at the Cearne, he had worked with Garnett to put together a book of poems, but after *Paul Morel*, Duckworth was in no mood to accept a poetry book, and Lawrence in no mood to hawk it around other publishers.

There were also distinct signs of a cooling off in his relationship with Garnett. Lawrence blamed him, in part, for the failure of *Paul Morel* and Duckworth's refusal to take the poetry book, and by the summer of 1913 the two men were writing to each other only occasionally.

For it had always been as a literary mentor that Garnett had been most helpful: and Lawrence's career as a writer was now in crisis. There had not been much left of the £50 for *The Trespasser* when he came back from Heidelberg (he had spent rather heavily there), while Duckworth's advance of £50 for *Paul Morel* was obviously not going to be added to (and Lawrence had debts to pay off, too). Before going to Germany, back in 1912, he had considered what he might do if the German expedition came to nothing – 'come back and work as a teacher' – and this is what, a little half-heartedly, he now felt obliged to do. Back in Eastwood, he went to live with his sister Ada in her lodgings in Percy Street. And he did his best to get into Secondary teaching, rather than the elementary teaching he had done so far – his German was now of a very passable standard. But he had no luck at all, wherever he tried. He spent the months between March and July 1913 in Eastwood, well aware that he could not afford to go on living with (or living off) his sister Ada. She was, anyway, getting married to Eddie Clarke in August, and there

10 *1L* 422.

was no way he was going to go and live with his other married sister Emily in Glasgow, or with his rather sanctimonious elder brother George in Nottingham. In a desultory way he tried to put together a volume of *German Sketches*, but that seemed rather pointless too. He seemed to have spent most of his time back in Eastwood drinking – 'Everybody in Eastwood is so jolly – I am always out' he told McLeod[11] – and railing against publishers. He also spent more time than usual with his father and seems to have got on quite well with him; but his father was shortly going into lodgings. Lawrence apparently made no attempt to get in touch again with Helen Corke, and although he remained on friendly terms with McLeod, in Croydon, at no point did he suggest going down to see him. Rather more significantly, there is no evidence of his attempting to see Alice Dax, only ten miles away in Shirebrook. Their affair had petered out before he went to Germany, and she had had her second child in October 1912; Lawrence may have felt that there was now no way back to the situation which had brought them together in the summer of 1911.

The drinking was, of course, nothing new in his life. In August 1910 it had been obvious to someone who had known him all his life that the 'temperate habits which his mother had tried to foster in him, had now almost gone'.[12] He had remarked in a letter 'I like very much the taste of vermouth'; and one of the things that had initially sealed his friendship with Garnett in 1911 had been drinking together ('wine in the ingle nook').[13] And at the end of the year after his mother's death, he had told Louie Burrows

> Sometimes when I have the horrors – the ashy sort – I drink a little – to mend the fire of my faith and hope,

11 *1L* 368.
12 *EY* 269.
13 *1L* 206, 315.

> you see ... The Good God made whiskey, as I have rather lately discovered ... too much whiskey is better than too much melancholies – and a drinking bout better than a bout of ferocious blues.[14]

Back in 1910 he had remarked 'Good Lord, I don't drink. Think of the paternal example.' But when thoroughly miserable, as at the time of his mother's death, he had drunk to ward off the 'ferocious blues': and in October 1911 he had written to a friend how 'night after night one stumbles up, half blind with work or with wastefulness'; he was drinking alone in his Croydon lodgings, and recorded writing letters 'towards midnight, with an empty glass at one's elbow'. [15] He had also drunk with his landlord when the opportunity presented itself: 'Pa Jones has had a bottle of whiskey for a christmas box, and we're just going to have a drop'. Visiting friends in Brighton in December 1910, it was natural for him to have 'a glass of Irish ... but I prefer Scotch'. May Holbrook, immediately he arrived in Germany in May 1912, had heard how he was 'already drinking my third pint of German beer ... Lord, these German mugs'.[16] He reproduced drunkenness – not just how it looks, but how it feels – surprisingly often in his writing, most notably in the scenes of George's drunkenness in *The White Peacock*.

His one public appearance in Eastwood during these months in 1913 was to address the Literary Society of the Congregational Church on 3 July, when he lectured on Germany; the account of the lecture in the *Eastwood & Kimberley Advertiser* says only that 'Mr. Lawrence sounded disillusioned with modern Germany; it is perhaps a pity that so many of our young men today are disillusioned with their lives, and we wonder what the future holds for them.' It was

14 *1L* 218.

15 *1L* 218, 311, 181.

16 *1L* 212, 218, 390.

an oddly prophetic remark. Lawrence sank into a more and more miserable state as the summer went on, failing to get employment as a teacher, and not writing. Back in 1910, feeling the onset of 'a blank space', he would 'begin to shut my teeth' and drink: 'Gott in Himmel! The nights are rather bad ...'[17] But at least he had then had Louie Burrows to talk to and, in his own way, to love. Now, in the summer of 1913, he seems simply to have gone from pub to pub: 'I went in the Golden Crown and a couple of other places'.[18]

What might have made a difference was the fact that he was seeing Jessie Chambers once again; she was still living in Nottingham. As Lawrence got depressed over the summer, he also started to go into Nottingham at weekends, and Jessie sometimes came out to Eastwood. They do not seem to have had a close relationship, however. Jessie simply wanted to encourage him to try and overcome his distaste for writing. In her memoir of Lawrence, she remembered her attempts to encourage him:

> He crossed to the hearth and sat there in silence, elbow on knee, his head resting on his hand, staring into the fire. It was the familiar spectacle; Lawrence in the grip of forces that pulled him with equal power in opposite directions. But what I saw at the moment was his utter loneliness, his separation, as it seemed from everything else in life ... Presently he said in a halting way, as if struggling to find the exact words, 'When we are not together, since we have been parted, I'm not the same man. *I* can't write poetry' ... his tone was the extremity of sincerity and of despair.[19]

17 *1L* 219.
18 *1L* 372.
19 E. T. 200.

He had gone to her for support, for comfort, to try and re-establish some kind of link with the days before his illness, and before his abortive trip to Germany: but deep down he knew, as he told his friend George Neville, that 'the old days have gone; gone altogether; gone beyond recall'.[20]

It has not often been remarked what a profoundly depressive character Lawrence had always been, from his earliest years, marked as they were by his bouts of inexplicable tears as a child: he once remarked that 'really, for me, it's been a devilish time ever since I was born'.[21] It is so easy to be impressed by his apparently effortless creativity when things were going well – though even then his manner could be what Jessie once called it, 'painfully bright'[22] – that we can overlook this intensely gloomy other self, regularly experiencing what he vividly called 'cold ashes of horrors'.[23] The word 'ash' – the sense of ash in the mouth – was in fact a constant reference in his writing and letters: it was very clear in his letters during 1911, for example, especially during the autumn, when he went through something similar to what he was now suffering during the long summer of 1913. 'I am a sad dog myself, pretty often',[24] he wrote, and person after person agreed: 'Lawrence often seemed very unhappy'; 'he was held back by the fact that he was not happy'.[25] He attended his sister's wedding on 13 August; but that was the end of his Eastwood life. He had to decide where to live and to eke out the little money he had left: something hard for a man now bout-drinking. He chose to go into lodgings in Jacksdale, three miles from Eastwood, where there was at least one woman (her name was Pauline) whom he had got to

[20] G. H. Neville, *A Memoir of D. H. Lawrence*, ed. Carl Baron (Cambridge, 1981), p. 155.

[21] *1L* 421.

[22] E. T. 200.

[23] *1L* 218.

[24] *2L* 29.

[25] Nehls, i. 65, 72.

know back in January 1912 – she may well have been the woman his sister found him 'kissing like nuts' there: but its real advantage was that it was 'simply snyed with pubs'.[26]

At all events, it was in Jacksdale, with Jessie's encouragement, that he actually started to write a story based on the life of Robert Burns (a working-class writer, of course, damaged by drink). He wrote some thirty pages before destroying the story; he told Arthur McLeod that it was not worth a ha'penny, of his or anyone else's time. Just a few pages of a draft survive, sent to McLeod, and perhaps significantly they describe the Burns character's drinking habits:

> He was by nature temperate. Being sensitive and emotional, his nausea prevented him from drinking too much. He felt, when he had drunk a certain amount, that his stomach was full enough, and the thought of further drinking nauseated him. But now, almost deliberately, with the greatest good-humour and apparent sanity, he began at twenty six to drink in order to get drunk ... he became a bout-drinker, having at intervals these bouts of three or four days of brandy drinking, when he was drunk for the whole time. He did not think about it. A deep resentment burned in him. He kept aloof from any woman, antagonistic.[27]

The connection Lawrence made there between alcohol, anger, separateness from others and depression was almost certainly true of his own life too.

In September 1913, his sister Ada felt obliged to start giving

26 *1L* 369, 372.

27 R MS version 27:14-17, 18:37-39

him money (in the first instance it could be disguised as a twenty-seventh birthday present); luckily her marriage to Eddie Clarke meant that she was financially a little better off than before. Lawrence survived in Jacksdale, in lodgings on the unlovely Alfreton Road, until the middle of October 1913. Very few letters survive from his time there: one extraordinary one, to McLeod, dated 9 October, described his feeling

> like a thing whose roots are all straining on their hold, and whose elemental life, that blind source, surges backwards and forwards darkly in a chaos, like something which is threatened with spilling out of its own vessel.[28]

Jessie saw him for the last time after he had hitched a lift into Nottingham in a cart on Saturday 12 October. For once he was not drunk – was, rather, in his own words 'cold-headed as mathematics'[29] – but he asked her, according to her memoir, 'What does it matter?' and answered himself '*Nothing* matters'.[30] Another friend had once heard him say – 'in a voice that broke as if strangled' – 'Then what does matter?'[31] He walked back to Jacksdale the same night, unable to afford a train, but this time in what the local paper called on the Monday 'a tempest of wind and rain'; he presumably arrived soaking wet. He was discovered dead in his room two days later. What had happened, we shall probably never know. Perhaps, as in 1911, the wet clothes in which he fell asleep led to pneumonia; though this time we can also blame depression and alcohol for his disregard of his health. The coroner held an inquest at the Nelson Inn in Eastwood on Tuesday 15

28 *LAH* 172:38–173:2.

29 *1L* 247.

30 E. T. 188.

31 Nehls, iii. 619.

October and decided that the death was due to 'natural causes'.

Lawrence was interred in Eastwood cemetery, in the grave where his brother Ernest and his mother Lydia were buried. His whole family attended: Emily came down from Glasgow, and Lawrence's father Arthur was there, of course, on the arms of his two daughters, while Edward Garnett came up from London; so did Austin Harrison of the *English Review*, and Walter de la Mare. Brief obituary notices appeared in a couple of London newspapers. His old friend George Neville travelled down from Staffordshire, but Pauline did not attend; according to Neville's unpublished memoir, Ada had told her in no uncertain terms to keep away.

After Lawrence's death, Edward Garnett persuaded Heinemann to bring out a volume of Lawrence's poetry, *Love Poems and Others*; it was published on Thursday 6 August 1914 (an inauspicious moment), and was completely ignored (only some 80 copies were ever sold, according to Heinemann). In September 1925, to mark what would have been his fortieth birthday, his sister Ada published privately that notoriously rare book, *Sketches of Germany and England,* a collection of her brother's travel writings. In the late 1920s, too, Duckworth republished *Paul Morel* and this time the book enjoyed reasonable sales; it has been in and out of print ever since that date, and Broadview Books have recently republished it in their series Twentieth Century Classics. *The White Peacock* and *The Trespasser* have however never been reprinted, and there are a number of plays in the hands of Lawrence's surviving relatives, as well as many poems and stories. Such a conference as this suggests that Lawrence's reputation may indeed be recovering, and it is my ambition with this brief biographical sketch to help encourage that recovery. In particular, Lawrence should be known as a letter writer, and it is a tribute to Frank Kermode's acumen that he should have included a 1910 letter by Lawrence in his *Oxford Book of*

Letters.[32]

We have to ask whether, if D. H. Lawrence had met a partner who could have helped him combat his tendency to depression, his life might have taken another path. Perhaps not: pursuing what he once called 'life single, not life double'[33] was probably what he was going to do in the end, come what may. Jessie Chambers apparently believed that she could, lovingly, have saved him, but that also seems highly questionable: it wasn't saving that he wanted. Perhaps a partner who simply, constantly, demanded relationship from him – who refused to *allow* him to be 'single' – would have helped most. If Garnett had stuck to him, or he had stuck to Garnett, that might also have helped him: we need constantly to look to Lawrence's problem with sustaining close relationships if we are to get any where near understanding him. The fact that he could be terrifyingly single and detached is perhaps the most obvious thing about him, apart from his equally tremendous, paradoxical and in the end nostalgic desire to be part of a group. Above all, if he could have continued to write, that would probably have helped him more than anything else. But it is, instead, the thread of a tragically brief, Single, un-diverging, non-convergent Life which we are here gathered to pursue ... and that would be as true if he had lived for another twenty years as it is of his death at the age of only twenty-eight.

Note

32 DHL to Rachel Annand Taylor (3 December 1910), *The Oxford Book of Letters*, ed. Frank and Anita Kermode (Oxford 1995), pp. 439-41.

33 *AR* 128:23.

Nothing in history before 3 March 1912 has been altered or added to. Extant documents subsequent to 3 March 1912 have not been altered, but events have been fictionalised, and new documents invented. All Lawrence's own words are authentic, although some have been re-assigned to earlier or later dates, works or contexts. Historical facts remain unchanged. The fiction attempts to inhabit the empty spaces existing between the surviving outcrops of history.

'Ways of Saying Goodbye': tech. script

D. H. Lawrence Pavilion, Nottingham, Friday 13 June 2003

I gave my retirement lecture in June 2003, and – after it – received a lot of criticism for my remarks about the School of English. My complaints that no one with specialised Lawrence expertise had been appointed to take charge of the D. H. Lawrence Research Centre might be thought to have been addressed twelve months later, when Dr Sean Matthews was appointed to direct the Centre, and I was assured that it had been Management's plan throughout to make such an appointment. It might however also be judged to have been in consequence of the storm of protest which this lecture generated that the appointment was made. And it was only in 2010, with the appointment of Dr Andrew Harrison, that the School of English Studies took on someone with specialist research expertise in Lawrence Studies. To that extent, my Jeremiad might seem to have been justified.

This is a lecture which, to have its proper effect on a reader, requires music and sound effects. I reproduce therefore the script in the hands of the technician on the evening of Friday 13 June 2003, in an attempt to reproduce a little of what happened.

[House lights full up: lights on stage as well if possible, in audience's eyes]
[Four minutes before start: music begins]
{*Luciano Berio,* rendering*: 'Quattro versioni originali della "Ritirata notturna di Madrid"' (1975). RCA Victor Red Seal 09026 68894 2: track 5 from start to 3.58'*}
[BLACK OUT]

[explosion, a.loud.a.p.] [cue smoke]

[JW enters stage right during black out]

[LIGHTS UP. JW at lectern. Smoke from lectern.]

I always wanted to make an entrance as the demon king: and I shall have few further chances.

That music was *inaugurating* music, if ever there was any. The late and great Luciano Berio's crazy and wonderful version of the Night Watch movement of Boccherini's guitar quintet was actually written as a concert *opening* piece for the La Scala opera house orchestra in 1975. I should really have let the Night Watch make its full pass-by, to its final retreat, fainter and fainter into the night – but decided to give you only the arrival. It takes me, however, straight into the Janus paradox at the heart of tonight: 'hail' is implicitly part of 'farewell'. I'm enormously pleased that you've all come, and I greet you happily; but I also feel extremely up-beat about retiring, and am not going to spend 40 minutes regretting doing so. I may be leaving, along with that Night Watch, but am not going gently into any kind of Good Night. Yet the opposite of an Inaugural lecture is, I reckon, a Decommissioning one: 'to take a ship or aeroplane (etc.) out of service, and especially to close down a nuclear reactor.'[1] In the next 40 minutes I intend to close myself down by finding ways of saying goodbye but also by extending the idea of goodbye into my own work on Lawrence.

The first, the saddest kind of goodbye I want to say is to Lawrence Studies in the School of English at Nottingham. I never imagined that when I retired, the School of English would not ensure that someone with interests in Lawrence would be appointed: not necessarily a Lawrence specialist – but with interests. The only question was at what level. Before I applied for retirement, however, just to be sure, I went to see the Pro-Vice Chancellor responsible for English Studies; and was assured by him that Management took on-going research in Lawrence in the School of English Studies very seriously, and would certainly safeguard it: I need have no fears. The advertisement put out by the School of English this spring for posts in Modern English Literature (*two* posts) – an advertisement constructed when I was away on research leave – made, however, no reference to Lawrence at all: a signal was thus being sent. The School failed to shortlist anyone with an interest in Lawrence for one post (as yet

1 *OED.*

uninterviewed), and last week failed to appoint the one Lawrence specialist it interviewed for the other post. (It appointed a very brilliant man whose research interests are not in Lawrence, but in Joyce, and especially in Joyce manuscripts: of which there is of course not one at the University of Nottingham.)

On the explicit instructions of my head of School, I have already turned away a number of Ph.D. applicants who wanted to come and study Lawrence at Nottingham, which has the best resources in the world for such study. Only last Tuesday afternoon I answered an e-mail from an American woman who had done an MA degree and who wanted to come to Nottingham (having looked at the websites of the Library and the Lawrence Research Centre): and I had to tell her that there was no point in her applying, as there would be no one in English Studies to supervise her. I suggested that she apply to a Midlands University – I mentioned Sheffield and Leicester in particular – and come and use the resources at Nottingham. As I am sure you know, library holdings are regularly used by colleagues from Nottingham Trent. I had to send another e-mail to a Japanese student who wanted to come to the University for two months next year with a scholarship, just to study Lawrence; I advised her not to come. These were heartbreaking things to have to do, after the work of the past ten years. The MA course on Lawrence and the Modern Age – which will have 4 to 6 students next year – will only run for one, maximum two years more, and that entirely because of the extreme dedication of Peter Preston (not of course in English Studies at all).

Turning down potential Ph.D. students is a bad business at the best of times: turning down Ph.D. students when you have the best facilities for their work in the country is absurd. I have been told that one reason why I am not being replaced is because I am irreplaceable. That's just a face-saving formula; supervising Ph.D. students is something any academic can do (even a young one, with joint supervision).

And it was only when I read the documentation which the

School sent to the candidates who applied for the recently advertised posts that I found that the D. H. Lawrence Research Centre (which Peter Preston founded in 1991) is, without a word of consultation with me or with Peter, its joint directors, about to 'come under the aegis of a new Centre for Regional Language, Literature and Culture'. That means the Lawrence Research Centre is being downgraded to being part of something else: which, considering that there will be no one in English Studies either to run it, or to take research students who would be part of it, is perhaps just as well. Neither Peter Preston nor I was, however ever informed of this decision, let alone consulted about it. I have (after demanding it) received a grudging apology for this.

But it looks to me as if the decision to let Lawrence studies go in the School of English was taken some time ago; and the failure to appoint anyone who will teach Lawrence is a natural concomitant of that decision. The School has, against the explicit commitment of Management, ensured that the magnificent and extraordinary library holdings will not now be of interest or use to any member of its staff. For a research-led University Department, this is astonishing. It is, obviously, a sign of my own political ineptitude that I have allowed things to get to this point; but I must say that I feel utterly miserable about it. All I can be grateful for is that Peter Preston, in Continuing Education, and my colleagues in the library at Nottingham – I must single out Dr Dorothy Johnston – have done far more than anyone in English Studies to promote Lawrence in the University. It was with Dorothy that I organised a series of Lawrence events to take place through the year, in this building, of which this is the last (and to none of which a single member of staff of English Studies ever came before tonight: welcome, colleagues). But even while I acknowledge that support, I realise that I have fundamentally failed in what I came to Nottingham for – to advance an area of study. That is, you will be glad to hear, the saddest story I shall be telling tonight: the only really regretful goodbye.

However, as there so many people here tonight connected with the study, the writing and the publication of Lawrence, who believe (as I do) that the teaching of Lawrence is something appropriate to a University School of English, and as there still *is* a D. H. Lawrence Research Centre (until it becomes merely an aspect of something regional), I intend to talk about Lawrence tonight; and I want to say a little about Lawrence and Farewell. It is arguable that John Keats and D. H. Lawrence are the two best letter writers in English, but when it came to farewell, Keats had skills which Lawrence simply did not possess. I have always admired Christopher Ricks' book on Keats, and how he dwells on the way that Keats – brilliantly – dealt in letters with the difficulties of saying goodbye:

> You know at taking leave of a party at a door way, sometimes a Man dallies and foolishes and gets awkward, and does not know how to make off to advantage – Good bye – well – good-bye – and yet he does not – go – good bye and so on – well – good bless you –

Keats learned from his own example: one letter to his young sister ends:

> — Good bye I've an appoantment – can't stop pon word – good bye – now don't get up – open the door myself go-o-o d bye – see ye Monday

And it was of course Keats who wrote in his own last letter (to his friend Charles Brown) how 'I can scarcely bid you good bye even in a letter. I always made an awkward bow': and that small joke is a wonderful way of saying goodbye, tenderly, in the very act of declaring that he could only do it awkwardly. As Ricks says, 'It must be the least awkward bow ever made.'[2]

2 Christopher Ricks, *Keats and Embarrassment* (Oxford 1974), pp.

By comparison, Lawrence's farewells either refer exclusively to the ending of relationships (all eleven uses of the word 'Good-bye' in his *Complete Poems* refer to lovers parting), or – in his correspondence – are either downright nasty – or non-existent. He never admitted his final illness, for reasons I shall be going into later, so in fact there is nothing valedictory in his correspondence. The first edition of his letters, published in 1932, however ended, rather wonderfully, with a postscript to a last letter which ran 'This place no good': [3] a final moving on. As is the way of scholarship, however, that 'last' letter has been replaced by four others, written six days later, none of which exudes the least frisson of farewell: one ends 'I'm in bed, a bit dismal', another ends with a compliment to the Aga Khan, who had just visited him in the sanatorium, the third says that moving out of the sanatorium is a good idea, the fourth (and longest) ends by saying that the clay head Jo Davidson had just modelled of him was 'mediocre'.[4] Nothing much there to research as a mode of saying goodbye. And when it came to saying goodbye to people in a more absolute way, Lawrence could be absolutely savage. We don't know how a very final letter to Katherine Mansfield ended, because the manuscript no longer exists, though the scraps of phrases which do survive are horrid;[5] but a farewell letter to John Middleton Murry is a real MOAB[6] of a letter. Murry had rejected some pieces of writing Lawrence had done for him, and in the most

---

215, 212, 219.

3 *The Letters of D. H. Lawrence*, ed. Aldous Huxley (Heinemann, 1932), p. 853.

4 *7L* 652-3.

5 *3L* 470.

6 *3L* 467-8. Cf. GBU-43/B, 'Mother of All Bombs' (or 'Massive Ordnance Air Blast'): the successor to the BLU-82 Daisy Cutter. Planned for use by the US Armed Forces in Iraq, and much discussed in 2003.

offhand way too. Lawrence wrote to him, on 30 January 1920:

> I have no doubt you 'didn't like them' ... But as a matter of fact, what it amounts to is that you are a dirty little worm, and you take the ways of a dirty little worm. But now let me tell you at last that I know it – not that it's anything new: and let it be plainly understood between you and me, that I consider you a dirty little worm: and so, deposit your dirty bit of venom where you like; at any rate we know what to expect.[7]

Wheewew. The very paucity of the phrasing – the way the horrid little phrase comes back, and back – is in its own way, of course, masterly. But I'd not want to get many letters like that. Lawrence's 'final' letter to Bertrand Russell in September 1915 had left Russell considering suicide [8] (which he congratulated himself, many years later, on not attempting).

But Lawrence's letters after the deaths of others – his participations in grief – are, over and over again, touching, tender, sympathetic. Just one, as an example: Sally Hopkin, the wife of an old Eastwood friend, had died while Lawrence was in America: and Lawrence wrote to Hopkin.

> Sallie had a fine adventurous life of the spirit, a fine adventurous life. And it's the adventure counts, not the success ... the rest of the journey she goes with us like a passenger now, instead of a straining traveller ... There will be another grave in that cemetery now, down Church Street [where Lawrence's mother and brother were buried]. It makes me feel I am growing

7 *3L* 467-8.

8 *2L* 392 & n.5.

old.

Never mind, one must strike camp, and pack up the things, and go on.

With love, that belongs to the old life.

D. H. Lawrence

England seems full of graves to me.[9]

Lawrence died too young himself for many of his contemporaries to have pre-deceased him; all the same, his writing about the death of Maurice Magnus is a classic; as is his letter to the widow of Harry Crosby, in January 1930, when he himself had only weeks to live. What *do* you say to the woman whose husband has died by shooting his mistress and then himself? Lawrence wrote to Caresse Crosby:

> don't you try to recover yourself too soon – it is much better to be a little blind and stunned for a time longer, and not make efforts to see or to feel. Work is the best, and a certain numbness, a merciful numbness. It was too dreadful a blow – and it was wrong.[10]

I think that is general where it needs to be, and precise where it can be. And Lawrence was himself dying.

But, as I said, one of the most remarkable things he did as a writer was not become the least bit valedictory about his own death. The reason is very simple. He did not acknowledge his own illness, in spite of being told in 1925 that he had TB, and gradually starting to show all the symptoms. His friend Earl Brewster noted: 'Never did he give me the impression that he thought his recovery doubtful.' Lawrence claimed in 1928 that in spite of 'delicate health', he had a 'strong constitution', and preferred to believe that a combination of living in the right place and

9 *4L* 327, corrected *8L* 127.

10 *7L* 634.

adopting the right attitude to life would lead to his recovery.[11] I want to spend a little time tonight with my biographer's hat on, thinking about this.

Lawrence went to stay with Maria and Aldous Huxley in Paris in the spring of 1929, with what was to them TB in an advanced state. They got him to go to a doctor, and tried to arrange an X-ray; but then Frieda arrived in Paris, and Lawrence went off with her to Majorca instead. Huxley was outraged; a letter to his brother Julian offered a straightforward way of summing Lawrence up:

> It's no good. He doesn't *want* to know how ill he is: that, I believe, is the fundamental reason why he won't go to Doctors and homes. He only went in Paris because he was feeling iller than usual and was even more frightened of dying at once than of hearing how ill he was.

What is more, the Huxleys told Mark Gertler, who had submitted to sanatorium treatment for T. B., that 'it is mostly Frieda's fault and ... it really seems almost as if it is she who is slowly killing him'. 'We've told her that she's a fool and a criminal; but it has no more effect than telling an elephant.'[12]

One of the difficult areas for a biographer is what happens between a married couple. Their conversation is not usually recorded; so unless (like the Tolstoys, with their multiple diaries) they make efforts to preserve what they believe is happening between them, we can only rely upon the presence of third parties for a sense of it. To me, all the rather limited evidence points to the fact that it was, in some way, important for their marriage that, to Frieda, Lawrence

11 E. & A. Brewster, *D. H. Lawrence: Reminiscences and Correspondence* (Martin Secker, 1934), p. 224; *LEA* 112:7-8.

12 *7L* 9; Mark Gertler, *Selected Letters*, ed. Noel Carrington (Rupert Hart-Davis, 1965), p. 228.

was not ill. And so Lawrence was *not* ill.

For Frieda did not bother about illness; it played no part in how she thought about herself or others. If anything, she was a kind of Nietzschean illness-snob: the ill were weak, second-class, inferior. Lawrence's own determination that illness was really *only* the result of mental attitude – he wrote how 'What is the matter with us is primarily chagrin. Then the microbes pounce' [13] – may well have been influenced, even derived from Frieda. Her attitude certainly meant that she was an awful nurse: impatient and intolerant. She did her best to ignore the ill person, but she was also awful in quite practical ways, such as not separating off Lawrence's tea-cup from those of guests, so that the chances were really quite high of being infected by Lawrence's TB, late on in his life. In the case of someone with what, from the seventeenth century, has been called galloping consumption, their saliva is extremely dangerous. But Frieda preferred to ignore illness. This attitude was possible because she also believed (and had been encouraged by Lawrence, among others, to believe) that her vitality was such that – with her – you were not ill: not ill, *really*. She cured you by being your virile (I use the word deliberately) partner. She once remarked about Lawrence, when he had been rather down, that 'I roused him into the determination to accept the challenge of my virility, he was not going to succumb.'[14]

Lawrence participated in her belief that she could do this: he told her how 'I could always trust your instinct to know the right thing for me.'[15] His bronchials, his asthma were

13 *6L* 409, vii. 440.

14 Martha Gordon Crotch, *Memories of Frieda Lawrence* (Edinburgh, n.d.), p. 7; see too Enid Hopkin Hilton, *More then One Life: A Nottinghamshire Childhood with D. H. Lawrence* (Stroud, 1993), pp. 53-4. Frieda's 'virility' is reminiscent of her claim to S. S. Koteliansky in 1923 that she was 'six times the "man" than any of you are!' (*Memoirs and Correspondence*, p. 230).

15 *"Not I, But the Wind"* (Santa Fe, 1934), p. 303.

small, irritating things; they were troublesome, that was all. His lungs were ok. He was not *ill.*

There would be times, of course, when this way of carrying on would be likely to break down: one came four days before Lawrence died, when he told her 'Frieda, you have killed me'. Meaning, I think, that their complex myth of her support and vitality, and his being kept alive by her, wasn't good enough: he *was* dying.

But another way in which I think Lawrence showed Frieda how unaffected he was by illness came in 1926, the year he wrote the first version of *Lady Chatterley's Lover*: a novel that started as a short fiction about class but which became a novel about sex. These things are hard to talk about; but almost exactly two years after starting the first version of the novel, Lawrence told a friend about being lonely, and went on: 'you think you have something in your life which makes up for everything, and then find you haven't got it ... Two years ago I found this out.'[16] He is unlikely to have meant Frieda's loyalty to him, which he had never had: in 1926 she had started the pursuit of Angelo Ravagli which ended in her becoming his mistress and (after Lawrence's death) marrying him. Lawrence might have meant Frieda as a sexual partner, but he is much more likely to have meant his capacity to experience desire: including (but not exclusively) sexual desire. He wrote a number of poems about this; it became a theme of his writing in his last years.

But not, of course, in his fiction after 1928: because there wasn't any. After *The Escaped Cock*, finished in July 1928, nothing. For Lawrence, whose fiction had always been *the* great resource of his life, to lose himself in that world of the imagination ... well, that links with something else he said to

[16] Nehls, iii. 258. Cf. DHL's comment to his sister Ada on 22 February 1929: 'The things that seemed to make up one's life die into insignificance, and the whole state is wretched. I've been through it these last three years – and suffered, I tell you' (*7L* 186).

Brigit Patmore in 1928: that although his writing had once touched and moved people, as he knew ('Once I could do that'), he now stated flatly: 'I can't any more'.[17] AS if the fact of desire, the losing of himself utterly in feelings that were quite outside his mental control – something in which he had come deeply to believe in, and which he had always linked with his fiction, which comes 'unwatched out of one's pen' – no longer happened: or at least not in the same way.

The second version of *Lady Chatterley's Lover*, however, started just two years earlier, had been the first sexually explicit book he had written.[18] What – as many people have pointed out – is striking is that Lawrence should late in 1926 have embarked on such a project as the *Lady Chatterley* novels just when Frieda had taken a lover, and when he was probably less sexually involved with her than in their entire life together.

Frieda was, however, very close to the writing of the book; she recalled reading every day what he had written. The following year, a visitor heard 'at intervals' Lawrence actually calling Frieda to his room, where he was writing in bed, to read to her: 'Sometimes they laughed together and at other times she would sound a little shocked and in her deep, throaty voice, said: "Lorenzo, you cannot say that".' [19] She was thus the first audience for the novel. Their own relationship had been unusual, in something of the way the novel was depicting, Lawrence working class and Frieda aristocracy, yet in many ways, when they met in 1912, Lawrence had been closer to the position of Constance (detached and inexperienced onlooker) and Frieda nearer that of Parkin/Mellors (instinctive, sympathetic, experienced married partner). And if there is one character in the novel

17 Nehls, iii. 258.

18 He may e.g. have been aware of the volumes of Frank Harris memoirs *My Life and Loves*, published in Paris from 1922, but there is no direct evidence of it.

19 Hilton, *More then One Life*, p. 53.

with whom Lawrence might have been expected to sympathise, it would of course have been Clifford Chatterley, demoralised by illness, whose wife wants more of her marriage than he can give her, and who is prepared to turn a blind eye to her taking a lover.

But instead, the novel takes the woman's point of view, and the sexually active woman abandons the sexually non-active but literary and intellectual husband for the non-intellectual gamekeeper. The novel shows less sympathy for the husband than would have seemed possible for a writer who must have been concerned by Clifford's predicament; and whose own lack of desire hurt him so much. The idea that Frieda might leave him for Ravagli must have occurred to Lawrence. How could he, then, be more like Parkin/ Mellors and less like Clifford?

And I think his answer was by writing the novel. If on the one hand its sexuality was an astonishing tribute to Frieda, and to how Lawrence felt about her feelings and her experience, the novel was above all a final tribute to the life of the body, male and female, which now occupied him more in imagination and re-creation than it could in actuality or in desire. It is not too much to say that the second and third versions of *Lady Chatterley's Lover* were verbal acts of love to Frieda, written in the words she would have read or heard each time he came back from writing, towards the end of a partnership which had started out as violent sexual attraction. The novels did what Lawrence could always do best, which was imaginatively develop the crucial experiences of his own life: and his sexual life had been overwhelmingly what he had shared with Frieda. The novel was, then, a way of insisting that he was not too withdrawn, ill or fragile to imagine making intense love to Frieda, as he always had done; and to experience (and to make his reader feel) what she felt. A critic called Edward Gilbert provoked Frieda in 1951 – twenty years after Lawrence died – into saying something unguarded about Lawrence: Gilbert (academics never cease to astonish me) had told Frieda that her husband was 'a sexual weakling'.

Frieda responded: 'It is just absurd to call L. a sexual weakling, anything but: with his intensity. You don't know how a man like he was, could give himself, body and soul. I experienced this miracle.'[20] It was the 'intensity' that she insisted on: the experience she had of his giving himself absolutely. She may even have envied him; she gave herself quickly and temporarily, to men like Harold Hobson and Cecil Gray, and sometimes with regret. Lawrence's final act of sexual giving, body and soul, was his writing of the second and third versions of *Lady Chatterley's Lover*; though they were also ways of saying goodbye to his own past. *The Escaped Cock* – its two halves written around the final *Lady Chatterley* novel – is a complementary other half: charting a progress from an utter lack of desire to reborn desire. But also celebrating what had gone: not sexual potency, whatever that is, but the actual power of overwhelming desire, which compelled and demanded and could not be resisted: in which Lawrence had believed: and now found himself without.

That is of course speculation. Something less speculative which I have had to consider, as a biographer, is how would Lawrence himself say goodbye, when he died on 2 March 1930? In his sanatorium in Vence in February 1930, he had been growing worse: he had started to suffer from pleurisy, and lost his appetite. By the end of the month he was in an appalling state of pain and dissolution, and Frieda told herself 'It is enough, it is enough; nobody should have to stand this.' She slept in his room, but this time he told her 'Your sleeping here does me no good.' She ran away and cried; such a remark undermined one of the central tenets of their joint life. When, however, she came back 'he said so tenderly: "Don't mind, you know I want nothing but you ..."' However true, he wanted to say it: and it was at least as true as it had been in Oaxaca in 1925, when – again – he had been on the point of death, and had said to Frieda: 'But if I die, nothing

20 *Memoirs and Correspondence*, p. 309.

has mattered but you, nothing at all.' Who or what else could he have wanted, at this point in his life? [21] He had no last words prepared beyond those. One account has his actual last words as 'I am better now': those commonest of last words, as the body floods with the relief of the relaxation that means death. The other version has him saying to Frieda: 'Wind my watch.' He would want to know the time during the night, when his coughing kept him awake; his watch was cheap and needed winding every evening.[22] But he also intended living on to the next day, and the small ritual of watch-winding had to be carried out. He made no goodbyes. He intended going on.

Lawrence has often been, for me, for the last thirty-five years, a way of keeping the real difficulties and problems of my own life at bay. He has not only been my companion in loneliness; he has given me another world in which to lose myself. As Julian Barnes put it, 'Perhaps this is the advantage of making friends with those already dead: your feelings towards them never cool.'[23] In fact, in many ways Lawrence has become the emotional and intellectual world for me. There is a positive side to this, of course. Go close enough to some things, and they constantly take you in other directions, like the ripples radiating out from a single pebble tossed into a pond. Because of Lawrence, I have read quite widely in the literature and history of the early twentieth century; that peculiar sensation of text and context continually overlapping is one which sometimes comes, and it is a way in which a tiny piece of the world's history can be, just a little, understood.

21 *"Not I, But the Wind ..."*, pp. 307, 308, 165.

22 David Ellis, *D. H. Lawrence: Dying Game 1922-1930* (Cambridge, 1998), p. 531; *"Not I, But the Wind ..."*, p. 309.

23 Julian Barnes, *Flaubert's Parrot* (Pan Books, Picador, 1985), p. 21.

On the other hand, I now feel that I have long been subservient to this utterly dominant personality, and have as a result been able to close down some of the real desires and needs of my own life. 'And whom shall I submit to?' asks Aaron at the end of *Aaron's Rod.*[24] I had that question answered from 1965. My devotion to Lawrence as a researcher, scholar and writer can in one way be seen as scholarly devotion of a rather old-fashioned but admirable kind; in another way as equivalent to an anorak's devotion to train-spotting; in yet another way as a considerable help to my School of English's research profile, sub-section international recognition; but in yet another way as an opportunity to ignore myself: to hide behind something else which was always more important than attending to needs of my own.

That is now coming to an end: not overnight, not suddenly, but as part of the process of retirement, and trying to live a little more actually in a world a little more real. The biography of Lawrence which I am going to hand in to Penguin Books in four weeks from now is going to be my last book on Lawrence; another kind of farewell, and another reason why I do not intend to continue as Professor of D. H. Lawrence Studies.

But I do not say farewell like Prospero. Tonight there will be no burning of books or breaking of staffs. My last book on Lawrence is one in which I have been at last able to say the things I was never able to say before, in the years when I was so strenuously clasping Lawrence to myself as a necessary friend and companion. I can now say what an utterly odd person he was; how depressive, how violent, how difficult, how esoteric in so much of his writing: but also what a spectacular writer. That more than anything: rich, compelling, extraordinary. No scales have dropped from my eyes: in ways I've always known all this. But only now have I

24 *AR* 299:19.

allowed myself to know it for real. It goes along with a realisation that I have hidden behind him for far too long; I've made him a kind of parent, I think, to whom I have listened all my life. People have admired the work I've done on Lawrence, and (this is something I have never said before) I can now say how proud I am of it, too; I gave him my best years. But there's been a price to pay; and it was only when I left Swansea and ventured into the wider worlds of Nottingham that I found how inadequately I was equipped to deal as an adult with most of the problems of life; and how much my reliance on Lawrence, with a concomitant escape into biography and editing and research, has been the great escape of my life. I certainly did the work; but at a cost. It's only been in the last six or eight years that I have discovered, firstly, how depressed I've been for a lot of my life, in ways that in the past I managed to run away from spectacularly well; and secondly how, if I really looked hard at Lawrence – into the darker and unhappier things about him which my CUP biography, to me now amazingly, managed almost completely to ignore – then something about my own life became apparent as well. The sensation has been, I recently found, described (as so much else has) by Jorge Luis Borges:

> *A man sets out to draw the world.* [To me this sounds rather like writing a comprehensive biography.] *As the years go by, he peoples a space with images of provinces, kingdoms, mountains, bays, ships, islands, fishes, rooms, instruments, stars, horses, and individuals. A short time before he dies, he discovers that that patient labyrinth of lines traces the lineaments of his own face.*[25]

The image I drew of Lawrence – not, I hope, just before I die – has shown me things I never sought to know about myself, but have learned by way of him.

25 Borges, *Collected Fictions*, tr. Hurley, p. [327].

But there is only so much knowledge one can acquire from book study. I like, again, very much the way Julian Barnes puts this:

> Books are where things are explained to you; life is where things aren't. I'm not surprised some people prefer books. Books make sense of life. The only problem is that the lives they make sense of are other people's lives, never your own.[26]

In my case, I am fairly sure that my quixotic resolution to live a better life has been bound up with giving up my reliance on Lawrence and dedicating myself – there still may be time – to my marriage and to my wife and to our friends, to life *with* others rather than burying myself in a life too busy to spend much time with them. And also to the writing of *my* work, not someone else's.

I hope this isn't maudlin or confessional; there are times when as a biographer I have felt uncomfortably close to Lawrence's friend and biographer John Middleton Murry, and the last thing I want to do tonight is bare my soul and wear my heart on my sleeve in the ways that Murry so horribly did. Saying goodbye certainly does *not* mean I shall never read Lawrence again, or somehow put a stop to all my interest in him. As Dr Dorothy Johnston put it, when I told her that I was retiring, if the library buys a new Lawrence manuscript, does my retirement mean that I shall not want to know about it? And the answer is that I most certainly will. While I have my knowledge (goodness knows how long that will last, with memory failing me as it currently is) I want to know, I shall comment and discuss and help. But I want to put on record tonight that my future work on Lawrence (because I shall be doing some) is going to be in the service of other people's books, not my own. There are some poems which Christopher Pollnitz needs help with annotating, for example;

26 Barnes, *Flaubert's Parrot*, p. 168.

Lawrence scholars will know which ones I mean.[27] There's a book Andrew Harrison is doing with which I'm helping.[28] Neil Reeve is doing an edition of Lawrence's reviews and introductions to which I am contributing.[29] Others may want to consult and involve me; I hope they do.[30] But Lawrence won't be the centre of my writing: or my life. There is a novel I need to re-write; there is a biography of Robert Schumann I want to research:[31] other books to write.

People ask me whether, in retirement, I won't miss being in demand, being an authority, being the D. H. Lawrence Professor. Margaret Attwood answered this nicely when she described herself as having reached 'the Helpful Granny stage':

> I can potter around with things that interest me, rather than worrying about what kind of impression I'm going to make at the party. I'm not entirely quaint yet, but I can see quaintness coming.[32]

I intend to potter with the things that interest me: I shall not worry a scrap about research (its ratings, its quality, RQA red channels etc.) I honestly don't think I'm going to miss the high life much: I never had much taste for it. There may be moments. I find Auden's poem 'Prospero to Ariel' very astute and very moving. Prospero is addressing Ariel: the wonderful, magical being whom he so much envies.

When I am safely home, oceans away in Milan [say,

27 The edition of *The Poems* will be published by Cambridge University Press in 2013.

28 *D. H. Lawrence's "Sons and Lovers": A Casebook*, ed. John Worthen and Andrew Harrison (New York, 2005).

29 This came out as *IR* in 2005.

30 Sean Matthews is for example responsible for the existence of the book in which you are reading this essay: see p. 19.

31 This became *Robert Schumann: Life and Death of a Musician* (2007).

32 Quoted in the *Guardian*, 2003.

> Oberhausen], and
> Realise once and for all I shall never see you again,
> Over there, maybe, it won't seem quite so dreadful
> Not to be interesting any more, but an old man
> Just like other old men, with eyes that water
> Easily in the wind, and a head that nods in the sunshine,
> Forgetful, maladroit, a little grubby,
> And to like it.[33]

My eyes already water, my head nods, my forgetfulness is legendary, my feet catch in more and more things; but Conni will save me from much grubbiness. And I also intend to like it.

So the moment of Goodbye approaches. Saying Goodbye, not just to this University community, but to the University communities with whom I have made my life, is very difficult, in one way; but mainly because it means that I shall need friends, more than ever. And I've not been good at making friends. So, those of you in this hall: don't give up on me, please. I need you, now more than ever. I think, again, of Auden and his 'Prospero to Ariel': Prospero a little glumly considering the ways in which he has wasted his life:

> If I peg away at it honestly every moment
> And have luck, perhaps by the time death pounces
> His stumping question, I shall just be getting to know
> The difference between moonshine and daylight ...
> I see you starting to fidget. I forgot. To you [Ariel]
> That doesn't matter. My dear, here comes Gonzalo
> With a solemn face to fetch me. O Ariel, Ariel,
> How I shall miss you. Enjoy your element. Good-bye.[34]

33 W. H. Auden, *Selected Poems* (1979), p. 134.

Great phrase, 'Enjoy your element': to friends, colleagues and collaborators all, enjoy your element. Good-bye. It was Auden who asked that Siegfried's funeral march from *Götterdämmerung* be played at his funeral; his closest friends stood and listened to it in his house before the ceremony, with the result that – when they appeared in public, to walk behind Auden's hearse to the cemetery – it was with their faces 'ravaged with grief'.[35] What a clever showman Auden was, to the end and well beyond it: no Hardyesque 'swift style'[36] of going, for him. No funeral, tonight, just the welcoming of another, better life. So, naturally, Conni and are going to a pub, just around the corner of the campus: the old Priory, now the Toby Carvery: there are maps in the foyer of how to find it. It would be great to see there anyone who isn't driving away immediately: though I shall be far too emotional to talk to you, as I would overflow with tears. Wagner's *Ring* was one of my leaving presents from the School of English; so what more appropriate than for me to leave, with Conni, not to the music of a funeral march but as the Gods enter Valhalla in *Rheingold.*

[Music start]
{*Wagner:* Orchestral Music from the Operas / *Klemperer / EMI Great Recordings of the Century 5678932 / CD2 Track 2:* Das Rheingold*: Entry of the Gods into Valhalla: start at 6.50'*};
[level faint, background: 2-3 on the scale 1-10]

To all of you, thank you so much for coming tonight: and remember, stay in touch with me, invite me, put me up: I need you badly. This kind of conclusion is the *Rasselas* kind in

---

34 *Selected Poems*, pp. 134-5.

35 Charles Osborne, *W. H. Auden: The Life of a Poet* (Methuen, 1980), p. 311.

36 'Without Ceremony', l. 12.

which I don't leave: I stay, in your hearts and minds, and spare bedrooms.

[Music louder, but so JW can still shout over it: 6 on the scale 1-10]

But the home of the gods is my forwarding address. And so, Goodbye: this is the final way.

[Music 10 on the scale 1-10. JW collects CR-W from front row of audience: bow: wave: exit together stage right]

[Music ends]
[Lecture ends]
[House lights up]

Lawrence in Moorgreen

Public Library, Eastwood, 17 July 2003

It was Emma Herrity who first asked me to contribute to the Eastwood Lawrence festival and – just a few weeks after my farewell lecture at the University – it was obviously a good idea to take up the role of speaking to a different constituency. I knew from many years in the D. H. Lawrence Society that nothing pleased a local audience better than a topic which was distinctly local; and the luck I had had the previous winter – when I had found the Holbrook house in Moorgreen – offered me a perfect subject. The evening upstairs in the Public Library turned out to be terribly hot; the audience was a good deal larger than expected; and of course the slide projector also gave out its usual quantity of hum and heat (I had to turn the bulb off after every slide, in an attempt to minimise this, and to stop the machine overheating). We had two fans going. At least I, up at the window end, had some fresh air. The lecture however went very well, with the audience at the end telling me things I really wanted to know – such as the fact that the farm next door had once been called 'Pear Tree Farm', fitting beautifully with my speculation about the identity of the tree at the end wall of the Holbrook house. I provide samples of some of the slides I used.

There is one building in the Eastwood area, with very strong connections with D. H. Lawrence, which has never had any publicity – to the extent that until very recently, no one even knew where it was: I think I am the only one of three people who do (and I told the other two). Everyone knows about the five Lawrence family houses in Eastwood (yes, five[1]). There are of course also the Lawrence family houses over at Brinsley, in particular Quarry Cottage and Vine Cottage (the 'Odour of Chrysanthemums' cottage). There are many other buildings with Lawrence connections, some of which we know he went inside, others we know from his recreations of

[1] Victoria Street, Garden Road [The Breach], Walker Street, Lynn Croft and (between February and May 1912) 'Bromley House', 13 Queen's Square.

them: the Hopkins' house in Devonshire Drive, for example (still with the tiles in the hall and the old mantel piece described in *Mr Noon*), the Three Tunns Inn, the Sun Inn, the Wellington, the Mechanics' Institute; and going further afield, the Board School in Beauvale, the Church and Vicarage at Greasley.

1. La H 49 (UN).

Yet the house I am concerned with has a haunting significance in his Eastwood life. Let me give you just four reasons for that significance. Which is the house which Lawrence visited, to see close friends, for their love and sympathy, the afternoon after his mother had died, on 9 December 1910? Which is the only house in the locality – apart from the Haggs – about which Lawrence wrote poetry? Which is the house where he last saw Jessie Chambers, in April 1912? And which is the only house in the region where he was able to carry on his affair with Frieda Weekley in April 1912, before they went off to Germany together? They are all the same house (or cottage); I am referring to the cottage at Moorgreen which Jessie Chambers' sister May rented with her husband, Will (or Bill) Holbrook, from 1909 to around 1913. There is just one, small and pretty tattered photograph of it, as it was in 1912. All there is, to help us identify it, is a note written in ink on the back of that little photograph: 'Cottage at Moorgreen, Newthorpe, Notts, 1912. May and Will.' I have been looking for it, on and off, ever since the late 1980s. I have at last been able to locate it: it's still standing, about a mile and a half away from us as we sit here. But more of the detective work later.

Jessie Chambers was the middle one of the three daughters of the Chambers family, and we know a very great deal about her: mostly because of her own writings, her surviving letters, and the fact that in the 1930s Emile Delavenay interviewed her and got her to answer many questions about her early life. The younger Chambers daughter Mollie I know (to my shame) very little indeed about; but May Chambers, the eldest, is fascinating. Three years older than Jessie, and two years older than Lawrence, at the age of 23 she got married to Will Holbrook, on 1 November 1906, while (of course) Lawrence was at the start of his teacher-training course in Nottingham. She had always been a bit of an outsider in the Chambers family: fiercely independent, training as a school-teacher (she was at the British Schools in Eastwood in 1903 when Lawrence himself was working there); and if you don't know them, I recommend you to read her memoirs, which arrived too late for Edward Nehls to include them in Volume I of his wonderful *Composite Biography* of Lawrence. But this was actually a wonderful piece of good fortune, because as a result he put the whole lot into Volume III;[2] and you will learn more about the Chambers family there than you will in the whole of Jessie's book. In the far distant past I speculated whether it might not have been the publication of her sister's book in 1935 that caused May to set down her own

2 Nehls, iii. 552-629.

memories, when she was living in Canada in the late 1930s.[3] May was always sharp with Lawrence, but she also stood up for him: when, for example, people in his youth thought that a boy interested in shopping and the price of groceries was 'Not right in the head' – 'You can't tell me he's right in his head. Anybody'll tell you the same' – May says she learned to answer this accusation 'with only one remark: "I wish I had his head!"'[4]

She had started teaching at the Beauvale School around 1904; but she and Lawrence still met at the Haggs when she was visiting her parents, and after Lawrence went down to Croydon in 1908 they stayed in touch by letter. Lawrence always adjusted his style of writing according to the person he was writing to, and you can learn a good deal about that person by seeing how *he* writes. His letters to May Holbrook reveal her as a wonderfully straightforward person: no nonsense, no fine writing from Lawrence, a lot of facts and details as well as clearly articulated feelings. In 1909, she and Will Holbrook moved into a rented farm cottage in Moorgreen, and – to start with – even Lawrence, down in Croydon, hearing the news, could not work out exactly where they had gone. He wrote to May:

> You will be happy now out at Moorgreen. I cannot quite understand where you are. Is it this side George's? Tell me – is it on the Moorgreen main road? I do not know Price's. I know Renshaw's, Mrs Rollings, Cunningham's, – no more.[5]

3 See John Worthen, 'The Chambers Memoirs of D. H. Lawrence: A Reply', *Renaissance and Modern Studies*, xix (1975), 102.

4 Nehls, iii. 571; cf. iii. 583 ('He's a sight more on his head than you have!').

5 *1L* 116.

Renshaws, Mrs Rollings and Cunninghams must all have been houses along the Moorgreen road, at various points. What he meant by 'this side George's' is, however, rather more peculiar. Could it be George Neville? But he wasn't living in Eastwood at the time. I *suspect* that Lawrence meant 'this side of the Ram Inn' – the old Ram Inn, of course, not the modern building. In his novel *The White Peacock*, Lawrence had made his hero George landlord of the Ram. The phrase 'this side George's' thus implies that May Chambers knew the text – or at least the story – of the as-yet-unpublished *White Peacock*. Which is striking in itself.

But Lawrence went to see the Holbrooks on one of his subsequent visits to Eastwood; and according to Will Holbrook, 'D. H.' became 'a constant visitor' to their cottage. It was, Will thought,

> much like a brother and sister relationship, as D. H. came and departed when the spirit moved him. I know he loved to come where he could do and say just what he pleased, even using strong language to win his point. But he had a hard antagonist to beat in my wife, who insisted that he was too young and inexperienced, in being so cocksure that what he knew and said was the Gospel. These ranglements would proceed all night and well into the a.m., each trying to prove himself the smarter of the two. I, of course, would fall asleep, which added more fuel to the fury, wherein D. H. would scream and shout:
>
> 'Look at that farm bumpkin, chaw bacon, hasn't the wit to keep awake. Then they say all men are equal.'
>
> I would mumble something about I'd done a day's work, when off would fly his lid:
>
> 'So have I, a damned harder day than you.' ...
>
> I want to say that to be in D. H.'s company was a

tonic. A more sincere friend one could not wish to find, with a most infectious laugh.[6]

The cottage is the setting of a number of the events in May Chambers' extended memoir of Lawrence. Lawrence went out there, for example, frequently during Lydia Lawrence's last illness, in the winter of 1910; he eventually came up to Eastwood for what he thought would be her final few days but had to stay for nearly three weeks. May Chambers records lengthy conversations with him during this awful period, about his mother and about his writing. If you don't know these, do look them up; they are beautifully written, and very revealing. And he actually went out there on the afternoon of 9 December 1910, at the end of his mother's long-drawn-out dying. As usual, May is narrating:

> A day or two later, Bert came in with a hurt and tender expression on his face.
>
> 'She's gone,' I said.
>
> He nodded. 'It's all over.' He turned as the door opened. 'Mother died this morning, Bill.'
>
> 'Your mother's dead, eh?'
>
> 'Mother is dead,' he repeated ... Suddenly I said:
>
> 'Let us help you. Can we help you? Is there *anything* we can do?'
>
> Then we all sat down to discuss immediate plans. Bill was to drive to the station for the flowers on the day of her funeral.
>
> 'I shall write little poems to her,' Bert said. 'She'd like that.'[7]

Those are the last words of May Chambers' memoir; it's a very great shame she didn't take it beyond that point. She and

6 Nehls, iii. 611.

7 Nehls, iii. 620.

Will were Lawrence's closest friends in the Eastwood region, and the Moorgreen cottage a kind of second home to him.

I first came across that little photograph of their cottage in the MSS Department at the University of Nottingham in 1988. I went round and round Moorgreen looking for the original, but I could never find it. It didn't actually seem very important: interesting, certainly, because the cottage told me how close he was to Will and May, but not much more.

And there the matter rested until January 2003 when, going through the photographs at Nottingham University again while looking for illustrations for my Penguin biography, and really checking everything, I noted an item I could not recall ever having seen before: it had the title 'Photograph of a cottage near Eastwood, where D. H. Lawrence once stayed.' That caught my eye. While he had family in Eastwood – which he did until 1913 – to the best of my recollection he had never 'stayed' anywhere else: why would he. I was intrigued: where was this place? So I asked to see it. This is the new picture the library had for me.

2. La Phot 2/86 (UN)

And I had no idea where it might be: just one clue – that church in the background. Could it be Greasley? But there's no detail at all: just a tower. I asked to see the old Holbrook cottage picture again: I'm not quite sure why – some kind of intuition.

When I put them side by side, there seemed no connection at all. The 1912 photograph showed a cottage shaded by a tree, and with plants climbing all over it; it feels very closed in. The new photograph (taken in the 1940s or 50s, by the look of the car parked nearby) showed a cottage entirely on its own, not a tree near it; distinctive mostly in having especially large chimneys. They must be different places. But the more I looked at the two very different photographs, the more I saw similarities. The same tiny panes of glass between the wooden window divides, which you can see especially well in the left hand top window, which is wide open and catching the sun (12 panes per half window); the same slightly curved top of the window embrasure; and most distinctive of all, that little window low down in the end wall. And then I realised that the low wall curving around the front of the cottage was an even better clue, and showed a gate in an identical place; and the gate even had the same pattern of bars and a cross-piece (it is open in one picture and closed in the other). I had discovered *another* picture of the Holbrooks' Moorgreen cottage. And this time with the clue of the church tower in it.

I went out to Moorgreen at once. It was a misty, snowy Saturday afternoon in January 2003. And what had looked like plain sailing became, as it so often does when you are trying to locate an actual place from a photograph, a real problem. Things never look as you want them to. All that new building was very confusing: I couldn't get a view of the church from anywhere, for example. Things just look very, very different. I never forget how, more than 20 years ago, I walked round and round the small Italian town of Picinisco with in my hand the xerox copy of a postcard Lawrence had sent from there, in 1920, which showed the ruined castle standing up clear over the market place.[8] And there was absolutely nowhere from where I could get that view; there were huge trees blocking my way wherever I went. I looked harder at the postcard ... and realised that there were tree saplings, tied up to stakes, all over the marketplace, which – sixty years later – had grown into enormous elm trees! So, in January, I walked up and down and up and down Moorgreen Road, trying to find my cottage with the huge chimneys and the two windows upstairs and the two windows downstairs. I asked the few people who were outdoors, but it wasn't the weather for gardening, and there weren't many people about. But there appeared nothing in the least like that house, in the whole row of dwellings running from the corner of the Moorgreen road at the *Horse and Groom* up to the old *Ram* inn; not a single house, either side of the road, with two windows upstairs, two down, a door in the middle and a pair of particularly large chimneys. I asked a couple of people who were in their gardens if they had heard any rumours of a cottage where Lawrence had once been, or people called Holbrook had once lived; and no one knew anything at all. I started to think that some houses must have been pulled down – and one woman confirmed to me that a couple of old buildings *had* been pulled down.

I had thought that asking people, and the names Holbrook and Lawrence, and that simple layout of four windows and two chimneys would do it. No good at all. I had to fall back on the – possible – view of a Church which *might* be Greasley.

There was just one place on the road where I could get a view out across the fields, as you can in the photograph, without having to go through someone's back garden; there was a derelict, modern-looking six windowed and three-chimneyed house, obviously not the one I was looking for, well back from the road, with a rough track beside it; this

8 *3L* 436: no. 1882.

might allow me a view over to the Church and its graveyard. Because if it *were* the tower of Greasley Church in the photo, then perhaps that was – below it – the outline of the hedge surrounding the extended graveyard at the church – the one that reaches out towards Moorgreen. I went down the track, thin snow over tufts of grass, to the gate; and there at least was Greasley Church the far side of the fields, though you could hardly see the tower for the trees. But remember Picinisco! Trees grow! I realised that it *was* Greasley in the second photograph, and the house I was after must be very near. And then I realised that there was a window, low down in the house's end wall beside me.

3. Holbrook Cottage, June 2003

I went back and looked again. And then, incredibly, everything fell into place. The whole left-hand end of the house, I realised, along with the third chimney, was a modern addition, and all the windows were modern windows. The roof, too, had been lowered and re-tiled, and the huge chimneys taken down.

4. Holbrook Cottage, June 2003

The cottage had at some stage since the 1950s been faced in cement, but the process of dereliction now showed the bricks under the cement; I could also see that the small modern chimneys were in coarse, modern brick, compared with the darker old brick of the walls (visible where the rendering was coming off) ... The right-hand end of the poor shattered house, with its dreadful wood and corrugated plastic porch, and horrid modern windows, was, indeed, all that remained of the Holbrook cottage at Moorgreen. The final proof was the round boss of a wall-tie just up and to the left of the front door, exactly as in the 1950s photograph: I had been unable to imagine what it was when looking at the photograph. This was the house: utterly changed: and yet the house. I went home exhilarated.

And it was at this point that I really began to look into the story of Lawrence's links with the house. Back in 1988, working on my first biography, I'd not done much – there had seemed no point. But finding the house made me want to go on with the history of Lawrence's relationship with it.

During 1911, Lawrence was most of the time in Croydon – and with his fiancée Louie Burrows in Quorn; he spent less time in Eastwood that year than in his whole life up to that point. I am sure he would have written to the Holbrooks, both Will and May; it looks as if he regularly wrote long and chatty letters to May right down to 1913, at least, though very few of them survive. There's a wonderful one about teaching in his school in Croydon, from 1908; and there's a superb one about life on the Lago di Garda from the winter of 1912 – so I suspect there were lots of others in between. Perhaps even more than usual – because Lawrence would not have been going round to see the Holbrooks as once he had.

In the winter of 1911-12, he fell severely ill in Croydon; he had to give up teaching, and after a month's convalescence in Bournemouth – and after breaking off his engagement to poor Louie – he came back to Eastwood on 9 February 1912. We can be absolutely certain that he very quickly renewed his friendship with the Holbrooks; there is one very simple way of being sure about this. Within a month of being back, on 3 March, Lawrence met Frieda Weekley. Within a week, he had written to her as 'the most wonderful woman in all England'.[9] And within three weeks of Lawrence first meeting Frieda, May knew all about her. We can be certain of this because the very first reference to Frieda in Lawrence's surviving correspondence comes in a letter to May Holbrook, in which he told her on 27 March – twenty-four days after meeting Frieda – 'I said nothing to Mrs. Weekley about coming over. Will discuss it further with you.' One reason was mentioned in that same letter: 'I suppose J[essie] will be at the cottage.'[10] So the idea of Frieda actually coming to Moorgreen had at least been discussed with May, and was on the cards, even if this was not the right weekend. But that suggests Lawrence's closeness to the Holbrooks; and also the problem that May

9 *1L* 376 [misdated to *c.* 20 March: it should be *c.* 7 March].

10 *1L* 377.

was Jessie's sister, and Lawrence did *not* want Jessie to meet Frieda. He did, you may remember, tell Jessie about Frieda: 'he told me it would do me good to know Mrs Weekley. I am afraid I replied that I was not very anxious to be done good to by Mrs Weekley ... Her name was not mentioned again.'[11]

But Frieda *did* subsequently come over to Moorgreen, and more than once. All I had remembered were memoirs of her meeting Lawrence out in the country, but the memories are actually more precise than that. A piece which her youngest daughter Barby wrote in the 1950s names the place: her mother took the two girls with her out into the country by train, and there they met Lawrence. This is our first direct sighting of Lawrence in Moorgreen with Frieda. Barby narrates:

> One day, Frieda, Elsa, and I were walking along a country lane outside Nottingham when we met a tall, pale, cross-looking young man, who took us to 'Holbrook's Farm.' My mother obviously knew him. It was Lawrence. A sister of Jessie Chambers, the Miriam of *Sons and Lovers*, had married the farmer. Mr Holbrook showed Elsa and me over the farm, and gave us a ride on a horse. I remember that, as it reared up, I slipped off and was caught by Mr. Holbrook.
>
> When we went into the farmhouse, Elsa and I found that everyone else had gone out. There was a plate of rock cakes on which Lawrence had printed a notice, 'Take One.' Later on we joined the others again in the parlour, where Frieda was standing by a piano, singing. Lawrence, still pale and preoccupied, was sitting near her.[12]

11 Emile Delavenay, *D. H. Lawrence: L'Homme et la Genèse de son Oeuvre. Les Années de Formation: 1885-1919*, 2 vols. (Paris, 1969), ii. 707.

12 Nehls, i. 163.

At this point, all kinds of things fell into place. That cottage I've been showing you: why was it there? Very simple. It belonged to the farm next door. There was a farm? Yes: some of its buildings are now incorporated in the doctor's house at no. 46 Moorgreen Road. And I believe that Will Holbrook, at least some of the time, was working at the farm; that would account for the fact that they were living in the cottage. Hence Lawrence's remarks about him as a farm bumpkin, in that argument when Will fell asleep. Frieda and Lawrence must have been out for a walk: May was probably at her teacher's job. It is striking that the Holbrook cottage was one of the only two places in England where Lawrence could go with Frieda at this time (the other being Edward Garnett's house at the Cearne, south of London). So this was the only place locally where he could go with Frieda; the Holbrooks were the sole friends in the region whom he could trust with his secret.[13]

But more happened there, I think, than a visit with the children. This gets very speculative: but let me try it out on you. Lawrence's references to the cottage show that he had peculiarly tender memories of it. A month later, when in Germany with Frieda, he recalled how 'Moorgreen seems sweet to me';[14] and from the Villa Igea in Gargnano, in Italy, he wrote to May Holbrook that 'we [that is, Frieda and he] often wish we had your cottage as well'.[15] Could that be just a

13 The rumour Keith Sagar uncovered in 1969 that Frieda came to Eastwood more than once, accompanied by her two children, and that Ada complained how often Frieda was coming over (see 'Lawrence and Frieda: The Alternative Story', *D. H. Lawrence Review*, ix (Spring 1976), 117-25) suggests that Ada too may have offered DHL and Frieda somewhere to go, during April 1912; a serious difference from the Holbrooks would have been that she would certainly not have offered them an empty house.

14 *1L* 397.

15 *1L* 500.

reminiscence of the day they went out there with the children, and Lawrence was so tense? I rather doubt it. There exist two poems dating from the period which Lawrence never tried to publish: 'She Was a Good Little Wife' and 'Pear-Blossom'. You probably don't know either of them; they're right at the back of the *Complete Poems*, in Appendix II. He sent them both to Garnett, along with a couple of poems which are like versified versions of scenes in *Sons and Lovers* about Paul making love to Clara and another one rejoicing about being brought to 'bursting and budding' by sexual experience. Both the poems I am talking about are sexual, and focus on an affair taking place under the influence of the 'pear-tree bloom': both are dated in manuscript 'c. 1912'. This is how 'She Was a Good Little Wife' starts – as it might be outdoors, in the garden:

> The hum of the bees in the pear-tree bloom
> Penetrated my blood.
>
> I looked in her eyes. The gloom
> In them did me good.
>
> I knew that she was waiting,
> Ah she,
> I knew that she was baiting
> Her looks, her bearing to me;
>
> For all her shyness, baiting
> Her looks with desire.
> And the bustle of bees in the pear-tree bloom,
> And their subtle, eager booming,
> Like a murmur of fire
> Passed into my blood.[16]

16 *Poems*, ii. 891.

The other poem, 'Pear-Blossom', starts with a kinds of continuation of the scene, but ends up very differently. I don't think this second poem really works – the switch of mood is so extreme and unpremeditated – and there is some fictionalising going on too (the person the narrator makes love to owns the cottage, and I really don't think there was anything between Lawrence and May Holbrook).

The pear-blossom is a fountain of foam
At your cottage-end; it falls back again
In sprays and spurts of foam.

Te flowers against your window pane
Are a 'poppy-show.' Peep, while you comb
Your hair, peer out on the lane!—

That year, when the pear was out, my delight
As you crawled nakèd over me,
Your small breasts clumps of white

Pear-blossom hanging! And one small knee
Dug firm in my breast as you reached out right
To the window and the white pear-tree!

And you climbed back nakèd over me
As I lay on the bed, and you sat with the flowers on your thighs,
And looked at me;

And as I lay and looked in your eyes
You wept, and the bed trembled under me,
I was faint with surprise —

I am terrified of the pear-blossom
Round and white as a small bosom
With a nipple centre of red.

> My God, to think it is gone for ever,
> To think that you are gone for ever,
> I am terrified you are dead.[17]

Remember *Mr Noon*, and the anguish Gilbert Noon feels, when he fears he has lost Johanna, and wakes up in bed in terror, looking at the empty pillow beside him, and feeling 'for a moment it was as if she was dead'?[18]

What value do poems have in biography? Especially poems worked over later (as I strongly suspect they were)? And why (anyway) should we link pear-blossom with Moorgreen? But here I do have an answer. Down in London at the end of April 1912, during the weekend when Lawrence went with Frieda to the Cearne, he sent Will Holbrook an odd little postcard from Kew Gardens:

> Oh Bill – it's ripping down here – slightly different from the cottage – Heaven on a lower plane, shall we say? By the end of this razzle, I shall sigh for peace under a pear-tree.[19]

The Holbrooks knew about Frieda – that much is certain. And there's a lot going on in that postcard, some of it bawdy. Another poem dating from that same weekend describes how 'At the Cearne', the narrator makes love to his woman in the garden: 'On the little bank, below the orchard.'[20] Will Holbrook was thus being asked to appreciate the fact that 'Heaven' at the Cearne with Frieda, down in the garden (it really does slope away: I went to look) was 'on a lower plane, shall we say' than it had been upstairs in Moorgreen.

The Moorgreen cottage was in the shadow of a tree,

17 *Poems*, ii. 891-2.
18 *MN* 230:11-12.
19 *1L* 387.
20 *Poems*, ii. 892.

indeed at the cottage-end. But is it a pear tree? This is where I am going to rely upon my audience, because I've never been able to show the picture so large, to so many people. Who can identify a pear tree? The leaves look right to me: but all apples and pears, being *Rosaceae*, have pretty similar leaves. It's almost certainly a fruit tree, that's all we can say: and a pretty big one, too. Of course the pear blossoms in April, which is when Lawrence and Frieda might have been in bed together, in the upstairs bedroom at Moorgreen. Although – fiction again – there is no way you could lean out of the window and gather the blossom: you'd have to be an acrobat.

It would seem, however, quite likely that May and Will at least once loaned the cottage – empty during the day, of course – to Lawrence and Frieda in April 1912, during the blossom time; and that this is bawdily confirmed by that postcard Lawrence sent to Will from London on 26 April.

The Moorgreen cottage was, however, rather uncannily, also the place where Lawrence met Jessie Chambers twice in the spring of 1912, before going away with Frieda. Her memoir records his arrival there on his return from Staffordshire on Sunday 31 March, after going to see his friend George Neville (the weekend he couldn't go with 'Mrs Weekley', because 'J' was going to be there). He slept in Eastwood that night, and then walked over to the Moorgreen Cottage again on the Monday, when he and Jessie walked out to Greasley, and she gave him her notes on 'Paul Morel'.[21]

And it was at the Moorgreen Cottage that she met Lawrence for the very last time. This was something I'd forgotten until I re-read her memoir. Lawrence was actually staying there for the weekend of 20-21 April 1912, with May and Will; this must have been the visit alluded to by that photograph caption about a cottage where Lawrence stayed. Jessie and her father drove over from Arno Vale, on Sunday 21 April. She and her father arrived unexpectedly, and

21 E. T. 206-12.

> for once I saw Lawrence tongue-tied. He didn't know what to say to us. He went outside and sat on the low garden wall, leaning forward and looking intently at the ground, in an odd attitude of concentration.[22]

What she couldn't know of course was that he would be leaving England with Frieda less than a fortnight later, or that he and Frieda had probably been upstairs making love in the cottage together recently (the Cearne weekend would come a week later). It was in fact the closest Jessie ever came to Frieda, and Lawrence must have been acutely aware of the fact. He obviously was not going to tell her anything. But it was the day they said goodbye for the last time. When Jessie and her father went back, Lawrence rode with them as far as Watnall Hill before getting out of the trap to walk back to Moorgreen.[23] Jessie continues:

> My sister said later that he returned to the cottage in a thoughtful mood. He carved the joint, and was subdued and gentle. In the afternoon he and her husband were lying out in the field on rugs, and Lawrence suddenly exclaimed:
>
> 'Bill, I like a *gushing* woman.'[24]

Frieda gushed.[25] Jessie didn't.

The tree at the end wall was cut down sixty years ago, at least, the cottage is utterly derelict; but (like history, like memory, like poetry) the relics of what happened in Moorgreen all those years ago have still not quite faded or vanished. Hunt in the long grass near the front door and you can still find the remains of that brick wall on which

22 E. T. 214-15.
23 E. T. 214-15.
24 E. T. 215-16.
25 Cf. *Mr Noon*, where the DHL character says to the Frieda character: 'Don't gush' (*MN* 213:37).

Lawrence sat, now very low indeed. Next time you are going along Moorgreen Road, glance down to the cottage, and give a thought to a place and a couple Lawrence loved to go to: where he used strong language to make his point; where he and the Holbrooks laughed and laughed; where he went the day his mother died; where he parted with Jessie: and where his relationship with Frieda was so happy, so full of promise. And the tree – a pear tree – blossomed. 'Moorgreen seems sweet to me ... '

'You Haggites see the Best of Me!'

Dora Phillips Hall, Eastwood, October 2003

Clive Leivers had asked me to be the J. D. Chambers lecturer for the Haggs Farm Preservation Society in 2003; I was very happy to agree. It was an afternoon talk in the Dora Phillips Hall, a venue where I had never previously spoken. It was also a relief to do my final talk of the year without heat, stress or technical problems; and it was, I still recall, a very happy occasion with a very appreciative audience.

I feel very honoured to be your J. D. Chambers lecturer this year; I've known the name of Jonathan David Chambers ever since I started looking into Lawrence's life, about forty years ago, and I always depended heavily on his writing about his family and about Jessie as a kind of counterweight to what Jessie herself wrote. I also owe Ann Howard my gratitude for supplying me (and Cambridge) with the best copy I have ever seen of the famous 1906 picture of the Haggs family, for the Cambridge biography. To give this lecture is, to me, an opportunity to speak gratefully and sympathetically and loyally in memory of a man, his life's work and his life's writing: whom I think of personally (though I never knew him) with great respect and affection.

This is going to be a lecture on Lawrence and the Haggs. I'm very conscious of all the possibilities lurking in my title, 'Ah, you Haggites see the best of me!'[1] Lawrence said it (according to Jessie) more than once: he said it 'whimsically': and it leaves me not only with the question 'why was that?' but with the more worrying question 'so what was he like when you *didn't* see the best of him?'

In pursuit of these answers I am going to start by looking again at one of the famous documents of all, of Lawrence's

1 J. D. Chambers, 'Memories of D. H. Lawrence', *Renaissance and Modern Studies*, xvi (1972), 12; E. T. 134.

relationship with the Chambers family: the letter he wrote on 15 November 1928 to J. D. Chambers himself: its very terms familiar to everyone who knows Lawrence. I don't think, however, that we've proved very good at reading that letter for what is there – as opposed to what we prefer to think is there (which is simply that Lawrence always loved the Haggs and the Chambers family). This is what Lawrence wrote, from the island of Port Cros in the Mediterranean:

> Dear David
> I hardly recognized you as J. D. – and you must be a man now, instead of a thin little lad with very fair hair. Ugh, what a gap in time! it makes me feel scared.
>
> Whatever I forget, I shall never forget the Haggs – I loved it so. I loved to come to you all, it really was a new life began in me there. The water-pippin by the door – those maiden-blush roses that Flower [the horse] would lean over and eat – and Trip [the bull-terrier] floundering round – And stewed figs for tea in winter, and in August green stewed apples. Do you still have them? Tell your mother I never forget, no matter where life carries us. – And does she still blush if somebody comes and finds her in a dirty white apron? or doesn't she wear work-aprons any more? Oh I'd love to be nineteen again, and coming up through the Warren and catching the first glimpse of the buildings. Then I'd sit on the sofa under the window, and we'd crowd round the little table to tea, in that tiny little kitchen I was so at home in.
>
> Son' tempi passati, cari miei! quanto cari, non saprete mai! ['There are times past, my dears! how dear, you will never know!'] – I could never tell you in English how much it all meant to me, how I still feel about it.
>
> If there is anything I can ever do for you, do tell me. – Because whatever else I am, I am somewhere still the same Bert who rushed with such joy to the

Haggs.
Ever. D. H. Lawrence[2]

And in a postscript he gives his London agent's address, so that they would be able to get in touch.

We all get involved in the myths of our own lives; we start to enact the feelings which we ought to have had; which we tell ourselves we should have had, because this WAS a time of sheer, unalloyed joy, this time at the Haggs.

But it wasn't ... not (as Frieda would say) by long chalks. However lovely the letter, I am struck all over again by a kind of overpowering, or devouring, nostalgia in it, of a kind in which Lawrence very, very rarely engaged (I cannot actually think of another example, not even in his writing about the ranch, which he regretted long and deeply): as well as the omission of an awful lot of things. Including, for example, actually expressing to David Chambers how dearly he still loved and remembered the Chambers family. He says it in Italian – and not many of the family, if any, would have understood that. And then he says he *couldn't* say it in English. Though they understood enough: enough not to dare to tell Jessie what he had written. (They only told her about that letter the week after his death: and they were right, as she confessed that if she had known about the letter 'I could not have kept from writing. But they never told me until now.'[3]) These are odd things. What exactly was Lawrence doing in that letter?

The context in which it was written helps us understand it. It was written in the late autumn of 1928: after the publication and distribution of *Lady Chatterley's Lover* earlier in the summer and autumn. Lawrence and Frieda had left the Villa Mirenda near Florence in June and spent July and August at altitude in Switzerland – where they were visited by

2 *6L* 618.
3 Nehls, iii. 452.

Peggy King and her mother – hoping in that way to harden up Lawrence's lungs and stop his TB in its tracks: a task made harder by the fact that Lawrence and Frieda had decided together that he was not suffering from TB at all, just from acute bronchitis. He had actually had a wretched summer in 1928, with small haemorrhages continuing, and unable to walk far because the place in Switzerland they'd chosen to go to, Gsteig bei Gstaad, at 4,000 feet, was on the edge of an Alp, and incredibly steep in all directions. Once up there, in the chalet Kesselmatte, Lawrence was in effect marooned: and they were there for more than two months. Finally, they came down, to see Frieda's mother in Baden-Baden; and while there the Lawrences finally decided to give up the Villa Mirenda, their current home. Although they had at first enjoyed living there, in 1926, the Mirenda was now irresistibly linked in Lawrence's mind with his haemorrhages of July 1927. Places he associated with illness (like Oaxaca and Mexico City) he never wanted to go back to, and he was now convinced that the Mirenda 'didn't suit my health'.[4] He had never been really happy there the previous winter; and now the peasant families they had got to know so well were being sent away, the Wilkinson family had left in March, and the place was starting to feel distant from the friends on whom they now depended particularly: Earl and Achsah Brewster, and Maria and Aldous Huxley. Frieda returned to the Mirenda to see to the packing up of their belongings; Lawrence waited for her in the Mediterranean port of Le Lavandou, near Toulon. They had been invited for the winter to the island of Port Cros, where Richard Aldington, Arabella Yorke and Brigit Patmore (whom they had known for years: she had played her part as 'Clariss Browning' in *Aaron's Rod*) had taken a house. This must have particularly appealed to Lawrence, after the failure of altitude to do him any good: sea air, the Mediterranean, would surely be better.

4 *6L* 573, *7L* 37.

Aldington was. however, both malicious and discreet when he commented that Frieda's task of giving up the Mirenda was 'a complicated process, since it involved a journey to Trieste'.[5] Frieda had seen rather little of Angelo Ravagli since April, and it is my understanding that – by now – she had started her affair with him; probably around April 1928. Lawrence could do nothing except sit and wait for her. He certainly knew what was happening.

The Vigie was a borrowed house at the top of the island of Port Cros: another place with the most marvellous view, of the kind that Lawrence chose to live in, time after time. But Lawrence's health was, by the autumn of 1928, a real problem. Aldington, who had not seen him since October 1926, was surprised how much frailer he had got, over the past two years. Although Lawrence liked the Vigie, and the island, and liked the people there, he was far too ill to take part in their expeditions, 'or indeed to rough it in so remote and exposed a place'. The steepness of the road from the harbour up to the Vigie meant that he was 'perched, as at Kesselmatte', and could not go with the others when they went down to the beach, to go swimming each afternoon. Aldington remembered how he would listen to Lawrence's 'dreadful hollow cough at night, and wonder what on earth I should do if he got worse'; they agreed that one of them should always stay with him when the rest of the party went off for the day or the afternoon. Frieda had come back from Italy (and Ravagli) with a cold, which of course Lawrence instantly caught. He also had 'two days hemorrhage' and felt 'rather rotten': 'this is worse than the Mirenda', he found himself thinking.[6] When Brigit took his breakfast to him in bed in the morning, and put a coat round his shoulders, 'I could feel his pyjamas soaked with perspiration.' He would give her one of his newly arrived, very splendidly produced

5 Nehls, iii. 253.

6 *6L* 593; Nehls, iii. 253; *6L* 598.

copies of *Sun*, inscribing it 'to Brigit / the angel in the Vigie'.[7]

It was while they were on the island, too, that Lawrence got a letter from his agent, which included some of the responses to *Lady Chatterley* which had been appearing in the English press during the autumn. There cannot have been much: *John Bull*'s notorious review, and a piece in the *Sunday Chronicle*. These had both appeared in mid-October. The group read them aloud, with shouts of hilarity: this is Brigit Patmore's account.

> 'My God!' one of us gave a shout. 'Here, in this one, Lorenzo, one of them calls you a cesspool!'
>
> He made a grimace which might have been a smile or slight nausea.
>
> 'Really? One's fellow creatures are too generous. It's *quite* worth while giving of one's best, isn't it?' Then, as if speaking to himself, 'Nobody *likes* being called a cesspool.'

In fact, we know what the press cutting had said: not that Lawrence was a cesspool, but that his novel was. The person who shouted out must have said 'one of them calls *Lady C* a cesspool!' And Lawrence must have said 'Nobody *likes* their book being called a cesspool.'

But various things went wrong at La Vigie, apart from those reviews. For one thing, Aldington was in the process of starting an affair with Brigit Patmore, and leaving Arabella Yorke, and both the Lawrences sided with Arabella, of whom they were very fond. And it also seems to have been at La Vigie that Lawrence was confronted by the fact that Frieda had started her affair with Ravagli, and that Aldington was helping her by concealing Ravagli's letters when collecting the

[7] Nehls, iii. 255; see *D. H. Lawrence*, Catalogue 51 (Simon Finch Rare Books Limited, 2002), item 75.

post.[8] Lawrence ended up violently angry with Aldington. His poem 'I know a noble Englishman', probably started at La Vigie, would assert that 'Ronald ... never wants a woman, he doesn't like women', because 'he's an instinctive homosexual'.[9] Aldington never, I think, forgave Lawrence for that ... and the party broke up months earlier than they had planned to. For another thing, the place was far more isolated than they had imagined it would be. But deepest of all, Lawrence was thoroughly depressed and miserable. One afternoon when the others were all off swimming – they all bathed, Aldington recalled with relish more than thirty years later, '*naked* daily together on one of the plages of Port-Cros, and then lay in the sun' – Lawrence told Brigit Patmore a little about his desolation. He described how 'you have something in your life which makes up for everything, and then find you haven't got it'. He might have meant Frieda: but she had *never* been loyal. I think he meant sexual desire. And whether they meant to or not, Frieda, Brigit and Aldington (and in her own way poor Arabella) were making horribly clear to him the continuing importance of sexual desire in their lives. Brigit felt that Lawrence 'was far away in a loneliness where nothing but what he desired could be of use to him'. She tried to tell him that his writing had mattered immensely to her in re-establishing her own sense of herself after she had been ill; but found she was only making matters worse. He replied: 'Yes. Once I could do that. But I can't any

8 Martha Gordon Crotch wrote in her 1935-6 memoirs how 'I believe there was a terrible scene once when Richard Aldington undertook to call at post office for letters Frieda was having sent there ... R. A. arrived with a missive in his pocket for F. found them all bathing except Lorenzo – He undressed to join them & threw his coat down carelessly – the letter fell out. Lorenzo found it & opened it. – It was from the Capitano' (Yale). Martha Crotch dated the event to Bandol, but the circumstances fit Île de Port Cros much better.

9 '[I Know a noble Englishman]', *Poems* 953-5 (variant version).

more.'[10] In the past, he could convey his experience of the body and its desires directly in his writing. He felt that that no longer happened; such writing was now inevitably either nostalgic or reminiscent.

And it was at just this point that the letter from Jessie Chambers' younger brother David came, and he wrote that famous response about the Haggs. Its nostalgia – for a time when he was well, active, young, hopeful – is palpable, and inevitably added to by the things that were happening round him. Its desperately nostalgic reminiscence of the old days – 'whatever else I am, I am somewhere still the same Bert who rushed with such joy to the Haggs'[11] – is that of a man who had left all that terribly far behind him, and who must have wondered whether he indeed *was* the same Bert any more. It's an odd formulation: 'Whatever else I am' – as if he feared that he *had* indeed changed, into something he didn't like very much. He actually uses it twice in the letter: 'whatever else I am' and 'Whatever I forget': suggesting that there was so much else that he would forget, if he could, and so much else he could be.

What is most remarkable, however, is how the letter keeps stressing how much at home he was at the Haggs ... in the group of people he loved. The whole subject of 'home' is something central in Lawrence's life and writing. He would, so to speak, come home repeatedly in his writing, as he recreated the people and the landscapes of the Eastwood region, even when living and writing hundreds of miles away: acknowledging how intimately he belonged to his family and its quarrels and its loving mother, even as he diligently wrote his way out of all such attachments (declaring that he rejected any idea of home, or love, and hated Eastwood and the past). But belonging to 'home' was always intensely problematic for

10 Richard Aldington to H. D., 17 October 1960 (*Richard Aldington & H. D.*, ed. Zilboorg, p. 251); Patmore 138.

11 *6L* 618.

him. In 1915 he would comment, about the Eastwood miners: 'I love them like brothers – but my God, I hate them too ...' [12] 'How many times have I packed our miserable boxes', he grumbled in 1919, as they engaged in yet another move to a borrowed house: but he still insisted on liking 'not to have a home'. This was in direct opposition to Frieda, who 'craved for a home and solidity'. In August 1923, about to sail to England with Frieda, he told Murry that, now it came to it, he could not bear the thought of 'England and home and my people': [13] and he did not go. When he eventually did, in December, one of the first things he did was write the caustic 'On Coming Home' for Murry's *Adelphi*. But later, thinking about the subsequent drunken debacle at the Café Royal, he wrote: 'That is what coming home means to me. Never again, pray the Lord.' [14] In 1925, once again in America, and thinking of visiting Europe, he had remarked, with grim irony, 'one's native land has a sort of hopeless attraction, when one is away'.[15] But where did he belong, now? He had always insisted that coming back was not 'coming home': 'I won't say home, it isn't home.'[16] And after coming back in 1925, and seeing the Midlands again, he had written, despairingly, 'Nothing depresses me more than to come home to the place where I was born.'[17]

So, in 1928, where was he now at home? He and Frieda had, literally, just given up their home at the Mirenda; he had no home. And though he was with a group at Port Cros, he still felt horribly isolated and cut off. The Chambers' farm had been one of the very few places in Lawrence's life where he had ever felt at home, and he never forgot it: it was the home he wanted to be in, as opposed to the home in

12 *2L* 489.
13 *4L* 483.
14 *5L* 46-7.
15 *5L* 312.
16 *4L* 520.
17 *LEA* 50:2-3.

Eastwood to which he belonged and continued to fight with himself about. In another mood from the one in which he wrote to David Chambers, he would have rejected the whole idea of home, or wanting to be there, or feeling nostalgic about home. We can be absolutely sure of this: on his last visit to England in September 1926 he had been for a walk with Willie Hopkin, and they had come in sight of the Haggs. We can construct what he thought then from what Hopkin remembered, and from what Lawrence used of that walk in the second version of *Lady Chatterley's Lover*, where Connie and Parkin actually come in view of the old farmhouse, in a walk described on the last page of the novel; they stop 'above the grey-green country. Across was Haggs Farm. Beyond, Underwood, the mining village and the mines.'[18] Hopkin and Lawrence went much closer; and Hopkin watched Lawrence when they got to Felley:

> he stood still and looked across to the Haggs. I went and sat by the pond. After a few minutes I turned and looked at him. He stood stiffly as a statue, and there was an expression of dreadful pain on his face.
>
> After a while he told me to come along. For ten minutes he never spoke a word, and then he broke out into a lot of brilliant nonsense.
>
> As we neared his old house [the Lynn Croft house, perhaps, but possibly the Breach house or the Walker Street house] he never gave it a glance. I asked when he was coming over again. His reply was 'Never! I hate the damned place.'[19]

In another version of his account of their time at Felley, as Lawrence stood looking across to the Haggs, Hopkin wrote how 'I have seen sadness on many a face, but nothing like

[18] *FSLC* 570:15-17.

[19] Nehls, iii. 93.

Lawrence's at that moment.'[20]

This is especially interesting in the light of that letter to J. D. Chambers. The warmth of the family and the time glowed all the more vividly not only because of the weakened physical state in which he now lived, but because it was both tantalising as an idea of what belonging to a group of people, happily together, might be like: and it also made him despair. Away from the Haggs he had never had that familial warmth, that love: he insisted he did not want it. But now, on Port Cros, at all times living the life of an invalid, cut off from the lively everyday concerns of the people he was with, cut off from Frieda, with those reviews of *Lady Chatterley* reminding him how much hatred was waiting for him in England, he must have felt more torn than ever. He had reacted badly to the visit Emily and Peggy had made a couple of months earlier, in August 1928: she would call him 'our Bert' but he was certain that 'I am not really "our Bert". Come to that, I never was.'[21] He had once been, for sure; but he was determined to be so no longer. On the other hand, Lawrence was sadly struck by the gulf, 'always yawning, horribly obvious to me', between him and his sister and niece: 'somehow it depresses me terribly'.[22] The reaction between belonging and independence went on being VERY actual in him. *He* didn't go swimming naked every day: he wasn't one of the happy crowd. And he was more distanced from Frieda than he had ever been, since 1912. Well, he wanted to be independent. But oh to be nineteen again

His response to David Chambers, therefore, tells us as much about Lawrence in 1928 as it does about the Lawrence of 1904; I would say, rather more. Both the joy and the despair underlying it belong to that very difficult complex of

20 Derek Britton, *Lady Chatterley: The Making of the Novel* (1988), p. 115.

21 *6L* 535.

22 *6L* 533.

feelings around home, and belonging, and being part of a group, and being independent, which had gone on in him since he was a teenager.

But what the letter does *not* contain, too, is very interesting. It contained not a mention of Jessie. This was perhaps tactful; he couldn't have helped realising that how he had treated her might still be a very sore subject in the Chambers family, who must have seen him – for a while at least – as someone who had left their daughter in the lurch, and her as someone who had never really got over him. And in their turn they were very careful neither to tell her they had been in touch with Lawrence, nor to let her know what he had said. But in his own recreation of the Haggs, in this extraordinary glow of memory, Lawrence simply left out the feelings of the years of strain and anxiety and (finally) emotional disaster with Jessie: even left out his own actual feelings in 1928. It was the still living actuality of the place and the family, the warmth and the home, on which he concentrated and (we might say) re-made: not the loss of them.

So what had he meant, so many years earlier, when he had said to the Chambers family, 'Ah, you Haggites see the best of me'? What was it that he was all too aware of, but which they didn't see? What, in fact, was the Haggs an escape from, that he re-created so astonishingly in 1928?

In the early 1890s, the Chambers family had occupied a house along Greenhills Lane, near the Breach, while the Lawrences were living there. The father, Edmund Chambers, a native of Eastwood (his father, 'Pawny Chambers', and mother had run a pawnbroker's shop), had a smallholding and a milk round in Eastwood. Edmund's wife Ann was, like Lydia Lawrence, a stranger in Eastwood, and a woman who never seems to have been especially happy there or anywhere; she had struck up acquaintance with Lydia at the Chapel in

Albert Street. Both of them 'hated the mining communities to which their husbands had brought them' and, according to Ann Chambers' son, they 'found in the Chapel ... the only place in which they felt really at home in an otherwise alien world'. The children of the two families met at Chapel and Sunday school: May and Jessie, the two eldest girls, remembered seeing Lawrence at Sunday school forgetting a poem he had learned for a recital, going white and provoking his sister Emily to hysterical giggles.[23]

In 1898, the Chambers family moved on from the smallholding, and rented the Haggs Farm near Underwood; an informally posed photograph shows them the first summer after the move. Seven children cluster around a mother who is only just forty but who also looks far older, and who is too busy dealing with her newest-born David to be concerned with the camera. The twelve-year-old Jessie kneels on the grass and seems almost the only one of the family to care much about the photograph; she smiles winsomely. May, already a pupil-teacher at the British School in Eastwood, is sixteen, and looks thin-faced and detached on the extreme left. The youngest daughter Mollie, aged three, stares open-mouthed. The three brothers are Alan (the eldest at seventeen, extreme right, elegantly waistcoated), eleven-year-old Hubert standing in front of him (a large-headed boy) and nine-year-old Bernard in front of May. The thirty-six-year-old father Edmund, elegantly dressed like Alan, in what looks like his best boater, is tall and thin and appears to have something in his hands which he has had no time to put down before being marshalled into the photograph.

Lydia Lawrence had a standing invitation to visit the Chambers family in their new place, but it was not until 1901 that she and Lawrence first followed the field paths out to the Haggs, on a half holiday in the early summer of his last year at the High School: he a 'tall, fair boy' with a 'swiftly changing

[23] Chambers, 'Memories', pp. 6-7; E. T. 15-16; Nehls, iii. 555.

expression', she a 'bright, vivacious little woman'. May Chambers, always an acid commentator, recognised how they came 'from the bricks and mortar of streets of houses where bay windows and front room furniture and new clothes were so very important'.[24] That was the world which the Chambers family prided themselves on having left, but which the Lawrences had risen into: the bay-window, the suite of mahogany and horse-hair chairs, the Brussels carpet rather than the usual rag rugs of the miner's house, the mahogany chiffonier and the oval table. But whereas Lydia Lawrence had always fought the dominating male figures of her world, whether her father or her husband, or her sons, Ann Chambers felt dominated by her men-folk; she had had her last child at the age of thirty-nine and would 'shudder when the subject of sex was mentioned'.[25] Mrs Morel, on an equivalent visit to the farm in *Sons and Lovers*, pities her friend: 'I'm sorry for her, and I'm sorry for him too.'[26]

For all its griminess, Eastwood was set in a surprisingly rural landscape. From the Walker Street house the family could look westwards to the monument at Crich Stand in the far distance of Derbyshire, nine-and-a-half miles away,[27] and Arthur Lawrence would gather mushrooms on his early morning's walk across the fields to work. To keep his mouth moist underground he would chew grass-stems. Although a town boy, Lawrence had grown up with a considerable knowledge of plants and the natural world. Arthur Lawrence, 'very good on wild life', according to his daughter Emily, not

24 E. T. 22, 24; Nehls, iii. 561.

25 Nehls, iii. 536. Miriam's comment – 'Mother said to me—"there is one thing in marriage that is always dreadful, but you have to bear it"' (*SL* 334:38-9) – suggests that Ann Chambers may have said something similar.

26 *SL* 158:16.

27 The present tower at Crich was built in 1923, replacing a monument 'sturdy and squat' erected in the 1820s, which Paul can see from Bestwood (*SL* 206:12-13).

only knew flowers, wild herbs and plants in general, and made himself a tea mixture out of the herbs he gathered, but 'watched every bird, every stir in the trembling grass'; on one occasion he brought home an abandoned baby rabbit.[28] He also worked the family allotment in the common gardens. His sons helped him; in 1900 Lawrence's acquisition of a standard flower-recognition book, *Our Country's Flowers and How to Know Them*,[29] suggests the direction in which his interests were growing, though he might have been happier learning from a book than from his father.

On his visits to the Haggs Farm Lawrence seems to have developed an altogether new awareness of the countryside and woods: its landscapes would dominate a great deal of his fiction, and as late as 1928 he would be recreating places and views he had first seen that day in 1901. His joy in going to the Haggs was not only, however, a reaction against the ugliness, narrowness and conventionality of his home in Eastwood. The Haggs offered something even more important: a kind of alternative family. In the spring and summer of 1902, an important part of his convalescence after pneumonia turned out to consist of going out to the Haggs and discovering how he could participate in life there. He 'could ride up in [Edmund's] milk cart and join his lads in the hayfield'; later, the walk there and back was thought to be good for his health.[30] Lawrence first made friends with the two younger boys, and then with Alan; he once claimed that the nearest he had ever come to 'perfect love' had been at the age of 'about sixteen', which would be before September 1902, and he was probably thinking of one of the Chambers' boys.[31] May was in the middle of a prolonged adolescent

28 Emily King, 'Son and Lover', BBC Third Programme, 8 May 1955 (UN: La Av 3/2); *EmyE* 201:16-29.

29 His second Mathematics prize at the High School, signed and dated 28 July 1900 (Jean Temple).

30 Chambers, 'Memories', p. 10; Nehls, iii. 578.

31 Compton Mackenzie, *My Life and Times, Octave Five 1915-1923*

extraction of herself from her family, and rejected the High School boy's offer of help with her homework; but the younger daughter, Jessie, seems to have been drawn to Lawrence from the start. Although his relationship with her would develop into one of the most important of his young life, when he first started going to the Haggs regularly, in the summer of 1902, she was no more than a rather immature fifteen; he was both better read and better educated, as well as eighteen months older, and did not spend much time with her. Her reaction to being surrounded by brothers who were physically active, and rather contemptuous of her, had been to shut herself away in a world of her own in which she was the heroine of poetry and romance; her younger brothers despised this and 'took delight in bursting in on her rhapsodical moods and shattering her poetical day-dreams in a wild scrimmage of slaps and bangs'.[32] Her brother David remembered her as 'equal to anybody'; nearly as tall as her elder brothers, she was equally broad-shouldered; solidly built, disciplined, dedicated, yearning. He also recalled how she would stand up to her younger brothers: she would 'wind a scarf round each fist and challenge them both to a fight'. Her 'lighter moods', however, were rare.[33] More often, she was simply angry with men for bossing her about or ignoring her. By contrast, Lawrence was someone serious; the realisation seems to have come around 1903, when he and she found themselves talking increasingly, and Lawrence came into her life as the person she believed would save her from her family. Eventually he offered to teach her; and together they worked on the very subjects, 'algìbbra an' French', which distinguished advanced education from

---

(1966), p. 168; Mackenzie however (knowing DHL's background) recalled him describing how he had loved a 'young coal-miner'.

32 Nehls, iii. 537.

33 See *EY* Illustration 21; Nehls, iii. 537.

ordinary.[34]

It is hard to overestimate how important the Haggs family was for Lawrence, long before he became close to Jessie. The coincidence of his return to life in the spring and summer of 1902 – and his new place in his mother's affections – with this discovery of another family to which he eagerly turned, and individuals whom he loved, suggests to me that he was reacting against the very intimacy which made such demands on him in Eastwood. Not for the last time in his life, a passionate emotional involvement (with his mother) had grown up in Lawrence simultaneously with a powerful desire to break away from the very object of his love. What many, even most people feel to some extent, in love and relationship, Lawrence lived through with an intensity that was surprising and often shocking. The way he turned to the Chambers family is perhaps its first clear instance. He had a deep longing for the normal: to *be* normal, himself. That seemed possible at the Haggs. At home, he was discovering, it was all too highly charged with tension and incipient conflict and demanding love.

For the anger, outbursts and loud quarrels of the Chambers family would have felt very different from the moralising, critical and emotionally demanding atmosphere of Walker Street. In Eastwood he was up against a household dominated by women: his mother and Ada (and until her marriage Emily), with his father largely absent or silenced. The Farm offered a simpler, old-fashioned world, in which men took precedence if they could, and women argued back: were not simply morally superior. The Chambers boys looked down on their sisters and tried to order them about; the girls fiercely resisted. But, for adolescents in particular, other people's families are nearly always easier to deal with than their own. The Chambers family seem to have felt a great deal more emotionally secure to Lawrence *because* of their

34 *SL* 96:6.

constant quarrels, their overt affections, their singing and boisterous intimacy, their jokes and laughter: 'He used to say that our laughter was Homeric.' He 'made us even happy with one another while he was there, – no small achievement in a family like ours!'[35]

The Chambers never forgot him: when he died in 1930, 'We all, as a family, mourn him, for the memories of old days were unspeakably dear to us all.'[36] Lawrence never forgot, perhaps never got over, this new experience of love and acceptance and family, which was why it was still so powerful in 1928. 'Whatever I forget, I shall never forget the Haggs – I loved it so.' In a life so full of radical changes, it was vitally important to him that, somehow, neither he nor the Haggs should change: 'whatever else I am, I am somewhere still the same Bert who rushed with such joy to the Haggs'. He had, once in his life, been capable of uninhibited joy: he knew that. For, perhaps above all else, the Haggs offered both devotion and companionship: something for which he would go on looking for the rest of his life. 'Then I'd sit on the sofa under the window, and we'd crowd round the little table to tea, in that tiny little kitchen I was so at home in.'[37] From 1902 to 1906, what mattered was discovering how much and how happily he could be 'at home' there: and he gave to the Chambers family as richly and lovingly as they gave to him. Ann Chambers loved him 'like one of her own', and he loved her; he was devoted to Alan; and with the family he could be the lively and cheerful son he found it so difficult to be at

35 E. T. 30; 'The Collected Letters of Jessie Chambers', ed. George J. Zytaruk, *D. H. Lawrence Review*, xii (Spring-Summer 1979), 58.

36 'Collected Letters', p. 49. The Ellis family at the farm at Wandoo in *The Boy in the Bush* (1924) was a later recreation of the Chambers family, in particular of their singing and laughter: 'the family! the family! Jack still loved it. It seemed to fill the whole of life for him' (*BB* 71:28-9).

37 *6L* 618. See too 'The Shades of Spring' (1914): 'To his last day, he would dream of this place' (*PO* 102:38).

home, though his good training at home would have made him even more welcome. At the Haggs, he 'set about household tasks, such as cooking, and even washing, and would help to prepare the family meal and lay the table. With Bert in charge, the meal was a family party.'[38] He could be an exhilarating companion, and probably first discovered this, too, at the uninhibited Haggs. Nearly fifty years later May recalled 'Bert with his mischievous grin':[39] his vivacity, his sense of adventure, his capacity for games and mimicry and fun were not only what he brought to them but seems to have discovered by going.

In retrospect, it all feels a little like Arthur Lawrence escaping Lydia Lawrence, and leaving behind the strictness of home and its moral absolutes for the farm and the 'wholesome happiness' of uncritical companionship.[40] It was at the Haggs that, not perhaps surprisingly, Lawrence seemed most like Arthur. He sang with the family (his father had been in the choir of St James's Church at Brinsley as a boy), and he demonstrated how he could dance 'in our little kitchen, and once while we paused for breath he said: "Father says one ought to be able to dance on a threepenny bit".'[41] Jessie, knowing Lawrence's hatred of his father, was surprised at that little revelation; but Lawrence also demonstrated his talent (his father's too) for mimicry. One set piece was a long-drawn-out row between his father and his mother which took Arthur's side and reduced its listeners to helplessness: 'even mother had to laugh'.[42] David Chambers, again, remembered: 'I think everyone loved him at this time; he combined with his vivacity a sweetness of disposition that was quite irresistible.'[43]

38 Chambers, 'Memories', p. 11.
39 May Holbrook to David Chambers, 25 March 1949 (Howard).
40 *1L* 103.
41 E. T. 30.
42 E. T. 32.
43 Chambers, 'Memories', p. 12; E. T. 134.

It was hardly surprising that his mother and his sisters grew jealous of his constant visits. Very soon after he started going, he confessed to May Chambers that, though he wanted to come one Saturday, 'They won't let me'; she also heard how 'We as a family were stealing him from his mother', while Jessie recalled: 'He told us rather shamefacedly that his mother said he might as well pack his things and come and live with us.'[44] The Lawrences resented his concentration on a family so unlike themselves; just as they would come to be deeply suspicious of the amount of time he and Jessie spent together. Lawrence was acutely aware of their disapproval but commented, sadly, 'If it wasn't this, it would be something else.'[45] But it was the farm and the family, not Jessie, which made the Haggs irresistible to him; and in that way his 1928 letter is utterly honest, too. Emily once even insisted on coming out to the Haggs with him, to see what was so marvellous about it, but all she found memorable was 'that awful walk'.[46] But her brother's visits to the Haggs remained a problem in the family for years; the fact that he kept going, in the face of the opposition he was up against, shows how necessary they were to him.

It is, they say, never too late to have a happy childhood, and Lawrence had (at the age of fifteen) at last discovered his at the Haggs: it was the place where he could be at his best, bringing the best out of others. And no one else ever again saw him quite like that. Which he knew, and regretted deeply. 'Whatever else I am', and he had been many other selves over the years, somewhere he needed to feel that he was still the happy, exciting and excited being who had rushed, with such joy, to the Haggs, before the damage of a lifetime started to accrue.

44 Nehls, iii. 565; E. T. 28.
45 Nehls, iii. 591.
46 Nehls, iii. 588.

Lawrence, Heseltine and the Inner Life

Montgomery, Sunday 18 December 2005

This lecture came about simply because – back in the 1980s – I had got to know Rhian Davies, who was now living in Montgomery and was organising a Peter Warlock conference there. She asked if I would come and talk and – after an initial hesitation, on the grounds that I didn't know enough to be of any use to Warlockians – I found myself taking part in a fascinating two day event centred on the beautifully restored Town Hall in Montgomery, one of the most fascinating small towns I had ever seen. I was put up for two nights by the owner of the local hardware shop in a wonderful eighteenth-century house; the Warlockians had organised music recitals, a church service using Warlock's settings, events in pubs, lectures and walks; they made me thoroughly welcome. My talk now seems a little elementary but it did its job for an audience who were not Lawrence specialists, and had indeed every reason to look askance at someone committed to singing the praises of a writer who disliked Warlock so thoroughly. But I was treated with great courtesy and unfailing attention; it was a wonderfully happy weekend.

If you know anything about D. H. Lawrence and Peter Warlock – or Philip Heseltine – you probably believe that Lawrence put a hateful, potentially slanderous portrait of Heseltine as Julius Halliday into his 1921 novel *Women in Love*: a portrait as offensive as the slightly later one by Aldous Huxley (as Coleman in his 1923 novel *Antic Hay*) would be cheerful and delightful. But there is so much myth and legend caught up in the Heseltine-Lawrence relationship that it needs a sober re-telling: and three recently discovered letters from Lawrence to Heseltine, two from very early in their friendship, and not available to Barry Smith when he wrote his biography, are a very good starting point. They help us understand how a relationship that began so well, and might have been productive for both men, went so horribly wrong and caused them both to react in ways that were revealing – at times horribly revealing – of them both.

I shall be referring to Warlock throughout as Heseltine,

the name under which Lawrence knew him. Their relationship falls into a number of phases. The opening one lasts from mid-November to the end of December 1915: the second from January to April 1916: the third very brief one in the summer of 1917: and the last follows the publication of *Women in Love* in the summer of 1921.

Heseltine was aware of Lawrence long before Lawrence was of Heseltine: Lawrence was nine years older, and by 1914 was the author of three novels and a book of poems, of which Heseltine had read *Love Poems and Others* by February 1914 and *Sons and Lovers* by October 1914. In fact, I believe that Heseltine set to music at least two of Lawrence's early poems. Neither setting unfortunately survives, but the fact that they even existed is a tribute to the power that Lawrence's work exerted over Heseltine when the latter was only nineteen.

When Heseltine came to London in 1914 he wanted to meet Lawrence, but the latter was only occasionally there until the late summer of 1915. Lawrence's return to London seems to have coincided with the twenty-one-year-old Heseltine starting his relationship with the dark-skinned model Minnie Lucy Channing, universally known as Puma. This period quickly turned out, however, to be Lawrence's unhappiest time for years. His novel *The Rainbow*, published 30 September 1915, got terrible reviews, at least two of which suggested police action (the book was seen as proclaiming lesbianism); a body called the National Council for Public Morals took the case up and made all the fuss it could. Copies were seized by the police at the end of October and the book's publisher, Methuen, was prosecuted for obscenity in a magistrate's court on 13 November; he pleaded guilty. The book was destroyed and Lawrence's career as a writer of fiction was in effect over for five years (which made it almost impossible for him to earn his living). There were tut-tuttings in the press about the serious work of a serious author being treated in this way, but very little actual support. Lawrence's friends in general did not like the book – his close friends Middleton Murry and Katherine Mansfield, for example, actively hated it. And even though her MP husband Philip Morrell managed to ask a question in the House of Commons, Lawrence's friend Ottoline Morrell also disliked the book. A planned letter of protest to be signed by the contemporary authors Walter de la Mare, E. M. Forster, J. D. Beresford, Hugh Walpole, Gilbert Cannan and Murry was never published and (I suspect) its text never agreed on.

As a result, the loyalty of a young man like Heseltine would have been especially nice. The coincidence of timing is exact. The novel was banned at Bow Street on Saturday 13 November, and Heseltine met Lawrence three days later, on Tuesday 16 November, when Lawrence was invited to dinner (it had been the young poet Robert Nichols who had effected the introduction).[1]

At this point, however, Lawrence was set on going away to America. He had planned this before the *Rainbow* prosecution, but the latter confirmed him in his plan. People talk grandly about Lawrence and his desire to found a community called *Rananim* but that is actually wrong; Lawrence only ever used the word Rananim about the original fantasy game played a year earlier with Koteliansky, Murry, Cannan and Mary Cannan. That had been a pure fantasy: what Lawrence hoped to do in the winter of 1915 was very real. It was to go and live and write in the southern states of the USA, not with an ideal society of friends about him, but with his wife Frieda – though if others *were* to come too, he would be extremely pleased. But he was not planning a colony; he wanted to go to a place which was *not* committed to war and destruction the way his own society was, a year and a half into the First World War. By the autumn of 1915,

1 *The Letters of Peter Warlock (Philip Heseltine)*, ed. Barry Smith, 4 vols. (Woodbridge, 2005), ii. 387.

Lawrence felt 'as if the whole thing were coming to an end – the whole of England, of the Christian era; as if ours was the age only of decline and fall ... I cannot bear it – this England, this past.'[2] 'I am sure I cannot do any more work for this country.'[3]

His first plan to go to America – and he nearly did go, on Wednesday 24 November – was delayed because the Society of Authors *did* after all seem to be mounting a protest about *The Rainbow*; but by then Heseltine had already done all he could in the way of being helpful by finding out from Frederick Delius whether the orange groves in Florida he had known in the 1880s would be suitable for Lawrence (the answer was that they certainly would not be).

But talking to young men like Heseltine – and Aldous Huxley, and Robert Nichols – was very encouraging to Lawrence, quite apart from the helpfulness that Heseltine had immediately shown. It was also, however, obvious to Lawrence that Heseltine was a very troubled and unsure person. And Lawrence from the start seems to have wanted to help him – or, as a friend said, 'rescue him'. [4] They were together again on Sunday 21 November (incidentally the day after Heseltine had moved into his flat at 12A Rossetti Mansions in Chelsea).

By the 21st, Lawrence knew Heseltine well enough to have heard the latter's cynicism about the Puma, with whom he had been linked since the summer – and at this point Lawrence attempted to counsel him: 'Above all be careful about losing the power to love really and profoundly ... to love a woman'. Lawrence wrote to him – Lawrence demanded a lot of his correspondents, but in general they would take this kind of thing from him, because he *was* amazingly wise and incisive and understanding – 'Only don't

2 *3L* 433.

3 *2L*. 441.

4 Juliette Huxley, *Leaves of the Tulip Tree* (1986), p. 48.

be cynical and self-sufficient: your face shows traces already.'[5] Heseltine's shell of cynicism in 1915 was both obvious and hollow, and his self-sufficiency a magnificently absurd and empty kind of self-assertion. And Lawrence seems to have seen through both, at once. He was good at that: terribly, even frighteningly good at an immediate, intuitive and deep insight into the people he met. But he also linked Heseltine's defences of cynicism and self-sufficiency with Heseltine's physical presentation of himself: he believed he could see such things expressed in Heseltine's face and body, and I think that this is important, given what he would one day write about Heseltine. It is also striking that, on so short an acquaintance, he should have picked up on Heseltine's deeply problematic relationship with women as central to the difficulties of his life.

Lawrence's own next letter to Heseltine – one of the three you almost certainly won't have seen – was written on 24 November 1915, while they were still waiting for Delius's reply about Florida. The letter is mostly about Robert Nichols, but it is also focused on an extraordinary analysis that – although provoked by Nichols – is, I suspect, written to Heseltine because (a) the latter would not object to its plain speaking about sex and (b) because Lawrence suspected that Heseltine was like this too. Nichols, said Lawrence,

> is the sort of Narcissus who not only watches his own reflection, but watches his own heart beat and his own bowels work and his own penis rise, and the woman is only the mirror in which all this is reflected. It sends me mad with opposition and fury. One wants to squash a certain evil self-soul in him, his self.

And, crucially, Lawrence added: 'For God's sake don't be like Nichols, and make the whole world your mirror to reflect

5 *2L* 448.

your own physical and mental self'.[6] That little addition confirms that the remarks about Nichols were indeed about Heseltine too, may even have been written for and about him in the first place. Lawrence saw Heseltine as innately narcissistic in his feelings, not taking the women with whom he was involved into account at all: and that worried Lawrence. Heseltine was doing all these things – having a passion for Puma, for example, and also being world-weary and full of distaste for her – in a kind of self-admiration, which the woman ideally reflected, but in which she played no actual part. It was Eric Fenby who later commented that Heseltine did not care 'that much [snapping his fingers] for women. He was using them.'[7] I think that Heseltine was capable of real friendships with women: sexually, I suspect that he always tended to hate them. He would for example write about the Puma, in 1917, that she was a woman 'with whom I had never had and could never have had any but a purely bestial relation'.[8]

But Lawrence for the moment continued fond of Heseltine, wanting to help him too: while Heseltine, in the first fortnight of their acquaintance, began to confess to Lawrence his own deepest feelings and anxieties, both when they met, and in lengthy letters. An arrangement to have dinner together on Saturday 27 November was replaced by an arrangement to have tea together the following day, but letters made up a little for the lack of an opportunity for a long talk. It was on the day that he got that letter about Nichols and narcissism that Heseltine himself wrote to Colin Taylor about Lawrence – 'whom I have long venerated as the greatest literary genius of his generation'.[9] But Heseltine wrote to

6 James T. Boulton, *D. H. Lawrence, Philip Heseltine and Three Unpublished Letters* (Birmingham, 2001), p. 11.

7 Barry Smith, *Peter Warlock: The Life of Philip Heseltine* (Oxford, 1994), pp. 109-10.

8 Smith, *Peter Warlock*, p. 108.

9 *The Letters of Peter Warlock*, ed. Smith, ii. 388.

Lawrence that same day, too, Thursday 25th, in an even more personal letter which (like every one of Heseltine's letters in this correspondence with Lawrence) has unfortunately not survived, but some of whose contents we can deduce from Lawrence's reply. Heseltine must now have confessed that the girl-friend he had mentioned before, the Puma, was pregnant, yet nevertheless that she was *not* someone to whom he could devote himself, and commit himself to loving, as Lawrence had (four days earlier) advised him to love his woman. Puma would give birth to Nigel Heseltine on 3 July 1916, suggesting that she conceived at earliest in the first fortnight of October 1915 – so that mid-November would have been exactly when she might first have known (or informed Heseltine) that she was pregnant. Lawrence may even have been among the first to know; Heseltine experts in the room will know better than me when first Heseltine himself knew.

Anyway, Lawrence's response to the news of Puma's pregnancy was rather astonishing for a man who was in so many ways innately puritan: I think it an example of his encouraging his correspondent by writing in part what they would like to hear: something he regularly did, and knew he did, and did not really like himself for doing. But that kind of sympathy is mixed with a repeat of the analysis of Heseltine's problems on which he had been engaged from the start.

> Dear Heseltine
> Don't trouble about this failure of this affair with the girl – it doesn't matter – one must fail often. Only let the child be born, and don't bother. Don't admit impediments, that's all. One cannot force love, and if one has a child by a woman one doesn't love with one's soul, what does it matter? It's merely a natural occurrence – let it be natural – it is not important – only let it be natural – don't try and force yourself – not a scrap. And don't let things of the outside be

> fetters – don't admit things of the outside to govern your inner life – even having children.[10]

From that, we may gauge that Heseltine had confessed to Lawrence that the Puma, and the coming child, really made him feel anxious and torn, and upset him horribly. It is also interesting that Lawrence should unerringly have put his finger on Heseltine's odd contradiction – on the one hand utterly unconventional, on the other oddly influenced *by* the conventional, to the extent of having to rebel against it constantly, in thought, word and deed. Lawrence wanted to help him stop that constant violent rebellion and reaction, by simply admitting that such things did not really matter. And he could do that better if he were concentrating on his own 'inner life' rather than on the outsides of things against which he was reacting so strongly.

Lawrence of course was a working-class writer who had never had any money, and who had made his way entirely by what he was able to earn, and who had never needed to compromise with the middle-classes or with middle-class respectabilities ... as opposed to Heseltine, a man constantly rebellious against and in reaction to the respectable and moneyed mother who paid for everything and kept (in every sense) a check on him.

But Lawrence's stress on the 'inner life' catches my eye. It was part of Lawrence's immediate understanding of Heseltine that, however energetic and in some ways lovable Heseltine was – obviously talented, full of wit and enthusiasm, naïve, wonderfully young, funny, intelligent, attractive, highly impressionable – he was also someone who was in some ways very unhappy, scared of himself, and lacking any kind of inner stability. Lawrence's short-hand summary of the area of Heseltine's deepest lack is in his 'inner life': that is,

10 Boulton, *D. H. Lawrence, Philip Heseltine and Three Unpublished Letters*, pp. 12-13.

somewhere where Heseltine *needed* to be himself, undeniably; and without which he was only the 'sort of Narcissus' who 'watches his own reflection' and 'watches his own heart beat'. (Lawrence would later call Heseltine 'empty, uncreated ... as if he were not yet born, as if he consisted only of echoes from the past, and reaction against the past').[11] Lawrence wanted Heseltine not to bother so much with the reflected, and what he was always reacting against, only with what he actually felt; but Heseltine would obviously have to work hard at finding out what that was.

As Lawrence had detected, knowing what he really wanted was a huge problem for Heseltine. But the younger man's at times rather comical flailings about did not stop Lawrence liking him. He got him an opening at Garsington Manor and an introduction to Ottoline Morrell, where he went the following week with the Lawrences and with his friends Hasan Shahid Suhrawardy and Dikran Kouyoumdjian. Ottoline did *not* like any of these new young friends of the Lawrences, at all, it must be said, or Lawrence for bringing them along, and she described Heseltine like this in her diary for 3 December:

> tall and blonde, soft and so degenerate that he seems somehow corrupt ...[12]

Those words 'degenerate' and 'corrupt' are, significantly (given that she was disagreeing with Lawrence about Heseltine) Lawrence's own language; a word like 'degenerate' being used neither as moral vocabulary, nor (as the mid-to-late nineteenth century began to use the word) to suggest some sexual and mental perversion, probably homosexuality. When Lawrence used a word like 'degenerate' or 'corrupt', it

11 *2L* 501-2.

12 *Ottoline at Garsington: Memoirs of Lady Ottoline Morrell 1915-1918*, ed. Robert Gathorne-Hardy (1974), p. 77.

was in an attempt to define the quality of unrealised, impure, echoing, old desires that engulfed the 'degenerate' person, who had to that extent lapsed away from the demands and needs of the potential 'inner self'. It was certainly not a criticism of immoral behaviour. Someone else, more moral, might have called Heseltine's attitude to the Puma 'degenerate'. Not Lawrence. To him, it was Heseltine's attitude towards himself that displayed his degeneracy.

The fact that Ottoline Morrell called Heseltine 'soft' and 'degenerate' and 'corrupt', however, strongly suggests to me that Lawrence had been talking to her about Heseltine, and that she was now using his language to convey her own reaction. It was, strikingly, the language that Lawrence would later use to describe his character Halliday in *Women in Love*: I quote from one of the very first descriptions of the character:

> Gerald looked at Halliday for some moments, watching the soft, rather degenerate face of the young man. Its very softness was an attraction; it was a soft, warm, corrupt nature, into which one might plunge with gratification.[13]

Let me stress again that this is *not* a language of moral criticism: it attempts to define the actual physical presence of someone lacking in that 'inner life' which so interested Lawrence, and who shows the lack in his body and face.

Heseltine, however, continued to admire Lawrence enormously, while Lawrence was prepared to spend time with Heseltine, and try and be an influence for the good on him. Of all his contemporaries, Heseltine could hardly have found one better qualified, for example, to understand the damage accruing from loving an overpowering and demanding mother than Lawrence. In conversation with Heseltine, Lawrence could strongly reinforce *Sons and Lovers*. Heseltine

[13] *FWL* 57:21-4.

would write to Delius about Lawrence a fortnight later, on 15 December 1915:

> I am convinced that the writer in question is about the greatest man in England at the present time. He is far greater than his books – which he himself accounts as nothing in comparison with what he wants to do.[14]

That was certainly an exaggeration: Lawrence was very proud still of *The Rainbow*. But in January, true to his word, Heseltine went down to Cornwall and lived with Lawrence and Frieda for six weeks in Porthcothan; and it was to Cornwall that, encouraged by Lawrence and Frieda, he invited the Puma at the end of the month; and Kouyoumdjian also went down. That was the start of the second phase of his relationship with Lawrence; the first had been marked by nothing except a kind of anxious hero-worship on Heseltine's part and a rather worried, analytical caringness on Lawrence's.

We do not actually know much about their time together in Cornwall. Lawrence was ill in bed a good deal, and Frieda enjoyed Heseltine's company. On 13 February she wrote: 'I like Heseltine, he is like a boy sometimes, and sometimes like the boy's grandfather!'[15] That was him exactly: the wonderful, energetic, naïve youthfulness – and then the world-weary, all-knowing and dismissive cynic. Heseltine's loyalty to Lawrence can however be gauged by the way he invented a scheme to be called *The Rainbow Books and Music*, which would – by subscription – raise the money to publish unpopular works, starting (of course) with *The Rainbow*. It was Heseltine who,

14 *The Letters of Peter Warlock*, ii. 392-3.
15 *Memoirs and Correspondence*, p. 199.

out of his own very restricted funds, paid for the printing and distribution of 1,000 leaflets to advertise the scheme.[16] Nothing came of it: but it was an extremely warm-hearted and generous act.

Neither Lawrence nor Frieda liked Dikran Kouyoumdjian and he had to be asked to leave. But Heseltine stayed on, and when the Puma came down at the start of February, the Lawrences liked her too. Lawrence, with his natural sympathy for the non-intellectual, called her 'very nice and very real and simple, we like her ... She is quite intelligent in her way, but no mental consciousness ... all intuition, in the dark ... But she is quite fine and subtle in that way, quite, and I esteem her there *quite* as much as I esteem him.'[17] The most intriguing note about their time together comes in a letter by Lawrence to a friend in which he says that 'At night we write a play, which is rather fun'[18] and of which he gave some details to Ottoline Morrell: 'a comedy for stage, about Heseltine and his Puma and so on'.[19] But none of it survives.

Heseltine and the Puma went back to London in mid-February; but then occurred the incident which permanently damaged Heseltine's friendship with Lawrence. Heseltine had, anyway, been growing increasingly restive under Lawrence's tutelage, and wanted to assert himself: he accused Lawrence of just wanting agreement. This would have been odd, given that Lawrence always liked best and got on best with those who disagreed with him. But it was what Heseltine preferred to believe. I think he was probably getting bored with being told about himself by Lawrence, and bored with Cornwall. What is more, he had been very struck, while visiting Garsington back in December, by the 'tall, slim, very pretty, shy, severe and composed ... almost absurdly young'[20] Swiss

16 Nehls, i. 348-9.
17 *2L* 539.
18 *2L* 508.
19 *2L* 501.
20 Huxley, *Leaves of the Tulip Tree*, p. 31.

girl Juliette Baillot (only nineteen), who was working there as a French-speaking governess for Ottoline's daughter, and who was known as 'Mademoiselle ('Mlle.'). At a party at Garsington back in December, they had both acted in the same sketch (Heseltine as The Beast, Juliette as Beauty) and they had started a correspondence; later he had invited her to visit him in London. Back in December, Lawrence had given Heseltine the cynical advice: 'Have enough of the other [i.e. Puma] then marry the little Swiss, properly.'[21] In a piece of profound insight into Heseltine's character, and into the paradoxes of desire and need, Lawrence had commented, while Heseltine and the Puma were both in Cornwall:

> He declares he does not like this one, the Puma, but he does really. He declares he wants her to go. But he is really attached to her in the senses, in the unconsciousness, in the blood. He is always fighting away from this. But in so doing he is a fool ... His affection for Mlle. is a desire for light because he is in the dark. If he were in the light he would want the dark. He wants Mlle. for *companionship*, not for the blood connection, the dark, sensuous relation. With Puma he has this second, dark relation, but not the first ... Perhaps he is very split, and would always have the two things separate.[22]

Everything we know about Heseltine's subsequent relations with women suggests that that was exactly true. Anyway, things did not work out with Juliette Baillot. Back in London, late in February or early in March 1916, Heseltine would see more of her, but when they spent time together, according to her, she

21 *2L* 481.
22 *2L* 539.

> became frightened and broke off our relationship, not gently but finally. A little later Ottoline questioned me about it, and I learned he had a mistress who was pregnant with his child. We never met again, and I burnt all his letters.[23]

It seems that Heseltine's relationship with Juliette had depended on his keeping her ignorant of the Puma and her pregnancy – and probably the Puma ignorant of Juliette, too; not only because they would each have reacted violently against the other, but because *he* was so split, too, and wanted to keep them in quite separate compartments in his life. Lawrence had told him that he *ought* to tell Juliette about Puma; and someone – it may have been Katherine Mansfield (it was not Lawrence in any surviving letter) – let slip to Ottoline (who of course felt responsible for the young woman she was employing as a governess) the news about Puma's pregnancy. And that was that. According to Juliette, this disclosure in itself was not the cause of the end of her relationship with Heseltine, but Heseltine chose to believe that what Lawrence had done 'very nearly landed me in the most fearful fix – indeed, it was calculated to do so'. He was, I think, blaming Lawrence for letting Juliette and the Puma know about each other. He was also determined that Lawrence only wanted disciples, and was a 'bloody bore'[24] (the old reaction and counter-reaction seems to have kicked in here too). For a while he was very angry and would have nothing to do with Lawrence; he wrote him at least one extremely nasty letter. However, the fact that in 1917 he rented a house very near where the Lawrences were then living, further west in Cornwall, near Zennor, and came down at least once with Puma and saw the Lawrences, shows that he had either forgiven Lawrence or had (perhaps) realised

23 Huxley, *Leaves of the Tulip Tree*, pp. 48-8.
24 Smith, *Peter Warlock*, p. 91.

that he could hardly blame him for what had happened. By 1917, however, it was Lawrence who was no longer interested by Heseltine. 'I don't like him any more, it can't come back, the liking', he remarked at the end of April 1917.[25] What had happened to change him, I think, was not that Heseltine had behaved badly in any new way, but that Lawrence had written his novel *Women in Love*: and had understood Heseltine in the way that writing a novel developing a character out of a real person had always allowed him to do. In my 2005 biography, I wrote in general terms about this habit of Lawrence:

> Writing fiction seems to have been his best way of freeing up the logjam of his feelings, of realizing in language what he was experiencing. It may well be true that it was not until he had *written* it that Lawrence had had an experience; and this would go some way to explaining why he used this recreative method so very often. People he apprehended intellectually, or as a mimic might remember them, came alive all over again as (in a deep, even tranquil sense) [26] he recollected them, and remade them. The habit of remaking did not make him especially liked or likeable. But in remaking people in a new language, he seems to have *experienced* them and their needs and feelings more fully than he had previously been able to do.[27]

I believe that that is what happened when he created Halliday in *Women in Love*.

He had written the novel between April and the end of

25 *3L* 122.

26 See William Wordsworth, 'Preface' (1800) to *Lyrical Ballads*, ed. R. L. Brett and A. R. Jones (1991), p. 266.

27 Worthen, *D. H. Lawrence: The Life of an Outsider*, p. 217.

October 1916. He thereafter revised it regularly until 1919, but the passages about the characters he named 'Halliday' and 'Pussum' were all of them written by the end of October 1916. Lawrence himself admitted that he had turned Heseltine and Puma into those characters: they may even have been remnants of that play they had such fun with early in 1916. But having created Halliday in the novel, it looks as if he could no longer like the real Heseltine: he had somehow written him *out*. The novel could not, anyway, be published – Lawrence's career could not be rehabilitated until after the war was over. But when it was, these versions of Heseltine and the Puma would come to light.

I have quoted the initial description of Halliday. Let me quote some more, so that on the one hand you can see how close it was to Heseltine – and yet, on the other, how it develops the enigmas of the young Heseltine into a serious character. Halliday is on the one hand – according to the Pussum – 'the most awful coward you've ever seen. He always faints if I lift a knife – he's *tewwified* of me'. On the other hand, where most other people are afraid of what people will think of them, Halliday is not: he is admirably uncaring. 'Julius doesn't care about that', [28] the Pussum admits. He invites everybody back to his flat: 'Do come, everybody, it will be *so* splendid.' Lawrence creates Halliday's voice in a way that sounds exactly as if had been Heseltine's: he had always been an extraordinarily good mimic. The Pussum spends the night with the stranger Gerald Crich, exactly as Heseltine would later describe in his own little poem about the Puma:

> You've heard of the promiscuous puma
> She is of a most generous humour
> She can't say no to anyone

[28] *FWL* 61:1-2, 6-7.

> Or rob a stranger of his fun.
> Because of this sad moral lack
> She spends her lifetime on her back.'[29]

After two days of this, however, Halliday turns violently against Gerald 'with hideous, imbecile animosity'; Gerald departs, 'leaving Halliday in a foolish state of gloating triumph.'[30] Lawrence really did know Heseltine horribly well, and disliked what he knew, the more he re-created it.

The passages about Halliday and Pussum were only revised in a few small details by the time the book was published in America in December 1920. Martin Secker published the novel in England in June 1921 in a version subjected to a few small cuts he had insisted on Lawrence making, and a few which he had made himself without telling Lawrence. What Secker was most worried about, following *The Rainbow*, was Lawrence's reputation as a writer about homosexuality – even the title *Women in Love* struck Secker as 'dangerous'. The parts he had cut himself had all been about Birkin's love for Gerald. Back in 1917, Ottoline Morrell (who had read the version finished in 1916) had made many protests about the character Hermione, and had claimed that it was a version of her, but by 1921 Secker appears to have been confident that she would not object legally to the published novel. So with no danger from that quarter – and the cuts he had made safeguarding the novel, he hoped, against sexual attack – he must have been especially distressed to find, in September 1921, Philip Heseltine's lawyers writing to him demanding that the book be withdrawn and threatening a libel action.

In a moment I shall go into what Heseltine was objecting

29 Smith, *Peter Warlock*, (1994), p. 109.

30 *FWL* 69:40.

to, but for the moment let me outline the sequence of events. Secker wrote to Lawrence some time before mid-September, saying that he wanted to incorporate changes because Heseltine was 'proposing a libel action'.[31] Lawrence responded 'Heseltine trying to make himself important',[32] but told Secker the address to send a marked copy of the novel. When he got it, with a very bad grace he made the requested changes, all designed to disguise Heseltine's fair hair and complexion, Chelsea flat and Hindu servant, and the Pussum's dark complexion and dark hair:

> The Pussum I have made a blue-eyed fair-haired little thing: Halliday black and swarthy: the manservant an Arab: the flat a house in St. John's Wood ... I think it all perfect nonsense – as if there weren't dozens of little Pussums about Chelsea, and dozens of Hallidays anywhere. But I do it since you wish it this way.[33]

A change subsequently demanded by the solicitors was that the name 'Pussum' be changed to 'Minette': given that the original's first name was 'Minnie', the demanded change looks maliciously designed by Heseltine to cause problems for Secker *and* to offend Minnie Channing. Secker issued an altered edition in December 1921, but two appearances of 'Pussum' in the text went unnoticed and remained in print for the next 60 years, baffling all readers who came across them.[34]

31 *4L* 88.

32 *4L* 87.

33 *4L* 93-4.

34 In *WL* at 233:8 and 380:31.

Lawrence had been sure from the start of his correspondence with Secker that 'the most likely thing is that Heseltine is trying to blackmail you. It is quite in character ... He is an impossible person. But money is at the bottom of it.'[35] That insight was exactly right; having exacted the textual changes, Heseltine's solicitor then demanded £50 damages and £10.10.0 costs, which Secker paid: he simply wanted the book back on the market, and was still fearful of a court action, which he reckoned would cost him three or four hundred pounds, whatever its outcome. But the news that Secker had paid up annoyed Lawrence more than anything: 'It makes me sick with rage to think that Heseltine got that money out of you.'[36]

For the whole action had, from the start, been a bluff, though extremely cleverly handled. Heseltine had made it clear to his solicitors that he could not afford to take a libel action which there was a good chance he would lose. He also know that – for a successful court case – he would have to get Puma into the witness box, and they were no longer on speaking terms. Consequently, and quite brilliantly, he used his solicitors to create the maximum pain and inconvenience for Lawrence and his publisher and to extract all the money he could possibly get without an action; and Secker fell for the bluff at every point. Heseltine commemorated his victory in exactly the kind of 'gloating triumph' which Lawrence had described Halliday showing in the book:

> Come, fill a vial with vintage, *vieux et sec*
> Fit for the King of Thule's golden *Becher*;
> Get half-seas-over – swamp the blooming deck.
> Swill swipes, swig swizzle, singing
> 'SUCKS TO SECKER'![37]

35 *4L* 113.

36 *4L* 129.

37 Nehls, ii. 94. 'Sucks to you' is recorded in *OED* as first used in

The only area where Heseltine failed was in attempting to take further the stir caused by a review in September 1921 in the jingoistic newspaper *John Bull*, which had called for police action against the book on the grounds that – like *The Rainbow* – it had advocated homosexuality. This was in some ways the most serious thing that Heseltine tried to do to Lawrence. This is what *John Bull* had printed:

> I do not claim to be a literary critic, but I know dirt when I smell it, and here it is in heaps – festering, putrid heaps which smell to high heaven ... The main episode of the novel deals with the relations of two men, Gerald and Birkin, and is nothing more or less than a shameful glorification of that state of mind which in practice, as every student of law is aware, leads to conduct which is condemned by the criminal law ... If *The Rainbow* was an indecent book this later production is an obscene abomination. The police must act...[38]

It is an indication of Heseltine's rage – or malice – that, in spite of his efforts for *The Rainbow* in 1915 and 1916, he should now have attempted to get *Women in Love* seized by the police. He wrote to his solicitors:

> I purposely left in certain passages which in other circumstances I should have insisted on getting omitted, in order that there should be no dearth of certain tendencies for which to get the book suppressed by the police. Will you please communicate

---

print in 1913 by Compton Mackenzie.

38 Nehls, ii. 90-1.

> with Scotland Yard again immediately ... if ever a book afforded grounds for prosecution on a charge of ... the glorification of homosexuality in particular, this one does.
>
> If Scotland Yard proves dilatory, could you not address a communication to the National Council for Public Morals, urging them to take the matter up and press for police action?[39]

Cecil Gray thought that request exuded an 'exquisitely subtle humour',[40] but it looks to me like an attempt to get the book banned and to wreck Lawrence's career for a second time. I confess I don't find that funny at all, just malicious, exactly as I would if Lawrence had ever attempted to wreck Heseltine's career. The fact that the book included a good deal about men's feelings for other men would however undoubtedly have brought out the worst in Heseltine: he was a savage hater of the homosexual.[41] The passages he mentions as having left in, to damage the novel still further, would have included those in Halliday's flat where the young men all go around naked in the morning.

It is worth asking exactly why Heseltine staged his attack on the book. It would seem likely that as early as January-February 1916, Lawrence had made clear to Heseltine the way he thought his emotional centre 'corrupt' and 'degenerate', and how this got into his physical behaviour and appearance. I don't think there would have been anything very new in what Heseltine would have read in the published novel, though he would have found offensive all kinds of

39 Nehls, ii. 93-4.

40 Nehls, ii. 94.

41 See e.g. Smith, *Peter Warlock*, p. 56.

small things – such as the word 'squeal' to describe his shouts of alarm when confronted by the Pussum; and he might have found unpleasant that description of Halliday, naked, as demonstrating a 'rather heavy, slack, broken beauty, white and firm ... The animal was not there at all, only the heavy, broken beauty.' [42] But, again, Lawrence had always told Heseltine that his desires were being driven by his self-image, not from his body, so there would have been nothing very new to him in such an analysis: though of course there would have been an element of public exposure in its appearance in a novel. And yet – Halliday/Heseltine did not in general care about what people thought.

At the back of Heseltine's attack was however, I suspect, a genuine anger on the one hand at being linked with a potentially homosexual novel in ways that might have made people wonder about *his* sexuality; and, on the other, the excellent chance of raising money: he was always chronically in debt. I never forget the story of the occasion in the 1920s when a church which he, Barbara Peache and Augustus John were visiting was struck by lightning just when Philip was about to ascend the tower. John had been making obscene suggestions about Barbara Peache being ravished on the altar when the lightning brought one of the tower pinnacles crashing to the ground. Where someone else might have been disturbed, or shocked, or amused, Heseltine's reaction was immediately to telephone a London newspaper and to make 2 guineas out of the story.[43] It is probably right to say that, rather than objecting, he would actually rather have enjoyed the notoriety of appearing in *Women in Love*, had it not been for what he thought was a homosexual slur. But the various baroque variations to the book's text which he was able to introduce – such as the change of Pussum to Minette (he did *not* demand that the name Halliday be changed), and the

42 *FWL* 66:22-4.

43 Smith, *Peter Warlock*, pp. 130-1.

appeal to the police on moral grounds – in addition to the money he managed to extract – would have been, to him, extremely pleasing; and above all the thought of annoying Lawrence profoundly would have delighted him. He deeply enjoyed practical jokes.

On the other hand ... one of the striking episodes in the novel is a passage where the Halliday character reads out a turgid, jargon-filled letter from Birkin in a terrible sing-song and sends it up something rotten.[44] Lawrence was in his own way paying tribute to the way Halliday was able to parody and guy Lawrence's own profoundest utterances; and he included that in the book. I hope you have heard enough already to convince you, if you were not previously convinced, of Heseltine's marvellously witty and ingenious word-play. Lawrence confirms that.

On the other hand, Lawrence was ruthless in conflating episodes in which Heseltine had appeared together with others when he had not been present. The description in the novel of the letter being recovered in the Café Pompadour was based on a real incident in September 1916 in which Katherine Mansfield had recovered a copy of Lawrence's book of poems *Amores* which was being mockingly read aloud in the Café Royal by friends of Heseltine – but Heseltine had not himself been present.[45]

You may well end up feeling that Heseltine was more than justified in trying to damage Lawrence in 1921, given the way he had been insulted and traduced by the novel. On the other hand, it was Lawrence's ability to strike right at the centre of a target's vulnerability which would have made the descriptions so painful. I'm afraid I would say that, so far as I understand Heseltine, Lawrence's insights into him are among the most profound ever offered, both those in his

44 See *FWL* 350-2.

45 See Mark Kinkead Weekes, *D. H. Lawrence: Triumph to Exile 1912-1922* (Cambridge, 1996), pp. 337-8, and *FWL* 352:38.

letters and in the portrait of Halliday. As always, Lawrence only created such characters because they fascinated him: they represented part of himself too. If in one way unforgivable intrusions into a person's life, they were also recreations in which the person continues to live a kind of posthumous existence, independently, vividly and brilliantly. To me it continues amazing that Lawrence could re-make someone so quickly, so accurately in sound and appearance, so frighteningly, if also so maliciously. It was a hateful as well as a remarkable gift; Heseltine hated him profoundly for it and in his own way returned the malice. Both died in 1930: too young, both of them.

Locating Lady Chatterley

Dora Phillips Hall, Eastwood 3 September 2005

What follows is the third of my Eastwood Festival talks, requested by Emma Herrity. In 2005, coinciding with the publication of my Penguin biography of Lawrence, there was throughout the country an especial celebration of Lady Chatterley's Lover, *eliciting both high-minded sniggering and predictable backlash: a group which had planned to do readings from the novel on the tram to Bulwell, for example, pulled out after threats of legal action were made against them. Emma asked me to say something about the novel for the Festival and, again, I tried to produce something that would be of local interest: the celebration accounts, perhaps, for the odd tone of my ending.*

The story has often been told of how, having spent the late summer of 1926 in England, Lawrence went back to Italy and started a short story about the Midlands which unexpectedly turned into the novel *Lady Chatterley's Lover.* All true, of course, and I shall tell that story again myself in a minute. But I would like to suggest that there is one odd fact about the book which might make us go a little earlier, in search of its origins. And it's this.

Like at least three of Lawrence's English novels, *Lady Chatterley's Lover* contains a fairly tight and almost completely concealed chronology. This may strike you as odd: was Lawrence really a writer to organise his novels in such a way? And it's true that the chronological structure in his novels is hardly ever visible – it runs along beneath the surface, like an underground stream, every now and then breaking surface with a random date. There's a date at the start of *The Rainbow*, for example: just one: 'About 1840', when everything changed and the Marsh Farm got cut off from Ilkeston.[1] The next implicit date most people will notice in *that* book is

1 *R* 13:20.

either the reference to Khartoum[2] (1898) or to the outbreak of the Boer War[3] (1899); the next actual date is Ursula's matriculation in 'June 1900'. [4] But in between the two there are births, and marriages, and of course the characters' ages are mentioned; and readers who know some history will also know when the Polish rebellion broke out in the 1860s, so they will know when Lydia Lensky comes to England ... and there is the occasional odd little detail – like Will marrying Anna Brangwen 'the Saturday before Christmas', which turns out to be Saturday 23 December 1882 ... and Tom Brangwen turns out actually to have been born in 1840, which feels right. Ursula is born late in 1883 and the novel ends in the autumn of 1905.

True, you have to be an exceptionally odd, not to say peculiar, reader to notice any of this, or to notice its tiny failures (at Anna's wedding, Tom is described as being '45': he is actually 44 and 8 months). But it's all there.

And there is a chronology in *Lady Chatterley's Lover* too. Easy to work it out at the start, of course; there's the war – and Clifford and Connie marry in 1917, that's on the first page;[5] then Clifford is wounded; and he and Connie come to Wragby in 1920.[6] But for most readers, that is probably that. And as we know that Lawrence began to write the book those sunny days in Italy in 1926, people probably assume that that is when it is set. But the novel is set mostly between 1922 and 1924. If you do the sums, then it turns out that Mellors leaves the army in 1922 and in June that year comes to work at Wragby (but Connie does not yet meet him). The playwright Michaelis visits Wragby in November 1922 and starts his affair with Connie – an affair which ends in the summer of 1923. (Connie has first seen Mellors in February

2 *R* 288:19.
3 *R* 303:18.
4 *R* 335:18.
5 *LCL* 5:11.
6 *LCL* 5:21.

1923.) But it is only in March 1924 that Connie starts to go out to the hut in the woods, and then in April actually starts her affair with Mellors; so that most of the action of the central part of the book takes place over the spring, summer and early autumn of 1924. It is in that way, oddly, an historical novel which Lawrence wrote some two years later, even if with a very recent history. There is one date that careful readers will certainly notice, on the letter which Mellors writes from the Farm right at the end of the book: 'Old Heanor 29 September'.[7] The year is not given in the text, but is clear from the chronology that it is still 1924 (29 September that year was a Monday, if you want to know). Connie's child by Mellors (expected at the end of the novel) is thus due to be born late in January or early in February 1925.

Now, you may say that you know the novel well, and have never noticed any of this, and that therefore it must be entirely irrelevant. And you may be right. But I still want to ask: was there anything about these years that might have made Lawrence want to set his novel in them? In particular, about the spring and summer and early autumn of 1924?

Well: Lawrence wasn't in the Midlands, for sure; he could hardly have been further away. Although he would come back here in the summer of 1925 and (famously) once again in the late summer of 1926, over the summer and early autumn of 1924 he and Frieda were 8,000 feet up at the Kiowa ranch in New Mexico, near Taos. No link there.

But it was in September 1924 that he began to do something – for him – distinctly unusual. It was eighty-one years ago this Thursday, as it happens, that he began to write autobiographically about his own early life. Not in his fiction,

7 *LCL* 298:10.

as he had always done – as in *Sons and Lovers*, for example – but in essays; and in this case in a very beautiful essay called either 'Introduction to *Bibliography*' or 'The Bad Side of Books', which he wrote for Edward McDonald as an introduction to the Bibliography of him which McDonald had recently completed. Let me read you just the first paragraph of that essay – one of Lawrence's very, very long sentences: but lovely for just this time of year. It's a long, contented gaze on a September morning, with a firmly expressed original direction that almost gets lost in the meandering – but doesn't quite.

> There doesn't seem much excuse for me, sitting under a little cedar tree at the foot of the Rockies, looking at the pale desert disappearing westward, with hummocks of shadow rising in the stillness of incipient autumn, this morning, the near pine trees perfectly still, the sunflowers and the purple Michaelmas daisies moving for the first time, this morning, in an invisible breath of breeze, to be writing an introduction to a bibliography.[8]

Lawrence wrote that on 1 September 1924: I'm so glad you asked me to give this lecture at the right time of year ... and the essay went on to include stories that you will certainly know: for example, the anecdote about his writing *The White Peacock* and his father asking 'what dun they gi'e thee for that, lad?' and Lawrence replying brightly 'Fifty pounds, father' – and Arthur Lawrence answering 'Fifty pound! An' tha's niver done a day's hard work in thy life.'[9] That's in the essay. And his memory of the copy of the novel arriving which his mother saw before she died: 'I think she doubted whether it could be much of a book, since no one more important than

8 *IR* 75:1-7.
9 *IR* 75:28-32.

I had written it'. And one of his sisters saying, about his early career, 'You *always* were lucky.'[10] And he also included reminiscences of his early days in publishing; and then of the *Rainbow* disaster.

Now this essay, started on 1 September 1924, and parcelled up for McDonald on 10 September, was the first time Lawrence had ever directly written about his family – that wonderful anecdote about Arthur Lawrence might actually have been lost for ever if Lawrence hadn't set it down then. But Lawrence would subsequently write about his own early life over and over again, during the next five years; essay after essay. Why did he start now?

Well, of course, I don't *know*. But I can speculate. One reason – entirely accidental – was the fact that McDonald had asked him to write the Introduction. Though of course he really didn't need to say anything about his father or mother or sister in it ... another thing that makes me wonder, however, is the fact that, at the start of August, just a month earlier, he had been rather seriously ill for the first time for a very long while, and had actually spat blood; he had probably had a small bronchial haemorrhage, which had been very disturbing. His tubercle-infected lungs were starting to 'move': this was the beginning of the TB which eventually killed him. He may perhaps have realised this: never underestimate him, or his encyclopaedic range of knowledge. Following that illness, he did a slightly out-of-character thing, which was to ask his American publisher Thomas Seltzer to start preserving his manuscripts for him; something he had never done in the past (as if he had at last realised their value and wanted to lay them down and preserve them). It would be his thirty-ninth birthday on 11 September; and so it was in September 1924 that he showed just a trace of a man digging in against illness, realising his age, making provision for the future. And becoming reminiscent about his early life; and

10 *IR* 75:18-20, 76:3.

about his father.

And the very day he parcelled up the essay for McDonald, the day before his own birthday on the 11th, Arthur Lawrence – back in Eastwood – died. Lawrence didn't hear at once, of course; but a telegram from his sister Emily came on the 13th. Lawrence wrote back to her the next day:

> I had your cablegram last night about father. It was the last thing I expected, Ada had just written he was as well as ever. – It is better to be gone than lingering on half helpless and half alive. But it upsets one, nevertheless: makes a strange break.
>
> When did he die – what date? The cablegram did not say. And when did you bury him. I hope it didn't rain ...[11]

There is an awful memory concealed in that last remark; the recollection of the two previous funerals at that particular grave in the Cemetery down Church Street: the first being that of his brother Ernest, back in 1901, and then his mother's funeral, in December 1910. On both those occasions it had rained and rained.

His letter to Emily went on: 'really, I thank God I wasn't there at the funeral. No, no more of that.'[12] He may not have wanted to think any more about it; but there was in fact going to be a *good* deal more 'of that'. Lawrence both feared and was impulsively drawn to nostalgia and reminiscence about his own early years. And during the last five years of his life, he would regularly revisit his memories of his parents, and of what had happened to him as a result.

There is just one other little fact about 1924 which interests me: Lawrence writing to his old friend Middleton Murry elegiacally in a letter three weeks later, linking the death of

11 *5L* 124.

12 *5L* 124.

Arthur Lawrence with the coming of autumn.

> The country here is very lovely at the moment, aspens high on the mountains like a fleece of gold ... The scrub oak is dark red, and the wild birds are coming down to the desert. It is time to go south. – Did I tell you my father died on Sept. 10th., the day before my birthday. – The autumn always gets me badly, as it breaks into colours. I want to go south, where there is no autumn, where the cold doesn't crouch over one like a snow-leopard waiting to pounce.[13]

That autumn breaking into colours also recalled the autumn of his mother's long-drawn-out dying. [14] That was something else, far off but unforgettable, belonging to the old world he had tried so hard to escape, and never quite managed to get away from.

Lawrence had responded all his life to his father's independence, his love for animals and nature, his dancing, and his practical outdoors knowledge (gathering herbs to make tea, for example),[15] not to speak of his determined refusal to listen to nagging women. Almost nothing is known about their relationship after Lawrence left England in 1912; there are just lots of records of Lawrence sending him money (he had done so for the last time at the end of August 1924). There is also just the occasional flash of memory, as when he had told Achsah Brewster in Ceylon that a workman there 'resembled his father – the same clean-cut and exuberant spirit, a true pagan. He added that he had not done justice to his father in *Sons and Lovers* and felt like rewriting it.'[16] A few months after Arthur Lawrence's death, in January 1925, Lawrence would

13 *5L* 143.

14 See e.g. 'Dolour of Autumn' and 'Brooding Grief' (*Poems*, i. 107-08, 110-11).

15 *Memoirs and Correspondence*, p. 131.

16 Nehls, ii. 126.

receive a photograph of their father from his sister Ada: 'It's very nice: I see a good deal of myself in it',[17] he would comment. And in his own last years, he would increasingly both write about his father as a man of warmth and unspeaking intimacy, belonging to 'the old wild England'. It was in that guise that Arthur Lawrence came to haunt Lawrence's later work. He became one of Lawrence's life-alternatives: not just a progenitor but a road not taken, which Lawrence now wanted imaginatively to travel down.

And – of all the kinds of influence his father had – I suppose the strongest of all is on the gamekeeper in *Lady Chatterley's Lover*, started in October 1926, when once again in clear autumn weather Lawrence sat outdoors and remembered Eastwood and the past. When the original gamekeeper Parkin, of the first two versions of the novel, became Oliver Mellors, some of Arthur Lawrence got lost; but he was there in Parkin all right. And Lawrence came to focus on September 1924 for the last part of his fiction. All these coincidences may of course be just that: coincidences. But I suspect, as Birkin does in *Women in Love*, that it all hangs together, in the deepest sense. A novel which celebrates so much that Lawrence now admired about his father would show *its* re-born working-class hero (of just Lawrence's own age, born in 1885) finding his partner in a woman from another class: and this time it would *not* work out like the Morels in *Sons and Lovers*, with the woman despising and looking down on the coarse, animal-like, working-class man. They would love and admire each other, and sex would be the most important thing they shared in the new novel.[18]

17 *5L* 208. See the cover of this volume for a photograph of DHL's maternal grandfather George Beardsall, in whom DHL might have seen even more of himself.

18 Connie's child would seem to be due in late January or (more likely) early in February 1925. This – again – may be entirely coincidental, but having given Mellors his own year of birth, 1885, DHL now gave Mellors' and Connie's child a birth-date exactly coinciding with when he had almost died himself, down

That was a real re-making of *Sons and Lovers.*

But that was still only one kind of return. When Lawrence wrote to his sister Ada about his father's death, he again commented: 'I hate to think of that Eastwood cemetery. I hate to think of Eastwood anyhow. Next time, you must come out here and see us: better than my coming back.'[19] That was what he had been feeling since 1919. But within six months of those remarks about Eastwood, and the cemetery, Lawrence was almost dead himself. The haemorrhaging up at the ranch was his TB becoming active: he had been first seriously and then desperately ill in Oaxaca and Mexico City, where a doctor had had him X-rayed, and had told Frieda that it was 'T.B. in the third degree' – i.e. active – and urged her: 'Take him to the ranch; it's his only chance ... A year or two at most.'[20]

And it had been at just at this point in his life that Lawrence had dictated to Frieda the first few pages of a new story, 'The Flying Fish': something he had never done before.[21] He really needed to write it. 'The Flying Fish'

---

in Oaxaca. I confess that I do not know what to make of that. It *is* the only DHL fiction to end with a pregnancy and an expected baby. The date of his own closest encounter with death may be simple coincidence. But a phrase from *The Winter's Tale* ('Thou met'st with things dying, I with things new-born' – III. iii. 112-13) reminds us how the two can – sometimes – provoke each other.

19 *4L* 126.

20 '*Not I, But the Wind ...*', p. 167; Frieda to Dorothy Brett, 12 August 1930, *D. H. Lawrence Review*, ix (Spring 1976), 101.

21 See *St.M* xxxiv-xxxvi. The manuscript is lost, so it cannot now be said exactly where Frieda's writing ended, but as she wrote almost a quarter of the whole (9 pages out of a total of 40: see E. W. Tedlock, *The Frieda Lawrence Collection of D. H. Lawrence*

fragment begins with its central figure, Gethin Day, desperately ill in Mexico, haunted by an intense nostalgia for the English Midlands. He wants 'to go home. He didn't care now whether England was tight and little and overcrowded and far too full of furniture. He no longer minded the curious quiet atmosphere ... in which he had felt he would stifle as a young man.' [22] It is probably not a coincidence that the remaking of England as a mythologised, rural world, came just when the sentence of Lawrence's own mortality had been pronounced; 'he felt that home was the place.'[23] This seems to me another step along the road to the re-creations in *Lady Chatterley's Lover*: himself now a resurrected man (like Mellors), and bringing his own father back to life as the man he *ought* to have been: not underground as a collier but outdoors, the wood his domain, not a terraced house; the man with red-brown eyes and 'the rather big, ragged moustache'[24] that he pushes out of the way of his mouth, and with colour in his cheeks, and that silky firm skin; at war with everything bourgeois; lonely and mature. A re-made Walter Morel: a new version of Arthur Lawrence, in which Lawrence would really be his father's son.

But after that illness down in Mexico, and recuperating up at Kiowa, in the early autumn of 1925, Lawrence came back to England for real, leaving the ranch behind (he would never see it again). And now he hated England all over again, for real. It rained and was foggy and cold: 'I hate it, the rain and dark and

---

Manuscripts, Albuquerque 1948, p. 55), it is probable that DHL dictated pp. 207-10 of the CUP edition.

22 *St.M* 209:40–210:3.

23 *St.M* 210:7-8.

24 *FSLC* 11:40.

dismalness here.'[25] Back in the Midlands, returning as Gethin Day had felt he had to, he recovered a bit; Ada and her husband Eddie Clarke took him out in their recently acquired car and they went 'all over my well-known Derbyshire'. But he still had awful problems with being back: 'I can't look at the body of my past, the spirit seems to have flown.'[26] 'I'm weary of past things – like one's home regions – and dont want to look at them.'[27] And it was in that mood that he left, going first to London and then to Italy. The real anguish of Lawrence's return in 1925 was, Catherine Carswell remembered, how 'especially on that visit, the horrors of his childhood had come up over him like a smothering flood'. This had been why he had found his 'home place ... more depressing to me than death'.[28] He had ended up with a profound dislike of mother love in particular, and rejected utterly the idea of a place that he might have called home.

His return in 1926 was rather different, though he had not been looking forward to it at all. He was not, this time, returning from the joys of the ranch; the weather in England was better; and the story is well known of how he came back and went to Mablethorpe and Sutton-on-Sea and felt that he had got 'into touch with my native land again, here – and feel at home.'[29] That was very unusual for him, and he took advantage of it to extend his stay. By the later 1920s, such feelings often linked directly with his health; he was 'at home' where he felt well. But it was the region in general where he felt at home. When he finally went over to Eastwood and Ripley (during the coal strike which was still

25 *5L* 316.
26 *5L* 318.
27 *5L* 319.
28 *The Savage Pilgrimage*, 1st edn. (1932), p. 229; *LEA* 54:11-12.
29 *5L* 534.

continuing: the General Strike was long since over), he didn't like them at all, feeling what he called 'devouring nostalgia' and 'infinite repulsion'. [30] Eastwood and the landscape around it may have been 'home to me' but it was also increasingly becoming bearable only in his writing about it.

And then, in spite of saying that he felt 'I'll never write another novel',[31] around 22 October, he started a story set in the Midlands. A couple of days later, having tea with their Mirenda neighbours, the Wilkinsons, the Lawrences had a row which helps us understand what he was doing in this new novel. This is the entry in the Wilkinson diary: 'The talk soon got on to Revolution & stayed there & was really impassioned. We all generalised a bit – but he did so tremendously & swears by his class & death & damnation to the other class. He's done with them. "They're hard – cruel cruel (crescendo)".' [32] Frieda, naturally, objected. But Lawrence was inventing his first working-class central figure in a novel since Aaron in *Aaron's Rod* in 1918: and arguably his first ever genuinely working-class hero. That was what he had brought to his fiction: a savage anger with the middle and upper classes, a completely new sympathy with the working-class: with, in fact, the spirit of Arthur Lawrence.

But the oddest way in which Lawrence returned to the Midlands in this novel was in his making and re-making of landscapes he had known since boyhood. More than any novel since *Sons and Lovers*, this book became rooted in the old places. There had been recreations of Eastwood and its surroundings briefly in *The Rainbow*, and then in some of the

[30] *LEA* 15:12-13.

[31] *5L* 559.

[32] John Turner, 'D. H. Lawrence in the Wilkinson Diaries', *D. H. Lawrence Review*, xxx, no. 2 (2002), 27-8.

scenes of *Women in Love*; and again in the early part of *Aaron's Rod*, and also in the early part of *Mr Noon*. And a lot – but not the ending – of *The Lost Girl* had been Eastwood-based. But in each of those last three novels, it had been crucial that the central characters should *leave* the Midlands, and stay away; exactly as Richard Lovatt Somers leaves the Midlands in the 'Nightmare' chapter of *Kangaroo*, and stays away. That was the pattern Lawrence's fiction had established.

The *Lady Chatterley* novels, however, were centred on the place throughout. The characters may leave for London, or Italy, but they always come back here. And that makes it all the odder that, after a writer's life-time of using the local places and local landscapes for recreations in his fictions, Lawrence should, in just this novel and in its predecessor by eight months, *The Virgin and the Gipsy*, have done something new and completely different. He re-designed the Midlands map.

The easiest places to identify in a fiction are, of course, those which keep their names.[33] Nottingham is named in the novel and – rather oddly, for this fiction – is just where Nottingham is today; it has a Trent river, a Mikado restaurant and an Empire Theatre for music hall (just as Nottingham used to). All serene. The same had happened in *Sons and Lovers*, of course, when Nottingham and Derby and Sheffield had all been where they are supposed to be, under their own names, although other places were disguised (so that we get the Knarborough road in Bestwood leading straight to Nottingham ...)

The next easiest to identify in the landscape of *Lady Chatterley* are the places simply disguised by a slight name change, as Lawrence had always slightly disguised places:

33 See *LCL* 453-62.

Bestwood for Eastwood, for example. In *Lady Chatterley's Lover*, Hardwick Hall becomes Chadwick Hall, more window than wall: Watnall becomes Whiteover, Kinbrook stands for Kimberley and Giltbrook. Sometimes the name simply changes in a less recognisable way: so Wingerworth Hall becomes Fritchley. But Lawrence had always done this.

But the next category – and these are a great deal odder – was quite new: places where there is a recognisable location, and a recognisable name – but the name is the wrong one, and actually belongs elsewhere. Connie goes to Marehay, for example, and to Marehay Farm, and she makes love with Mellors in Marehay wood. Marehay is 1 mile s.w. of Ripley; but the place Lawrence is recreating is almost certainly Coneygrey, just north of Eastwood. There *is* a village of Teversal, quite near Hardwick Hall; but when Lawrence describes Tevershall, he is recreating Eastwood. On the other hand, we hear of Bestwood Hill at one point – and that is Eastwood too, under its old, *Sons and Lovers* name.

But things get even odder than that. Just consider the Chatterley family home 'Wragby'. The name perhaps comes from the village in Lincolnshire through which I believe the Lawrence party would have passed on their way back from the coast in 1926. Forget the name: at times the house is apparently located exactly where Lamb Close House is, in Moorgreen, about a mile and a half from where you are sitting tonight: the home of the Barber family, the proprietors of the colliery company Barber Walker. This Wragby is (most of the time) situated near a mining village called Tevershall (for which we may read Eastwood); and beside Wragby (most of the time) lies the wood which is the focus of so much of the novel, and which certainly originates in High Park Wood. (It contains a spring called John's Well; High Park contains Robin Hood's Well.)

And yet, when Connie leaves her home Wragby in Chapter XI, and is explicitly travelling 'south',[34] we are told that she is going towards the Peak district; on her left she can see what Lawrence calls 'Warsop Castle'. Hold on to your seats. That name comes from the town of Warsop you doubtless all know and love, on the edge of Sherwood Forest, just to the east of Shirebrook. But there is no doubt that the house is a creation of Bolsover Castle. And you can see Bolsover when driving south from Eastwood? Pull the other one.

It gets worse. Where exactly is Stacks Gate colliery? In Chapters V, IX and X, the colliery of Stacks Gate is within three miles of Wragby – indeed within sight and hearing of Wragby wood. Clifford of course runs it. Mellors complains about the colliers from Stacks Gate who set snares in his wood. To me, assuming that Wragby recreates Lamb Close House, Stacks Gate probably recreates Underwood colliery; or perhaps Moorgreen. But in Chapter XI, Mrs Bolton assumes that Clifford – far from running it – has never even seen Stacks Gate colliery: and the description of it confirms that the novel is recreating the colliery (new then) at Hollingwood, just south of Sheffield, at Staveley.

Some of this oddity is certainly caused by having Wragby sometimes where Lamb Close House is, in Moorgreen, and at other times where Renishaw Hall is, in Derbyshire. Lawrence had got to know the Sitwell family in Florence, in 1926, and when he came back in the summer he went to call on them in their house at Renishaw, on one of his excursions with Ada and Eddie. They weren't at home – but he certainly saw and remembered the house, as at times Wragby recreates it. Did you notice that Wragby is a 'long, low old house in brown stone'?[35] Well, that's Renishaw. Lamb Close is neither long nor low and is built of grey stone.

This leads to problems, however. When Wragby is Renishaw, you would indeed see Bolsover – or Warsop –

[34] *LCL* 153:40.

[35] *LCL* 13:5.

where Connie sees it, driving south (though you would not actually be running towards the Peak district at the time: that is still wrong). And Staveley/Stacks Gate would be just where the novel sets it. When Wragby is Lamb Close House at Moorgreen, however, then obviously Staveley/Stacks Gate is miles away, and Clifford Chatterley has never seen it (even though he owns it), and its colliers certainly don't set snares in High Park Wood.

But the use of Warsop in the wrong place – and Teversall in the wrong place – and Marehay, and many others – suggests that more is going on than Lawrence protecting himself against the wrath of the Sitwell family for having used their house in his fiction, and consequently mixing places up (I don't think he'd have bothered about the Barber family; they were old enemies). He certainly knew where all these places were; he had actually refreshed his already excellent memory on his car journeys through Derbyshire in 1925.

My conclusion is that, in these late works of Midlands fiction, he was enjoying being perverse and confusing his local readers; people who thought they had cracked his system (Bestwood = Eastwood, etc.) would get it wrong – and local people would also get it wrong – and Stacks Gate could never finally be pinned down; and the landscape was entirely re-made, but this time with Lawrence's kind of malicious pleasure at mixing it up. Gentle malice is the best phrase I can find for it. It remains local, it remains Midlands, the names are fine: but it has been re-shaped. It's a kind of subversive undermining of the mapped landscape.

But if the landscape is at times perversely remade, what word should use for another and in its own way far more malicious example of a way in which Lawrence returned to the Midlands in this novel?

George Chatterley, born 1861, died 1940, was one of the

most well-known and highly thought-of local figures in Eastwood. He had worked his way up to being a senior figure in the colliery company of Barber Walker. Lawrence would have known of him for years, and his father Arthur Lawrence would have known him even better, but Lawrence would have been unlikely to have met him, except in the street: George Chatterley had become firmly middle-class. He had joined the firm when he was 'about twelve'[36] as an office boy, in the 1870s, and had worked his way up: at first a clerk, later promoted to manager of the general office staff, and finally becoming Secretary when the firm became a Limited Company in 1918. He also served as an accountant to the Barber family, and was a close acquaintance of the company's managing director Major Thomas Barber: for many years he 'kept the books of his estate'. I know only one other thing about him: 'in middle life he was conspicuous for his luxurious moustachios which he removed suddenly, to the dismay of his wife and the surprise of his colleagues'. The only picture I know of him shows him clean-shaven, sadly.[37] He retired in 1931, at the age of 70 and went to live in Bournemouth. I wonder what people down there made of him and of that now notorious name, and if anyone jokingly asked him if he were related to Constance Chatterley: and what happened if they did.

For it was not just a question of Lawrence using the well-known local name and subjecting it to scandal and notoriety. Even more to the point, George Chatterley had two daughters, one of whom was, astonishingly, named Constance. She had been born in Eastwood in 1883, so she was two years older than Lawrence; the other, Winifred (not Hilda, at least), had been born in 1886. In 1924 the real

[36] These and other biographical details come from G. C. H. Whitelock, *250 Years in Coal: The History of Barber Walker and Company Limited* (n.d. [1957]), p. 245.

[37] The photograph appears in *250 Years in Coal*, p. 244.

Constance would thus have been forty-one years old. The novel's Constance is twelve years younger, being born in the middle 1890s, and so is twenty-nine in the novel's chronology; and she of course is the daughter of a Scottish painter, not of an Eastwood Colliery Company official. And she only acquires the Chatterley name by marriage. And yet Lawrence's use of the name is breathtaking, given what notoriety he must soon have realised the novel would attract.

And here I have chosen to be ignorant. I don't know when or if the real-life Constance Chatterley married; I don't know where she lived when married – locally or away; I do not even know the name of her mother. It should not be too difficult to find the answers; it would take 2 or 3 hours work in the Births, Marriages and Deaths. I was in London on Thursday but have an odd hesitation about researching her, I confess.[38] I have the peculiar feeling that I don't want to expose her any more than she has already been exposed. What happened in 1928 when the book was finally published would have been bad enough. What I am, however, sure about is that – given that George Chatterley was a friend of Major Barber, the then director of the coal company – the latter's anger with Lawrence for having used family details in *Women in Love*, and then again in that wicked, scandalous, shocking novel *Lady Chatterley's Lover*, would have been increased still further on hearing that the name of his friend's daughter had been taken straight over into it, as that of its central character. Local people had a lot to forgive Lawrence: and in this case they didn't forgive him. There was no forgiveness from the Barbers. I don't know what the Chatterleys thought, but I guess it was unprintable.

[38] Seven years on, I have still done nothing to uncover the facts.

But how does all this add up? In any way you wish, of course. Some people – and I respect this – will say that the writer's imagination transcends any local effects of date, locality and place: and that any biographical account of how Lawrence came to write *Lady Chatterley's Lover* is simply a non-starter, because the needs within the writer in which such a book is rooted are so deep, so profoundly linked with imagination – in a way, they are a proof and product of individual consciousness itself – that all this speculation about events and places and dates and causes is simply scrabbling about on the surface, *pretending* to explain what is far, far richer and more complex and utterly resistant to straight-forward explanation.

On the other hand, other people will say that the study of a life and of its chronology, at the greatest level of depth and complexity that we can, allows us to trace many of the crucial experiences of that life (as many diary writers will agree): and that a writer so imbued with the habits of writing biographically and autobiographically as Lawrence was, by long practice and inclination, is going to use his experience constantly: and at times in ways of which he himself may not even be conscious. And that what we see in *Lady Chatterley's Lover* is a return to place, to origin, to father, to class, far stronger than any Lawrence himself would probably ever have admitted to. So that the man who looked across to the Haggs with that look of dreadful pain on his face, when walking through the area again with Willie Hopkin in 1926 on that last visit, was recognisably the man who showed Parkin and Connie, in the second version of the book, looking at an identical landscape:

> Across was Haggs Farm. Beyond, Underwood, the mining village, and the mines. The old, old countryside where Byron walked so often, and Mary Chaworth. Now colliers straying with their lasses, from ugly Underwood, from Eastwood, from Hucknall. And the mill-ponds at Felley lying so still, so

> abandoned, abandoned like everything that is not coal or iron, away below. The dead country-side! – and the grisly live spots, the mining settlements![39]

That description is the only one in Lawrence's fiction which gives those places the right names and sets them down like that: Haggs and Felley and Underwood. But it's a pretty grim description, too, and if the narrator of that *Second Lady Chatterley* novel had been able to, I think he might well have replaced Byron and Mary Chaworth with D. H. Lawrence and Jessie Chambers, as the ghosts who perpetually and grimly walk *that* particular landscape, so full of miserable memory for Lawrence. If this was, for Lawrence in 1926, the country of my heart, it was also the country of a heart that he had hoped long dead, but had turned out to be only unquietly slumbering.[40] The novel – especially the second version – revisits this landscape with just that combination of nostalgia and utter repulsion which matches Lawrence's reaction to Eastwood when he saw it in 1926.

But other readers still will say that in the long process of his own dying – of which Lawrence was terribly conscious from the moment when the Mexican doctor had 'rather brutally' said: 'Mr Lawrence has tuberculosis' and (Frieda remembered) 'Lawrence looked at me with such unforgettable eyes'[41] – that in that process of dying, Lawrence was impelled to celebrate the most life-giving and restorative of all his own life experiences, his falling in love with Frieda in the Midlands and his sexual experience with her, the more urgently in 1926 because Frieda's attraction to Angelo Ravagli at just that time had warned him that he was actually in danger of losing her, and he must do and be everything he could to remain her

39 *FSLC* 570:16-23.

40 See Emily Brontë, *Wuthering Heights*, end of chap. 34.

41 *"Not I, But the Wind ..."*, pp. 166-7; Frieda to Dorothy Brett, 12 August 1930, *D. H. Lawrence Review*, ix (Spring 1976), 101.

husband and mate ... and writing this novel as a tribute to Frieda and her sexuality was one of the most inspiriting things that a dying man could do. That feeling haunts the book from end to end. Of all Lawrence's work since *Sons and Lovers*, *Lady Chatterley* became the most reminiscent of his own youth, and of the crucial experiences of his own early life; in particular, how he changed from a person in a dead-end relationship with Jessie Chambers which was barely sexual (or not sexual at all, most of the time) into a person for whom a sexual relationship was the most important thing in life itself. And that was because of Frieda.

Or other readers might just want to say that *Lady Chatterley* is a novel that works – or doesn't work – because of what it is. All we have to talk about is what it is really about – and that, we shall have fun for the rest of our lives agreeing and disagreeing about.

I refuse to arbitrate. I want the richest possible reading experience, and I rule nothing out and I rule nothing in. I'm fortunate. I have neither to pass examinations nor to write critical essays to convince people. I can just read and sometimes experiment with a few thoughts, as now. So let me end with Lawrence, not with myself: Lawrence this time at the end of that same 1924 *Bibliography* essay, thinking about how evanescent – but also how haunting – books are. He had started his essay on that September morning, with those flowers around him, and with his own wonderings about writing. He ended the essay like this: thinking of the trees up on that hillside at the Kiowa ranch where his own little memorial stands today.

> To the vast public, the autumn morning is only a sort of stage background against which they can best display their own mechanical importance. But to some men still the trees stand up and look around at the daylight, having woven the two ends of the daylight together into visible being and presence. And soon, they will let go the two ends of the darkness again, and disappear. A

> flower laughs once, and having had his laugh, chuckles off into seed and is gone. Whence? whither? who knows, who cares? That little laugh of achieved being is all.
>
> So it is with books. To every man who struggles with his own soul in mystery, a book that is a book flowers once, and seeds, and is gone.[42]

I would say: let *Lady Chatterley* flower, as it has done this year, and in this Festival, and seed, in the minds of its readers as it has now done for three-quarters of a century: and then – be gone. Achieved.

42 *IR* 78:1-10.

Paper and ink in a digital age

October 2006, Tulsa, Oklahoma

This is not a lecture. I wrote it to explain to myself why seeing an original Lawrence manuscript (that of 'New Eve and Old Adam') was so important. I had actually edited the story in question for the CUP Love Among the Haystacks *volume in 1983, but I had worked from a xerox copy: I had never seen the original. Now I had the chance to do so – Holly Laird had invited me to a Modernist Studies conference in Tulsa – and I could spend two mornings with the manuscript of a story which I had admired for a long time and which I would also discuss in my paper for the conference, but which I had never seen.*

It was, as usual, a chastening experience. I found that the word I had printed as 'stretched' should have been the word 'sketched', that the phrase 'braided plait' should have been 'banded plait', and so on. One simply sees *so much more on an original! Day 1was spent clearing up such textual errors.*

On Day 2, however, I could look at something else. The work I was doing was also a kind of preliminary to working seriously on Frieda. At that date, I still hoped to be writing a biography of her fairly soon and I wanted to know what she thought of this story; in particular, what rights she might have believed she had over the central woman character. And I found something of an answer.

I am at the McFarlin Library in the University of Tulsa. I am here to see a manuscript: a very long way from anywhere, it feels. The library pretends to be a European fortified manor house of the sixteenth century: it even has crenellations. Inside, of course, it is a modern building, with lifts and air-conditioning. I go to the reading room, show my credentials, and am admitted to the oak-panelled reading room, where I am quite alone. The oak-panels look as if they came from ... a European manor house of the sixteenth century. Perhaps they did.

They bring me the manuscript I have come to see. It is the story 'New Eve and Old Adam', written in the spring of 1913. I have of course already seen a xerox of the story: first saw it, indeed, in 1981. I have also, courtesy of the McFarlin Library, downloaded on to my own laptop a beautiful colour digital image of the manuscript, where I can zoom in and out again, focussing on every letter of every word. What an advantage for the working scholar and editor! Why would one ever again need to cross half the world, just to see a manuscript?

But I have still had to come to Tulsa, to the McFarlin Library, to see this one. I now have it in my white-gloved hands.

The first lines are easy. They contain the story's title. Lawrence first wrote 'Eve': that was his first title, complete. Then he added the word 'Renegade': 'Renegade Eve'. Then he crossed most of it out and wrote 'The New Eve and the Old Adam'. Then he crossed out bits of that and ended up with the title the story had when it was published: 'New Eve and Old Adam'. But I don't need to be in Tulsa to see any of that. That was all clear on the xerox.

What I have come to see in particular, this morning, is in the second line of the story. I know Lawrence's writing well, and he first wrote

> 'I can't see it was so wonderful of you, to hurry home to me, if you are so tame when you do come.'

A wife is complaining to her husband, as he sits in the room with her after returning from a journey. The interesting thing, however, is that the word 'tame' has been struck through and another word inserted: 'cross'.

My xerox and my digital image have already been enough to make me pretty certain that the word 'cross' is not in Lawrence's handwriting. It is, I can now be certain, the writing of his partner (in 1913 not yet wife) Frieda Weekley. Frieda felt quite strongly that, whatever Lawrence wrote about the woman in the story, he was really writing about *her*. So when Frieda read that sentence, she felt she had the right to change 'tame' to 'cross'. *She* knew what she would have said. She crossed out the word 'tame'.

But – and this is why I have actually come to the library in Tulsa this morning – that was not the only change made in the first three lines of the manuscript. In line one, another word has also been crossed through: 'maddeningly'. And in line three, the word 'bitingly' has also been deleted. I want to know who it was who deleted those words. Was it Lawrence or Frieda?

And no xerox will help with such a question. Nor will even the most beautiful colour digital image. I need the actual paper: I need to see it under the strongest light and with the most powerful magnifying glass I can get, to see whether 'maddeningly' and 'bitingly' were crossed out in the same ink and in the same way as the word 'tame'. It's not just a question of ink colour, though that might help (on the other hand, Frieda might well have picked up Lawrence's pen and used it herself). But how did the deleting pen – whoever was holding it – dig into the paper, as the person inscribed the deleting line? Did it dig in deeply at the start and taper off, or did it dig in consistently? I *know* that Frieda deleted 'tame'; I have that deletion with which to compare these deletions. Can I be sure that she deleted 'maddeningly' and 'bitingly' as well?

This is a good example of what one has to do, at times, in an archive. I have stared and stared at the front of the paper. I have turned over the page and looked hard at the back, too, to see if these particular crossings out were done so hard that they came through the paper, or at least marked it. And I have looked at other examples of crossings out as well, throughout the manuscript, especially ones which I am confident are Lawrence's own, to serve as some kind of comparison.

The matter is at last clear. I have the answer. I have handed back my magnifying glass, along with the manuscript and the white gloves, to the archivist who has provided me with my materials. I can now go away happy.

For I am confident that Frieda deleted all three words.

Only she deleted in just that kind of a way, with a thickish kind of slightly wavy line, pressing pretty hard. She clearly felt she had the right to do that, in this manuscript. She believed she was the woman in question: she obviously didn't think she would have been maddening, and she did not believe she would have used the word 'tame'.

Thirty years ago I would probably have regarded Frieda's contribution to the story as a corruption of, an interference with, Lawrence's text; I would probably have treated her changes and deletions in the same way as I would have treated those of a typist who failed to transcribe what Lawrence wrote. I would have attempted to remove them. I would have re-instated 'tame', I would have brought back 'maddeningly' and 'bitingly' into the text. In the early 1980s, we Cambridge editors thought we were establishing a text that was Lawrence's alone. The CUP edition elected to evade Frieda's contributions to *Women in Love*, for example, made when she was copying from one typescript to another.[1]

Twenty-five years on, I now think it would be wrong to deny Frieda her role of collaborator with Lawrence. He gave her that role and she happily accepted it. She was not just a typist making mistakes.

It is just as well I did not come to Tulsa in 1981, and have seen what I now have seen, or I might have tried to adjust the CUP text of 'New Eve and Old Adam' in an attempt to remove Frieda's influence. Luckily, I didn't know that the deleting hand was Frieda's, so I let the changes stand.

Being twenty-five years late with one's textual research sometimes has its advantages.

1 See *WL* lix-xli.

The Memoirs of Frieda Lawrence

Public Library, Eastwood, Wednesday 9 April 2008

In April 2008, the D. H. Lawrence Society in Eastwood lost its scheduled speaker 72 hours before its Wednesday meeting. Ron Faulks rang me up on the Monday morning with the news, and I offered to stand in. I already had to hand a longish piece of writing about Frieda's memoirs, compiled in the reading room at the Humanities Research Center in Texas, where in the autumn of 2004 I had gone through masses of Frieda papers and had tried to make sense of them. In 2008, I used this piece of writing as the basis for a quickly prepared talk, and incorporated on a handout some of the materials I had seen.

Not all readers of Lawrence will know that, after Frieda published *"Not I, But the Wind ..."*, her biography of Lawrence, in 1934, she then worked at writing the story of her own life, and continued with the project until at least 1955 (the year before she died). She had thus written for many years longer than she had spent on *"Not I, but the Wind ..."*. But she published no book as a result of these labours. She died in 1956; and Angelo Ravagli, by then her husband, sold her papers and draft memoirs to two North American universities.

As a result, the nearest, up to now, that Frieda's memoirs of her life have got into print have been in three very different forms: two of them almost completely inaccessible. First – in 1957-58 – came the publication in a rare magazine called *Manuscripts* of a notebook into which she had written some extensive memories of her life; the notebook itself is in the library at the University of New Mexico at Albuquerque. And the magazine is very hard to get hold of; it's actually rather easier to go and read the original in Albuquerque. I shall call it the Albuquerque notebook.

Nearly all the rest of Frieda's surviving memoir material came to find itself at the University of Texas; and in 1961 in Britain, and in 1964 in the US, came the book which E. W. Tedlock edited, *Frieda Lawrence: Memoirs and Correspondence*, which reprinted nearly all of the Albuquerque notebook, though in a different order, but heavily interleaved it and overlapped it with extracts from the extensive material assembled at Texas. This created a wholly new kind of text and narrative, one which Frieda herself never put together; but it is the only form in which most people today can actually read Frieda's memoir material.

And thirdly, in 1976, came a Ph.D. thesis done by James Elery Holland at Texas, which assembled many of the same materials in a very different form. For one thing it kept the Albuquerque notebook material strictly separate, as an appendix only, though for the first time in its three appearances in print the Albuquerque notebook material was put into a strictly chronological order. The thesis also printed a good deal more (though by no means all) of the material at Texas. But this thesis was never published.

Since 1976, no one has attempted to do anything else with the materials, except to draw upon them (Janet Byrne's 1991 biography of Frieda, for example, uses Tedlock and Holland and some of the unpublished Texas material).

I was in Texas in 2004, doing a project on Frieda's German correspondence for which they had paid my fare and living expenses, and I took a look at Frieda's memoir material. It survives in various large boxes, and in various folders in those boxes, and has been catalogued almost entirely at random. There are about 600 pages in all, some in notebooks, some loose-leaf; some of then published, some of them nothing to do at all with her memoir writing project (for example, the Lawrences' original 13 July 1914 marriage certificate, in which 'D. H. Lawrence', 'Father: Coal Miner', marries 'E. M. F. J. Weekley', 'Father: Officer in the German Army'). Some are just scraps of random recollections. On your handout are four anecdotes about Lawrence from a single loose-leaf page: so far as I know all completely unpublished and unknown, and you are the first people ever to see them.

> He loved people so much more than I did. I had my doubts about humanity. 'If one gave you some children and animals you would be satisfied,' he once told me a little scornfully. 'Flowers I want too' I said.
>
> There came a letter to me saying: 'I would have died for you.' 'Those phrases! Lawrence said scornfully: you cant die for anybody, we each have to do our own dying & living too.'
>
> I would watch with what ingenuity he would try to write so as to get people's interest aroused ... 'How can I put it so that they get what I mean.' He was not so much interested in producing a work of art, that was by the way, but in rousing his readers to a greater zest in living ...
>
> I remember offering him, when my father was dead, and they gave me his ring with the Richthofen arms on it. It was a pretty ring & I said to Lawrence: 'Do you want it? I give it you.' He looked at it, because he liked nice things, for a little while. 'No,' he said, 'that isn't for me.'[1]

But that is an unusual page; there is not very much about Lawrence in these memoirs. Anyway, I had a good rifle through all these materials, and typed up about 130 pages of copies of the unpublished bits, which I have with me tonight.

The fact is that Frieda's memoirs are really in a very odd condition. All three of the printed versions I have mentioned are in their own way unsatisfactory, because the material –

1 Box 1 Folder 1 (q) (HRC).

even the Albuquerque notebook – is in an extraordinarily fragmentary state of incompletion. Frieda experimented with many different ways of presenting her memoirs, including different kinds of structure; it was going to be a book called *And the Fullness Thereof*; it was going to be called *What's the Big Idea*; it was going to be written as a letter to Kurt von Monbart. At other times she did not know how to shape it. She adopted various fictional names for herself and the central figures of her life (and then changed them all): she was Gisla, Paula and Manya and then 'I' again; her first man (the young soldier Kurt von Richthofen) is Olaf, Ulrich, Karl and Mark. Some episodes were more fictionalised than others; some were jotted down memories; some were designed as passages to be inserted into an idea she had in the late 1930s of a memoir structured around a visit she paid with Angelo Ravagli to South America, into which she would insert flash-backs of her childhood and her later life.

Holland, in 1976, was probably correct in deciding that the Albuquerque notebook material should not be mixed in indiscriminately with the other materials, though that is exactly what Tedlock did throughout his edition of the *Memoirs and Correspondence*, which is how most people come across it today. The Albuquerque notebook memoirs are markedly more fictional than the Texas material; but what is striking is that they supply a great deal of detail not in other versions of the early-love episode with the Olaf/Ulrich/Karl/Mark figure, for example. However – apart from that single case – all the other Albuquerque notebook episodes are concerned with events not dealt with elsewhere in the hundreds of pages of memoir material. At least one of the Albuquerque episodes is fictional: it's a third person narrative of how the Frieda character drowns herself in the Lago di Garda, because of the suffering she experiences at the loss of her children.

The materials at Texas are – in one way – more objectively reliable; even if they have the names changed, they are not fictionalised. But they mostly appear to be written rather later; and some of the more 'finished' materials at Texas – notably those included in two decorative notebooks labelled *Book I* and *Book II* by Frieda herself – present a much clearer, but also much less detailed, record of events covered elsewhere, and would seem to me to have been probably created relatively late in the process of memoir writing.

What I discovered as I worked through all these memoirs was something I had not at all expected, from the coherent published form which Tedlock had given them in the *Memoirs and Correspondence* book: that there were numerous episodes of which Frieda had actually written multiple versions, with no indication at all of which was the final one; and as most of them recreate memories with different details, and nearly all are undated, there is in general no objective (or even subjective) way of telling which was written either first – or last – or which is superior – or which might be preferable to all the others. What I want to do in this talk is ask what this plethora of material might tell us about Frieda, and about memoir.

It is easy to gain the impression – from these materials – that after childhood nothing was quite so real to Frieda, ever again. Her famous 'childishness' was that of someone who continued in memory to inhabit her childhood world very vividly indeed; the tree-climbing, untidy, fair-hair-sticking-up-all-over-the-place, loving and lovable brat was one of the selves she was determined never to grow completely out of, and she went back to it and used it extensively in her memoir materials – and in life too. She obviously told Lawrence all about it soon after meeting him, and his versions of Anna Brangwen growing up on a Midlands farm in *The Rainbow* actually draw heavily on Frieda's memories of growing up in

Metz. Anna's uncontrollable fair hair [2] was Frieda's as a child, too; while Anna's protests that it *is* hair [3] were also Frieda's. Frieda's writing about childhood is one of the best things she did, as a writer; but she also went on recreating and recreating it, into old age, in a way that seems oddly compulsive.

This probably had something to do, of course, with her later relationship with her parents, in particular with her father, whom she loved so very, very much and with whom she hated quarrelling; but with whom she did quarrel badly, during 1912-13, about leaving Weekley and taking up with Lawrence. Her old relationship with him never had a chance to re-establish itself. With the outbreak of War in August 1914, too, she lost touch with her family, and was unable to go over to Germany during her father's last illness, in the winter of 1914-15; nor even to attend his funeral after his death on 29 January 1915 (it was some while before she even heard that he had died).

But about these sad, later developments, the memoirs are entirely silent. For Frieda as memoirist later in life, her father continues to exist in this sunny garden in Sablon, and in his beloved study; he is utterly loving, caring and understanding. The earliest of all the fragments of her memoirs were actually inscribed in English on the back of two pages of the manuscript of Lawrence's story 'The Prussian Officer', thus almost certainly dating from the early summer of 1913 – and they too are about the father she loved so much. Characteristically, they are two different versions of the same memory. Here is one of them:

> He bent down over the little mound of earth in the asparagus bed. Firstly, he scraped the earth with his asparagus knife and a little white head appeared – Gisla come and look he cried – A little girl of 5 came

2 *R* 31:25-7.

3 *R* 84:19-28

> and looked with awe at it. The first asparagus, he said. He walked on gingerly. Are there more than one? she asked.[4]

So there is Frieda from the start telling alternative stories about her father. And Lawrence developed them into the story of Ursula in *The Rainbow*, helping Will in the garden.

Yet on the other hand ... the re-telling and re-telling of her memoirs, over the next forty years or so, the more I found of it, the odder it became to someone (like myself) on the look out for the 'real', the 'true' story of a childhood, to put into a biography. What Frieda produced is almost perversely the opposite of what one expects memoir to do. It is as if she were compelled by the very nature of the material to re-draft and re-draft, to tell the same stories over and over again in very slightly different ways ... and never, never reach a 'final version'. The plethora of materials telling the same story seems to support this.

Here are two examples of anecdotes, to show exactly what I mean. 1) Her father would catch flies and throw them into the spiders webs that draped the vines which grew in his garden. Frieda told this story herself on new fewer than four separate occasions. Each draft is in full, covering many pages in all; each is slightly different; each appears to have been composed without reference to any of the others. Why on earth would she do that? 2) Another of her early memories is that of her father coming home from work before the family has lunch out of doors, under the trees; the manservant Wilhelm, in white gloves, doles out the soup from a tureen, and Frieda's father complains that it is too hot. Frieda started this lengthy anecdote no fewer than seven times in her

4 E326.5, back of p. [8], originally 7.

memoir fragments. All have some details not in the others, some are long, some short, none are dated. Here is a short version from notebook 7:

> I came home and lunch was set under the cherry trees ... I ran along the garden & watched at the little gate at the end of the garden. There was father coming along with his quick, light steps. He was thinking & absorbed, his fist shaking nervously. I ran to meet him. When he saw me a warm smile welcomed me. 'Putzli' he called, he had lots of wonderful names for me.[5]

Here however is how notebook 13 presents it:

> Paula had just rushed home from school as she always did & found the lunch table set under the cherry trees, soon it would be too cold to eat out-of-doors. She skipped down the garden path along the wall where the spiders made such beautiful webs in the vine, the dogs came rushing, followed her in great bounds barking, she ran out of the little garden gate by the plum trees. The yellow plums were rotting on the ground, there had been such a lot & a swarm of wasps flew up with a scented honey as she ran. Paula watched the road, no father yet, she waited impatiently, finally she saw him and a flame of recognition went through her – He came along so quickly, absorbed in his thoughts, lightly shaking his right hand as if in argument with somebody. He took off his hat & the air waved through his thick hair. 'Papa', she called & ran to him, & a bright look came into his face at the sight of her, 'Polly putzli' he said & took her hand in his while the dogs fussed round them both.[6]

5 Box 1 Folder 4 (b) Notebook 7 (HRC).

6 Box 1 Folder 9 (a) (i) Notebook 13 (HRC).

Just the same – only quite different.

So how are we to view this multiple memoir writing?

One rather plausible argument would be that Frieda wrote all these alternative versions, and never finished her book, *because she did not want to finish it*: because she preferred to keep this childhood and adolescent world separate, continual – as it was constantly in her own mind.

In one sense, you see, to finish a memoir of childhood is to be untrue to it: to fix into a single and permanent shape something that is, by its very nature, quite different. How can someone who would like to write about her childhood do so while remaining true to the memories? Writing our memoirs always actually encourages us finally to shape and confine and order stuff that is in reality kaleidoscopically shifting; sometimes this memory with that one – sometimes differently, always differently remembered. Frieda's multiple drafts of her memoirs might therefore be considered – oddly – as ways of being honest and true to the actual ways and kinds of remembering that we do; so that by their very plethora of versions they resist being shaped into any kind of final narrative. Those of us who wish to make a final-version narrative out of them – as we do when we write a biography, say – will plunder them for details ... but in a way that is radically untrue to the nature of the material, which has – in a sense – been left in the state of memory itself: of neurones firing and links being made but never the same links, never the same shapes, never *exactly* the same account: longer, briefer, and so on.

This is an attractive way of thinking. It is in a way attuned to the nature of the material, which certainly gives one a wonderful idea of what Frieda was like; rather short attention span, entirely spontaneous, her mind jumping from this to that, times of intense creation and re-creation, but no grand and overarching narrative, not even of her own life. The reason she left all these alternative versions of her life might conceivably have been because she actually preferred it that way: because that *was* what she was like; and anything else, that was finished and polished and complete, would have been untrue to what she was like and to how she thought about herself and – of course – how she remembered her childhood.

But I have now come to distrust such a way of thinking, attractive though it is. For one thing, I suspect that she had learned from Lawrence what 'being a writer' was and involved – and that meant writing spontaneously to the moment, and making multiple drafts (just as we can see her doing on the back of 'The Prussian Officer' manuscript). In his case, at some point the drafts issued – they were obliged to issue, because he was a professional writer – as a finished work: his original and deliberately cultivated spontaneity always ended up as something finished and completed. Frieda could afford to stay at the level of writing to the moment, of constantly being spontaneous, and leaving the drafts. And that is what she did. I also suspect that she had no filing system, and that she preferred to re-create rather than to dig out old papers.

Now, in so doing, in one way she constructed the best possible kind of monument to her own life; rich, varied, and incapable of being turned into a single narrative: so that it remains something that retains the very quality of the life and memories, the very *feelings* of childhood, that were so precious to her.

But there is another way of viewing this multiplicity of materials. The memories – however compiled – are not just instinctive recollections. They are a loving, even compulsively loving, re-working of very nearly the same materials. There is, despite the plethora of versions, actually a very limited range of memories and anecdotes. Frieda may have been guided by a compulsion *not* to pin anything down, certainly – but not simply because that is what memory is like. No: it is because the material (limited, but loved) is so precious, such a reflection and construction of self-image: and Frieda loves telling and re-telling these stories. Her activity is less like reproducing the nature of actual memory than its complete opposite: like polishing precious objects in your hands, and seeing them slightly differently as every time you do so; and never wanting to stop. You go over and over.

This oddly becomes clear in Box I, folder 1 at the University of Texas (which for some reason known only to librarians starts with notebook 46). This is an extract from that folder which – for once – we can date, to 1934 ('after 4 years that he is dead' Frieda notes of Lawrence).

> pictures rise before my eyes – pictures that remain so fresh forever. My sister Nusch's heartshaped child's face, so mysteriously beautiful, my father's intense look of tenderness under his long grey curling eyebrows, my mother's bathingdress black lace over red satin, when I first thought: she is beautiful – My sister Else going to her first ball with snowdrops in her hair & I struck by her virginal quality – All these things come up out of the sunken past – Past & dead & yet alive in me – I see Lawrence's white body made of light & power, delicate bones pure white skin. *Forever must I love these visions. [crossed out]* My son's baby throat, that falls back as he laughs & laughs when I dart my face into this cradle from behind the curtains with the red cockerels – saying 'bonjour Monsieur' alas the flowering plants that bloomed in Lawrence's room at the Beau Soleil – and give me a pang of grief[7]

Here Frieda is being perfectly explicit about the randomness

7 Box 1 Folder 1 (a) Notebook 46 (HRC).

of her memoirs: they are the precious pictures which memory has selected, the visions to which she likes to return and return, as if caressing and turning them over in her hands.

Because the recollections are by no means as naive as their randomness and multitude of versions might encourage one to think: and as I thought when I was first typing them up. There is nearly always a real point to the telling; they do not just represent a random dredge of memory. There is for example a repeated memory of her getting her school report and showing it to her father (three different versions), and there are descriptions of her hatred of being told to be humble (of which there are no fewer than six accounts). These all have as a sub-text her validation of her life-long insistence on her own worth; they are a way of asserting that she has been 'her self' from the time when she was very young, in spite of the efforts of others to prevent her.

Frieda is in fact insisting that she has been a natural aristocrat from the start; other people are always likely to have proved themselves her inferiors. You don't need to go prancing around being triumphant about this, but you just know it, as you always have; and here is the childhood memory to prove it, which again you polish, and turn over yet again, and feel in your hands, like a lovely old stone, and confirm the nature of yourself as you do so. This is how you have always been. I suspect that this way of thinking is truer to the situation of Frieda's multiple memoir drafts than the attractive, neurone-randomly firing account of how we might be true to the nature of memory. Even the lunch-in-the-garden memory is a loving recreation of her very special closeness to her father: of their particular love. She wrote it out again and again because she loved it, and it was a way she deeply enjoyed thinking about herself.

There also seems however something just a bit obsessive about Frieda's constant insistence on her own happy childhood, on the absolute preciousness of home and mother and father. There are certainly reasons why such an obsession might have grown up. Her own horribly frustrated desire, between 1912 and 1923, to be a caring mother to her own children, after leaving them behind with Weekley when she went with Lawrence, suggests one good reason. She struggled for years to be allowed to see her children, and eventually got a small number of 30 minute visits in the offices of a lawyer (and once in Mark Gertler's Hampstead studio). Her ex-husband, Ernest Weekley, was determined to punish her so far as he could: as she put it in one of these memoir fragments (dating from 1955): 'My immorality had to be punished but it was not that really, it was revenge.' [8] In the eyes of the law, nevertheless, Frieda was almost a criminal. She, of course, could never see this; she felt herself to be as doting and loving a mother as ever, constantly frustrated by the inhuman refusal of her ex-husband to allow her to see the children she loved (and by her second husband's regular failures to sympathise sufficiently with her need).

For someone who believed so deeply in the freedom and joy of childhood, in home as so wonderful, and in the love of the parent so crucial, the loss of the childhood of her own children, and the damage she must have thought she had done to them, must have been awful. No wonder she went on mourning it all for years – and annoying Lawrence so much. In later life, however, she preferred to go back to her own childhood, and re-live it and re live it. In that way, her own desire to have her *own* children back, her constant pursuit of them, was totally validated. Of course she had been right and Weekley wrong!

So, as well as polishing, sometimes she went over and over memories like an oyster covering grit with pearl, over and over and over, until the pain was swealed away, the guilt assuaged, the wonder of childhood reasserted.

8 Box 2 Folder 15 (a) Diary for 1955 (15 January) (HRC).

However, the end result is that we get many of the same details repeated over and over in draft after draft. To read them is a little like being in the hands of a raconteur who constantly repeats him or herself, using almost the same words to tell almost the same stories. Whatever Frieda's motives and feelings were, producing this material, sometimes all that I can imagine doing as a biographer is simply culling, stealing and using every detail I can to build a 'final' memoir as rich and full as I can. I cannot prove it but I have the strong feeling that Frieda did not re-read her old pieces when writing the rewrites. Again, I think she was doing what she liked to think Lawrence did: write it new every time. (There is actually extensive evidence of Lawrence using and depending on his own previous drafts when creating later ones.) But Frieda preferred to forget her own previous attempts, and liked to do it all over again. I think she was, deep down, rather bored in the 1930s and 40s. She had relived her Lawrence years in *"Not I, But the Wind ..."*, but now she was going to dwell on the distant past – home and parents and sisters and marriage and parents-in-law and Otto Gross. And this is what she did.

But, however, she was not going to revisit other things, which had also happened in those years, but which did not contribute to the memories and self-image she was now polishing. There are enormous gaps in her memoirs. Just to take the period 1899-1912 (her first marriage): although she writes several times about how she came to England, and what it was first like, her years of growing disillusionment with her husband Ernest Weekley are completely omitted; her affair in 1905 with Will Dowson (and why she started it) is not there: her affair with Ernst Frick in 1911 is left out; and every detail of her life in Nottingham between 1907 and 1912 is totally excluded. And the lives of her sisters and their influence upon her are also totally excluded after early childhood: there is no Else, no Johanna, no Edgar Jaffe (Else's husband). The same is true of English influences: no Madge Bradley; no Lily Kipping. And there is practically nothing in all her memoirs about all the years she spent without her children, 1912-23.

In fact, in the memoir materials that survive at Texas there is an almost total cull of the bad things. They simply vanish. She creates a resolutely up-beat way of telling her early life story. On the other hand, the chapters in the Albuquerque notebook – which I think she wrote first, probably in the middle 1930s, fictionalising things, before abandoning the project – do get anxious about a few of the bad things that had happened to her. In the rather later Texas memoir materials, the failures are got over (because now she knows better); the anecdotes are lovingly polished; the boredom, the anger, of English marriage (for example) is missed out completely; the loss of the children is never mentioned.

There is also a great deal of self-mythologizing going on in the Frieda of the 1930s and 1940s when she recreates her early life. When she crosses out 'high-spirits' in a memoir of her early life in Berlin, and substitutes 'vitality',[9] that is her way of putting her finger exactly on it. Nearly all the memories she recalls celebrate her vitality and her aristocratic difference, the way she overcame her difficulties, the way she was instinctively opposed to all the hypocrisy and 'highfalute'[10] of her society. The Texas memoirs are up-beat in just the way that real-life is not, as they constantly recreate and reinforce that self-image. At the age of eighteen, although provincial and ignorant, she apparently knows enough to be able to see that court society in Berlin is absurd, ridiculous, doomed – or at least she does in her memoir. And the older she gets, the more that is reinforced: she grows increasingly unconventional, independent, flouting convention, damning

9 Box 2 Folder 4 (a) (i) Notebook 1 (HRC).

10 Box 2 Folder 4 (a) (i) Notebook 1 (HRC).

society, going her own way with her own opinions unaltered by experience. I suspect that living with Lawrence had a great deal to do with that.

What would not allow her to draw this inference, or re-enforce that persona, is simply omitted. But what *does* re-enforce it is repeated, over and over and over again.

So the job of the biographer might be to cull and select the very best possible, richest and fullest details from the materials surviving; to use them very carefully, being constantly aware of why Frieda loves them – and using the Albuquerque material with extra-special care, because of its fictional quality – and above all filling in the gaps. And all the time being very, very cautious about accepting any of Frieda's apparent revelations about how she thought when she was young. What often turns out to be most reliable in the memoir material is the incidental detail, *not* the considered opinion or belief or reaction. One often has to read the memoirs shutting oneself off from the point about her life she is trying to make, in fact.

This can at times pay dividends. In Texas, I read and compared and (at least twice) typed out accounts of her father's study at Sablon, with its guns and its plants. Here is one of the drafts I typed:

> There was her father's study, that her mother condemned as the dog kennel because the dogs were allowed to lie on the old sofa, over it all the guns were arranged in line. On the big writing desk lay a meteor, of a strange porous substance with a perfect pattern of dents. There was sealing wax & seal & a bowl of roman coins & pencils all neatly sharpened, great big ones & small ones a box of delicate instruments – In the windows bloomed the many cactus plants, red & happy. There was the big coo-coo clock that the other children Paula brought home admired so & insisted

> on watching for what seemed an endless time for the coloured bird to come out from behind its door.[11]

And here is another one:

> She dashed right into her fathers study. The study was full of light & flowering plants at the windows, that her father with his green hand cared for himself. In the spring there were fat blue & pink & red & white hyacinths; there were cacti red & purple, so flourishing & shiny leaf plants & it was gay. There were heads of deer with many antlers hung on the walls & the guns on their racks; on the large desk a meteor as a paper weight & broken shell splinters on a malachite base that had wounded him in the war & silver boxes & – There was the big sofa, that her mother scornfully called the dog sofa, covered with a rough blanket.[12]

The crucial detail, to me, is that object beside the meteor. Friedrich von Richthofen kept, on his desk, the splinters from the shell which had wrecked his career as an army officer when he was wounded in the hand during the Franco-Prussian war: he kept them mounted on a malachite base. They were why he had a civilian job in Metz: why his career had gone nowhere: and, incidentally, why he shook his hand as he came up the path to the garden ... I find that astonishing and fascinating – but that is the only one of the four versions of the study's appearance to include the detail. Her father's pain was also Frieda's, and the memoir's job was not to record it.

11 Box 1 Folder 13 (a) (i) Notebook 9 (HRC).

12 Box 2 Folder 6 (a) (i) Notebook 20 (HRC).

The reasons, perhaps, that Frieda did not finish her work on writing her life story were both because she did not want to – that wasn't the point of doing it – and because she did *not* want to go into the things that were more troubling. Gaps remained and were never filled; and the more such a way of thinking dominated her, the more certain it was that they never would be filled. Instead, the writing became a constant process of re-enforcement: I *was* like that, I *am* like that. There is something akin to boasting in it; the constant re-telling of the same story, in which you always come out on top, or take the right attitude, or instinctively have the right reaction.

This, if nothing else, might convince us that her memoir writing was not what I at first speculated – memory which had 'been left in the state of memory itself'. That may be how the memoir writing now comes down to us, but that was no part of her own writing project.

The memory and its recreation as the memoir had, in Frieda's case, acted as a talisman: it warded off any sense of loss; it kept constantly new what might otherwise have become old or got lost. Telling the story of our lives can be – and in Frieda's case, certainly was – a way of asserting that, what we once were, we are essentially and will always remain. Deep into old age, Frieda was – to herself – still the wide-eyed tomboy in the summer garden. Here she is yet again: this is the final item on your handout.

> She ran to meet her father. She ran along by the south wall where the grapes grew, where the spiderwebs hung and where the father would feed the spiders deftly with flies. Then past the plumtrees called mirabelles, where in the autumn the bees swarmed over the fallen fruit on the ground in the hot sun & there was a scent of honey & decaying fruit. Out through the small lower garden gate & she saw her father coming absorbed in some thought, he was shaking his fist about something, he came along on

> light, fast feet. She ran to him with a protective tenderness for him, child that she was, as if she wanted to make up to him for something, she did not know what ... She took his hand & he said 'Paulaputzli'.[13]

I guess 'Friedaputzli' in real life. The lovely, damaged, deeply beloved father is still coming up the path towards her, his hand shaking, and life stands still in that perfect, beloved memory, from which all the pain of loss (his loss, her loss) has been expunged. In writing it, Frieda liberated herself into childhood again; one of the reasons, I am sure, why she wrote.

13 Box 2 Folder 2 (a) (iii) Notebook 27 (HRC).

Baroness Frieda

Beinecke Library, Yale, Friday 7 November 2008

In the autumn of 2008 I was lucky enough to be awarded a Fellowship by the Beinecke Library at Yale, to go and study their Frieda Lawrence materials. On the day I arrived, the co-ordinator of the program, Priscilla Holmes, explained that I could – if I liked – give a talk about the work I was doing. And after a couple of weeks, I did: primarily to make myself start to draw things together that would be helpful in suggesting directions for my research during my final two weeks. The talk I gave, to other Fellows and some library staff, necessarily goes over some old ground – my audience were not Frieda or Lawrence experts – but was my first attempt to explain to myself why I might be writing a biography of Frieda. Never before had I felt so unlike her: never before had I seen so clearly how I might be able to use that to write about her. I am very sad that the biography project remains on hold; I cannot find a publisher for it.

I am planning a biography of Emma Maria Frieda Johanna Freiin von Richthofen Weekley Lawrence Ravagli – to give her all the names she ever officially had[1] – and that very list immediately introduces some of the problems, as well as the excitements, of the project. She was born von Richthofen: she was the daughter of a baron, and so – in the German system – was a baroness in her own right (hence the Freiin); and she was married three times, to Ernest Weekley, D. H. Lawrence, and Angelo Ravagli.

Frieda Ravagli was her name when she died in 1956: she had lived with Ravagli unmarried for the best part of twenty years before marrying him in October 1950; in 1955 she actually started using notepaper with a bold 'FLR' (standing for Frieda Lawrence Ravagli) printed across it. There are sev-

1 Fritz, Fritzli, Fritzel, Fritzle and Friedele were common in her family, and at different times she signed herself 'die Weekley', 'Frederika', 'Friederike', 'Euer Kättche', 'F'Kättche', 'Eichfried', 'Frieda' and simply 'F'.

eral examples in the Beinecke archive.[2] But search your Beinecke database, the electronic one or even the old card catalogue, and you will find no trace of Frieda Ravagli or even of Frieda Lawrence Ravagli: that person does not officially exist in the archive here.

Nor will you find any reference to Frieda Weekley in the archive or the database, although she was married to her first husband for thirteen years.[3] In the Beinecke database you *will* find references to the von Richthofen name – for example in the listing of the start of Box 23 in the Mabel Dodge Luhan archive – but only in the slightly weird form of 'Frieda von Richthofen Lawrence': a form which neither she nor (I believe) anyone else ever used, but which is the official Library of Congress allocation of her name, to be used by archivists.

Don't get me wrong: I'm not attacking archivists. The problem of identifying someone with three husbands, and who acquires their names, is normally insoluble. The date of the archive and its provenance will be a clue to how it was set up and what it describes: and it was as the wife of D. H. Lawrence that, quite naturally, Frieda originally entered the archive. Once in: that's how it stays.[4]

Frieda herself, however, would very much have approved the Beinecke database's reference to her as a von Richthofen.

2 E.g. Frieda to Dudley Nichols (11 March 1955), Yale Lawrence Vault.

3 The name Frieda Weekley appears on the title-page of two little school anthologies she published in 1902 and 1906 respectively: Schiller's ballads and Bechstein's *Märchen*.

4 I hate Jane Austen's biographers' assumption of intimacy that makes them call her 'Jane'. But what can I call my subject? It would be absurd to call her 'Frieda Lawrence' during the first 33 years of her life, when she had never even met him. Just 'Frieda' is inevitable unless I call her 'Frieda von Richthofen', 'Frieda Weekley', 'Frieda Lawrence' and finally 'Frieda Ravagli', according to date.

If you wish to visit her grave, you will have to find your way nearly 9,000 feet up into the *Sangre de Cristo* mountains in New Mexico; but you will find – cut into the granite slab – the name 'Frieda Lawrence Ravagli', her dates, an inscription – 'In Memory of twenty five years of incomparable companionship – Angie' – and (of all things) the von Richthofen coat of arms. Angelo Ravagli, her third husband, had had the organising of the grave-making (though not of the Beinecke archive), and did what he – and she – wished.[5]

For Frieda never forget that she was, as she once put it, 'a beastly "aristo" ',[6] and she didn't like anyone else forgetting it either.[7] She herself recalled a moment in the summer of 1912 when – having gone away to Germany with working-class Bert Lawrence, to the huge anger of her family – her old 'aristo' self returned with a vengeance:

> One day, in Munich, seeing all the elegant people in the streets I had an aristocratic fit. I bought some handkerchiefs with an *F* and a little crown on them. When I brought them home [Lawrence] said: 'Now I'll draw *my* coat-of-arms.' He drew a pickaxe, a school-board, a fountain pen with two lions rampant.[8]

Good move ... but on my very first day in the Beinecke I was

5 Angelo Ravagli wrote to Frieda's children immediately after her death: 'I will lay on the grave a full length of granite stone with her name, date of birth, and death, plus her coat of arms. Do you agree?' (*Memoirs and Correspondence*, p. 378). Presumably they did.

6 *1L* 476.

7 Returning from a visit to her parents in September 1913, Frieda had brought with her a stack of good quality notepaper with the von Richthofen coat of arms on it; DHL apologised for it ('please excuse it') and denounced it ('This coruscating notepaper') to his correspondents (see *2L* 79, 106).

8 *'Not I, But the Wind ...'*, p. 57.

reminded of Frieda's insistence on her title. I was looking at her letters to the hostess and writer Mabel Luhan; it was Mabel (another person with an interesting list of names: Mabel Ganson Evans Dodge Sterne Luhan) – it was Mabel who had invited the Lawrences to Taos, late in 1921, and whom Frieda answered enthusiastically in a letter written late in December 1921 which ends 'Best wishes to you / Frieda Lawrence / geb. von Richthofen'.[9] 'Geboren' simply means 'born': 'born von Richthofen'. Added not simply because Frieda liked it, or because she was a snob: not simply as a proof to the world of her status: but, I want to argue, as part of her identity as an independent woman.

I will come back to that. But let me move forward by sharing with you one of my major problems as a biographer of Frieda. Compared with many lives – and with all those I have so far written – Frieda's is remarkable not for how much she did, but for how little, in the conventional sense. Her friends were very aware of this: 'has she ever done anything but lie on a bed and smoke', one of them remarked in exasperation.[10] Well, she also read a lot while lying there smoking: throughout her life, letters were sent off either asking for books to be sent or thanking people for having sent them on. Not just novels either: she read voraciously. But the life of such a person – whether reading, or smoking, or lying – is actually very hard to turn into a biography.

So what makes her important? One conventional answer might be 'her writing': another might be 'her relationships'; a third one would be 'how she lived'. Let me start with the writing. She wrote one book, which she called *"Not I, But the Wind ..."*: her memoir of D. H. Lawrence. It is in fact a rather remarkable production. Lawrence died in March 1930; a

9 Frieda to Mabel Dodge Luhan (?28 December 1921), Yale 196 / 23 / 640)

10 Dorothy Brett to Alfred Stieglitz (2 June 1931), Yale / MSS 85 / 7 / 157.

number of authors were already at work by April that year, and by 1933 there had been published no fewer than eight biographical and reminiscent books on him (two by John Middleton Murry, one apiece by Lawrence's sister Ada, Mabel Luhan, Catherine Carswell, Dorothy Brett, Helen Corke and Earl and Achsah Brewster), while Aldous Huxley had contributed a long biographical preface to a volume of Lawrence's letters. It seemed as if everyone who had ever known Lawrence was climbing on this particular bandwagon; but obviously Frieda would bring something special even to such a crowded market. She was at work on her own book by November 1931 and it finally came out in July 1934.

She had had her problems. A friend had remarked back in 1931 that, although Frieda 'has been writing her Memoir, of all the years she seems to remember but little'.[11] Unlike most of the other writers, Frieda had very few letters from Lawrence to herself to help enrich her narrative; and (unlike at least two other of the memoirists) she had no diaries to help her either. But she had other materials, and she drew heavily on them. She included early drafts of Lawrence poems, essays, and great sheaves of letters which he had written to Frieda's mother and sister. Frieda's own linking narrative, which tends to ignore the periods for which she has letters, occupies however only 117 of the book's 311 published pages, making her book – in spite of its impressive weight and bulk, especially in its original Rydal Press edition – actually one of the slightest of these early lives.

That was her only finished book. She spent the years between 1936 and 1955 working on the memoirs of her own life outside her years with Lawrence.[12] What survives is a great rat's nest of memoir material, which never reached the stage of having a framework, title or even running order.

[11] Dorothy Brett to Alfred Stieglitz (16 November 1931), Yale / MSS 85 / 7 / 157.

[12] I discussed it in 'The Memoirs of Frieda Lawrence'.

Her own writing – her book, her fragmentary memoirs, her essays and especially her letters – is nevertheless of enormous interest, and my biography should be the first book to take it seriously. At the Beinecke I am taking my chance to go through the collections of four of the most important batches of her letters: those to other figures in whom the Beinecke specialises: Mabel Dodge Luhan, Dorothy Brett, Dudley Nichols, Alfred Stieglitz: and also to track cross-references between these people as they discuss Frieda (Brett's letters to Stieglitz, Spud Johnson's letters to Luhan, etc.). At times Frieda writes with wonderful sensitivity and brilliance, even though she had decided to make her book on Lawrence ignore most of the problems of life with him. Their quarrels, for example, her feelings about her children, her jealousies of other women, her affair with Angelo Ravagli – are all ignored in *"Not I, But the Wind ..."*. Other parts, however – especially the section culminating in his death – are written with such sensitivity that I don't know anything to touch them.

That Frieda was a writer, there can be no question. However, although I am thinking of devoting a chapter each to her two main writing projects, there's an awful lot of her life which neither project gets anywhere near. I shall spend the rest of my time trying to explain in what Frieda's peculiar fascination and difference consists, in her relationships and in how she lived.

In Frieda biography so far, her life has most frequently been constructed as one lived through and for the various men who mattered to her. Just as the life of Mabel Dodge Luhan can be discussed as that of a social hostess who brought people together, as much as in the terms of the person she *was*, so the life of Frieda has up to now largely been constructed as either that of Lawrence's wife, or that of a kind of *sexual* hostess, to whom interesting men came. She has been seen as a kind of poor man's Alma Mahler, though she really cannot compete with a list of lovers such as Gustav Mahler, Walter Gropius, Franz Werfel, Oscar Kokoschka, Gustav Klimt and Alexander Zemlinsky. Frieda was not in that league, but her conquests were interesting. Her first was her first husband, Ernest Weekley, the Frieda husband most usually written off as dull and boring, actually no such thing.[13] Fourteen years older than Frieda, he fell devastatingly in love with her in the Black Forest in 1898. He was – for that date – that almost unheard-of thing, a self-taught academic, who – the son of lower-lower-middle-class parents – had gone to university as a mature student (as we now call them: incredibly rare in the 1890s) after educating himself through night-schools and correspondence courses: within eight years of starting as an undergraduate, he had been appointed to the Chair of Modern Languages at the University College of Nottingham. He was a brilliant linguist. He was also – for the period – an utterly unusual one, because he wrote popular books on language which in time made him a household name in England. He and Frieda had three children.

Frieda, however, was bored. She moved on to her conquests: the first a local lace manufacturer in Nottingham, the second the fascinating and compelling Otto Gross, pioneer psychoanalyst and cocaine addict, the third a Swiss anarchist painter called Ernst Frick ... all while staying married. Then came D. H. Lawrence, a young and hardly recognised writer when she first met him, but in the throes of writing *Sons and Lovers*. She thought he would be just another affair, but her relationship with him brought her first marriage to an end, and she lost her three children, to her utter and continuing distress. There are two or three other young men who got caught up in Frieda's skirts around the same time, including the young writer David Garnett. But she

[13] See my *Cold Hearts and Coronets: Lawrence, the Weekleys and the von Richthofens* (Nottingham, 1995), pp. 19-25.

mostly kept her hands off other men until 1926, when she fell for an Italian Bersaglieri captain called Angelo Ravagli, twelve years younger than herself, extremely practical and active; eventually she got him into bed, while (as I have described[14]) Lawrence had to be content with writing *Lady Chatterley's Lover*. As soon as Lawrence was dead in 1930 she accepted as her lover John Middleton Murry, once the husband of Katherine Mansfield: Murry had wanted her for years. But Frieda needed a man to help her survive in the place where she wished to live, at the ranch near Taos which she and Lawrence had acquired in 1924. For that, Murry was useless. She persuaded Angelo Ravagli to come with her. Angelo's wife knew all about it, but I think was pragmatically prepared to accept the idea that her husband was changing career. Their hope must have been that he might go to America for some years with this rich older woman and come home with a good deal more money than he would have earned in the army. So off he went; and after various return visits over the years – and marrying Frieda in 1950 – eventually Angie did come home again after Frieda's death, with half the now very considerable Lawrence estate in his pocket; his reward for many years service ... to rejoin the wife and family he had left twenty-five years earlier.

Well, that is a potted biography. Most Frieda biographies have, however, concentrated almost entirely on her years with Lawrence. The real situation is that she spent her first 20 years unmarried, 13 years married to Weekley, 18 years partnered by Lawrence, and 26 years partnered by Ravagli: so that less than a quarter of her life was spent with Lawrence. But the quantity of information available about him during their years together is enormous, and Frieda in previous biographies has inevitably become the adjunct of a famous man leading a richly documented life. This does something, too, to make up for the lack of achievements in her life –

14 See above, 'Ways of Saying Goodbye'.

books or essays or poems or social good works.[15]

I intend not to shipwreck on this particular reef. My chapters about her years with Lawrence will, I hope, concentrate almost entirely on their travels, and on the use he made of her in his work; and I plan my biography to give a great deal more space to her life before and after Lawrence than to her years with him.

So let me put the fundamental question like this. What should the biography of an independent woman like Frieda be like? Because that is the person whose biography I hope I will be writing: not that of a woman who was a man's partner before she was anything else. An independent woman who married three times, you ask me, ironically? Absolutely. To try and define Frieda's very particular kind of independence, let me read you a paragraph she wrote about herself while trying, in the 1950s, to understand her own life. (This document is not here but in the HRC in Texas.)

> Sometimes she lost herself in the past, and it bowled her over – She would have liked to grasp the meaning of her long years, of the changes, why she was compelled to do this thing and not that, the out of the way places many and varied she had seen and all the people she had cared for and those not cared for and how she had wanted to save people and had been

15 Of the existing five books which count as biographies or partial biographies, 84% of Jacqueline Gouirand-Rousselon's *Frieda von Richthofen* (Paris, 1998) is devoted to her years with DHL; 83% of Michael Squires / Lynne Talbot's *Living at the Edge* (2002): 75% of Janet Byrne's *A Genius for Living* (New York, 1995): 74% of Robert Lucas's *Frieda Lawrence* (New York, 1973): 60% of Kirsten Jüngling & Brigitte Roßbeck's *Frieda von Richthofen* (Berlin, 1998).

> fanatic about it and now she was contented and peaceful leading this quiet busy life – Anyhow she had achieved that and a thought came, then another the very opposite, but often she just went on in a vague, secretly joyful way, as if she did not want people to know how happy she was ––

Such writing is perfectly characteristic of her. She uses fewer full stops than most people, while her dashes at times out-sprint Emily Dickinson's – and some might think her prose a little meandering. [16] Yet I believe it is actually a careful construction, worthy of Virginia Woolf: lucid, honest, thoughtful, and entirely to the point.

And, happy as she was – perhaps *because* she was happy – she was not a person who in the course of an extraordinarily varied life ever did or thought anything especially influential.

[16] Her published memoir material has been heavily edited; E. W. Tedlock not only cut and pasted different drafts to make a generally coherent text, but imposed upon her writing his own kind of punctuation; and occasionally he rewrote her in ways that changed her meaning. One of her early meetings with Ernest Weekley is a case in point. Frieda wrote:

> He did not know anything; he was nothing by himself, his sole being was in that approaching pink and white girl. His emotion almost paralysed him. Gisla felt slightly uncomfortable; she went up to him. He took her in his arms. Gently, tenderly, repressing his passion, so as not to frighten her. "My sunflower," he said. (HRC Box 2 Folder 7)

Tedlock reproduces this as follows:

> He did not know anything, he was nothing by himself, his sole being was in that approaching pink and white girl. His emotion almost paralysed him. Paula felt slightly uncomfortable, she went up to him. He took her in his arms, gently, tenderly, repressing his passion, so as not to frighten her. "My snowflower," he said ... (*Memoirs and Correspondence*, p. 70-1)

Before 1913 or so, as she says, she wanted to save people: not in a religious way but by sleeping with them, and thus liberating them. Lawrence however did not believe in such mass conversions, and for the most part she gave them up. What she exhibited instead was a quality which hugely impressed Lawrence: a kind of richly uninhibited latent sexuality, a huge capacity for pleasure and happiness, for spontaneity and directness, for being herself. It was because she lived so happily in her own skin that she was mostly unconcerned with where and how she actually lived in the world, and was so remarkably adaptable to different ways of life. She took life for what it was and just got on with it: she was herself. If you read Lawrence's fiction, you keep coming across attempts to describe a person like this: so utterly unlike the troubled, introspective figures of his heroes and narrators. Here's the kind of thing I mean:

> She drew away, and looked at him radiant, exquisitely, glowingly beautiful, and satisfied, but radiant as an illumined cloud.
>
> To him this was bitter, that she was so radiant and satisfied. She laughed upon him, blind to him, so full of her own bliss ...[17]

The negative side of this quality, of course, is likely to be some blindness to others: some lack of interest in what other people actually feel. Dorothy Brett, who knew Frieda well, and envied her deeply, once asked, bitterly, cattily and as negatively as possible:

> Has Frieda ever loved anyone ? Lawrence used to say that he never saw Frieda look affectionate, except when looking at herself in the glass ...[18]

[17] *R* 282:19-22.

[18] Dorothy Brett to Alfred Stieglitz (2 June 1931), Yale / MSS 85 / 7 / 157 / 1.

But it is this quality which I identify with Frieda's belief in her own aristocracy: her attitude of (on the one hand) unthinking difference, and (on the other) of letting other people serve her.

Aristocracy is an unfashionable subject, usually seen as merely a subset of a larger grouping called Class Distinction, sub-section Snobbery. We'll have to change that. What Frieda got from her upbringing was a belief and happiness in her own self that survived bourgeois marriage, the loss of her children, Lawrence's demands, their quarrels, his death. When she came to write her book about Lawrence, of course, her own deep attitude was not going to change. Let me draw your attention to the title-page of her book *"Not I, But the Wind ..."*. For a modern publisher, that would be a useless title for a biography: nowhere in it appears the name of the person the book is about. The phrase *"Not I, But the Wind ..."* is a line from a poem of Lawrence's which Frieda especially liked ... but how many people know that? The only place the name 'Lawrence' actually appears on the title page is in *her* name: 'by Frieda Lawrence'. But of course she does not stop there. The name on the title page goes on: 'geb. Freiin von Richthofen'. That's what hits you. That's who she is: not just born 'von Richthofen'; but born 'Baroness von Richthofen'. Her name, in effect, twice. His name nowhere.

And then the eye naturally travels to the facing page, the frontispiece. What leit-motif for the book would most appropriately appear there? What would Frieda choose for a life of D. H. Lawrence?

It's a coat of arms. It's the von Richthofen coat of arms. As a child, sitting in a railway train, Frieda had confided in her mother: 'Mummy, do you think the people in the carriage know that I'm a baroness?' All her life she ensured that people knew. Most of her family – including her intellectual elder sister Else, who had a long relationship with Max and Marianne Weber and Alfred Weber – laughed at her for being a snob. But I don't think she was: she was declaring that she was and felt different. She was not just an aristocrat, but one of life's aristocrats. No pictures of phoenixes on *her* biography of Lawrence: not even a picture of him: but what enrooted her. When she signed the private press edition of the book, she signed right across the coat-of-arms, as if validating a stamp or seal.

The early twentieth-century liberation of women is not simply a matter of political freedoms gained, but of a change in mind-set: in particular a new consciousness of the role of sexuality in the ways in which women are themselves. Frieda exemplified and practised a kind of aristocratic and sexual self-confidence and superiority: her 'fundamental self-assertion'[19] was a new kind of toughness and insouciance. Someone who met her in 1955, only a year before she died, acutely described her 'overbearing and yet tender-skinned offering of herself'.[20] It was because of her receptivity to others, that the fact that she remained self-proclaimedly an aristocrat was neither overpowering nor overbearing. She was 'unaffectedly affirmative'[21] in a way that made people either tolerate her aristocratic claims or see them as something else altogether: as emotionally real.

Of course, as the daughter of a Baron she also took certain things for granted. In her marriage to Ernest Weekley, the cook and the maid did the household work – and as for the children, their nanny took care of *them*. In her second marriage, to Lawrence, he did most things – cooking, floor-scrubbing and so on – but Frieda started to do the washing: and at the ranch she did some cooking – and took care of the chickens. Those were *her* specialisms. To an outsider, however, she always looked like someone who spent most of time lying on her bed smoking; Dorothy Brett, catty as usual, wrote how Frieda's creed was 'never to do anything for

19 Martin Green, *The von Richthofen Sisters: The Triumphant and the Tragic Modes of Love: Else and Frieda Von Richthofen, Otto Gross, Max Weber, and D. H. Lawrence* (Basic Books, 1974), p. xvi.

20 Martin Green, *The von Richthofen Sisters*, p. [xv].

21 Martin Green, *The von Richthofen Sisters*, p. [xv].

herself if she can find some one else to do it for her'.[22] That was written as a denunciation. We might read it differently: it defines a kind of independence.

In Lawrence, too, she had a husband who not only stood up against her – hence their constant quarrels – but who also dramatised what he felt was her implicit aristocracy and independence to their contemporaries. She was a woman whose feelings – and her liberation – were made vivid to countless readers of Lawrence's work. Her influence, in that way, was surprising.

I hope I've not made her out to you as selfish or uncaring. But the extraordinary way in which she finally laid Lawrence to rest – or, in another way, disposed of him – is the last story I shall tell you, and it is very characteristic. I have learned new things about it while I've been here at the Beinecke.

It is in many ways a comic story – though not for Lawrence who, as Aldous Huxley remarked, hated 'having his own intimate life exposed'.[23] Frieda was less troubled. Lawrence had died in March 1930, and had been buried where he died, in Vence (regularly misprinted as Venice, where of course artists go to die). It was however Frieda's idea within four days of his death that, when she went back to New Mexico, she would 'come <u>with</u> Lawrence and have a great funeral with drums at the ranch and we'll make him a place there'.[24] She even knew the site: 'at the Ranch, high up beyond the

22 Dorothy Brett to Alfred Stieglitz (22 April 1930), Yale / MSS 85 / 6 / 153.

23 Dorothy Brett to Alfred Stieglitz (6 August 1930), Yale / MSS 85 / 7 / 160.

24 Frieda to Spud Johnson (?15 March 1930), Yale Uncatalogued MS Vault 133.

spring'.[25]

But months went by as she wrestled with the fact that Lawrence had left no will ... and the only good time to come to the ranch, at that altitude, was in late spring or early summer. She resolved to come in the spring of 1931 ... though when she *did* come, she brought not Lawrence but Angelo Ravagli. It was not until 1934 that she finally decided to 'bring Lawrence' back to the ranch: and it would, naturally, be a man's job to sort *that* out. So Angelo was despatched back to Europe, to see his wife and family, and to arrange for the exhumation, cremation and transport of his predecessor. An interesting job for any man: but Frieda never troubled about such things. She knew what she wanted, and she knew the man for the job. Basta! as she – and Lawrence – would have said.

In fact, Angelo – who had almost no French – was by no means the right man for the job. He had terrible trouble getting the business sorted out, and relied heavily upon Lawrence and Frieda's friends in the south of France. But finally, in April 1935, together with the box provided for the ashes, he got on a boat to New York, took the train south from there ... and ended up in Santa Fe, where Frieda was: waiting – one might say – for her two men to arrive, one in the box. Let me tell the next part of the story via a horrified letter which Dorothy Brett wrote to Alfred Stieglitz:

> did I tell you of ... Frieda meeting Angelino in Santa Fe … of the tea-party with the Ashes on the table .. and Frieda pointing giggling to them and saying 'Here is Lawrence' … and how even Santa Fe hard-boiled as it is was shocked …. most of the tea-party a bit drunk too …. and then the drive up with the Ashes resting on Mrs Fechen's feet and Angelino leaning over from the front

[25] Frieda to Dorothy Brett, copy in Dorothy Brett to Mabel Dodge Luhan (?March 1930), Yale / MSS 196 / 4 / 120 / 2.

> seat saying 'This is Lawrence ' to scandalised friends …. and their finally forgetting them for a whole week at Mrs Fechen's house …… She being Russian . . emotional … made a little altar for them under an Icon … and put candles round them[26]

So much myth has grown up around the story that it is good to read at least a second-hand account. You hear stories of Lawrence's ashes being abandoned on station platforms, and so on. None of them seem to be true, or Brett would certainly have included them.

But finally Frieda, Angie and the box got to the ranch ... and it was (of course) Angie's job to house the ashes. A very practical man, Angie ... he had acquired some bricks, and he built a kind of shrine on the site which Frieda had chosen. It was about 10 feet long and 8 feet wide and 8 feet high, with a pitched roof. Brett was cutting about it:

> It is so vulgar so far from Lawrence that everyone is disgusted and laughing ... the ugly cold desolate chapel of fire-bricks ...[27]

When the building was done – except for the decorating – the box of ashes was placed in it. But Brett relented sufficiently to help decorate the little building with her paintings. The opening ceremony – should that be closing ceremony? – was planned for mid-September 1935.

I have learned from the materials I've seen here how, back in July, Brett had been sounding off to lots of people – though not to Frieda – about how awful it was for Lawrence to be stuck in this ugly little brick building, and how the ashes

[26] Dorothy Brett to Alfred Stieglitz (19 July 1935), Yale / MSS 85 / 7 / 160.

[27] Dorothy Brett to Alfred Stieglitz (19 July 1935), Yale / MSS 85 / 7 / 160.

should have been scattered ... and how she wouldn't mind stealing them herself. But she never did it. To her it was just a pleasing fantasy. Nevertheless, a couple of days before the ceremony on 15 September, Mabel Luhan told Frieda's daughter Barby – who was there for the summer – that Brett had been making such plans ... and all hell broke loose. Frieda denounced Mabel for a lack of friendship in not telling her before, and declared their friendship at an end ... (the two line letter is here in the archive): she loosed off a torrent of abuse towards Brett ... and she and Angie conferred. Lawrence must be safeguarded! The solution they came up with was concrete. Angie was a dab hand with concrete and building: and a kind of altar was built up (about 2 foot by 3 by 4) into which the contents of the box were mixed.

So Lawrence's last resting place – perhaps – is in a solid block of concrete, 9,000 feet up in the foothills of the *Sangro de Cristo* mountains: with Frieda's tomb just outside the little shrine.

Mabel Luhan never plotted to steal the ashes. Brett never plotted: just fantasised loudly. The evidence – here in the Beinecke – is very clear. As Brett pointed out to anyone who would listen to her, she had had ample chance to steal the ashes during the long hours she had spent painting decorations in the shrine, when the box was sitting on the floor. But the story of the planned theft is a good one, and will doubtless be told again.[28]

So the Lawrence ashes story is also one in which Frieda von Richthofen finally got him where she wanted him, on her ranch. There is a final twist, but I've gone on long enough.[29] I

28 A few years ago, a campaign started to 'bring Lawrence home' to Eastwood, because of press reports that the shrine was not being cared for (in fact it was being cared for extremely well). What no one in England apparently realised is that it would take heavy lifting gear to lift the lump of concrete off the mountainside.

29 See Emile Delavenay, 'A Shrine without Relics?', *D. H. Lawrence*

wanted to describe the kinds of materials I've been exploring, and to demonstrate why it was important for a potential biographer to come here: I am very grateful indeed for the Fellowship that has made it possible.

Review, xvi (Summer 1983), 111-31. In old age, and in his cups, Ravagli claimed to a friend that he had grown scared of the expense of transporting the box containing the ashes to Villefranche, where he was due to sail to the USA, although Delavenay has demonstrated the extent to which Ravagli was exaggerating the problem. It does seem likely, however, that he did *not* transport the ashes across the Atlantic, but abandoned them somewhere in the south of France; in which case (as he also confessed) he must have filled the box (or another box) with ashes acquired in North America. What is preserved in the shrine near Taos is likely to have no connection with DHL at all.

Publications and productions 1970-2010

A. Selected articles and review articles

'D. H. Lawrence: The Critical Heritage', *Cambridge Quarterly* (Spring-Summer 1970), pp. 104-9

'D. H. Lawrence and Louie Burrows', *D. H. Lawrence Review*, iv (Fall 1970), 253-62

'Sanity, Madness and *Women in Love*', *Trivium*, x (May 1975), 125-36

'The Chambers Memoirs of D. H. Lawrence: A Reply', *Renaissance and Modern Studies*, xix (1975), 98-107

'Beginnings and Endings: Edward Bond and the Shock of Recognition', *Educational Theatre Journal*, iv (December 1975), 466-79

'D. H. Lawrence and Families', *Journal of the D. H. Lawrence Society* (1985), pp. 13-19

'Short Story and Autobiography: Kinds of Detachment in D. H. Lawrence's Early Fiction', *Renaissance and Modern Studies*, xxix (1985), 1-15

[with Lindeth Vasey] '*Mr Noon*/Mr Noon', *D. H. Lawrence Review*, xx (Summer 1988), 179-89

'New Materials in the Biography of D. H. Lawrence – I: Catalogue of Some Letters and Postcards Relating to the Lawrence Family, 1897-1910', *D. H. Lawrence Review*, xx (Fall 1988), 269-274

'Lawrence and "the Woman of a Lifetime"', *Meridian*, vii (October 1988), 99-115

[with Lindeth Vasey] 'Rejoinder: The Cambridge *Women in Love*', *Essays in Criticism*, xxxix (April 1989), 176-84

'New Materials in the Biography of D. H. Lawrence – II: Catalogue of the Louie Burrows Papers', *D. H. Lawrence*

Review, xxi (Spring 1989), 47-53

'Lawrence and Frieda Weekley', *The Swansea Review*, no. 6 (July 1989), pp. 23-44

'Problems in the Biography of D. H. Lawrence', *Transactions of the Leicester Literary and Philosophical Society*, lxxxiii (August 1989), 18-19

'Never Too Late for a Happy Childhood', *The Guardian* (8 August 1991), p. 30

'No End to the Intercourse of Talk', *The Guardian* (9 August 1991), p. 30

'*Sons and Lovers*', *The Independent* (5 September 1992), p. 18

'Coal Comfort' [Review of Ken Russell's television film of *Lady Chatterley's Lover*], *Times Literary Supplement* (1 July 1993)

'Check the fact-checkers', *Times Literary Supplement* (7 January 1994), pp. 11-12

'Orts and Slarts', *Review of English Studies*, xlvi (1995), 26-40

'The Spirit of Place: A Re-definition', *Appropriations and Impositions: National, Regional and Sexual Identity in Literature*, ed. Igor Navrátil and Robert B. Pynsent (Bratislava: Národné literárne centrum, 1997), pp. 28-41.

'D. H. Lawrence's Theatre of the South-West', *The Journal of the D. H. Lawrence Society* (1998), pp. 8-36

'Towards a New Version of D. H. Lawrence's *The Daughter-in-Law*: Scholarly Edition or Play Text?', *The Yearbook of English Studies*, xxix (1999), 231-46

'Dramatic Punctuation: The Case of *The Daughter-in-Law*', *Études Lawrenciennes*, xix (1999), 65-79

[with John Turner] 'Ideas of Community: Lawrence and "Rananim"', *D. H. Lawrence Studies*, viii (July 1999), 135-71

'In Bed with Sara Hutchinson', *The Cambridge Quarterly*, xxviii

(1999 [2000]), 232-48

'D. H. Lawrence: A Single Life', *Journal of the D. H. Lawrence Society* (Autumn 2001), 119-33

'The Date of Birth of D. H. Lawrence's Father', *Notes and Queries*, l, no. 3 (September 2003), 327-8

'Open Letter to George Hyde', *Journal of the D. H. Lawrence Society* (2004-2005), 141-4

'Frieda von Richthofen and Karl von Marbahr', *Journal of D. H. Lawrence Studies*, i, no. 2 (2007), 119-27

'Afterword' to 'Fanny and Annie', *Journal of D. H. Lawrence Studies*, i, no. 3 (2008), 73-7

B. Contributions to Books

'Introduction' and 'Note on the Text' to D. H. Lawrence, *The White Peacock*, ed. A. Newton (Penguin Books, 1982), pp. 11-33

Entry on D. H. Lawrence in *The Fontana Biographical Companion to Modern Thought*, ed. A. Bullock and R. B. Woodings (Fontana, 1983), p. 429

'Lawrence and Eastwood', *D. H. Lawrence: Centenary Essays*, ed. M. Kalnins (Bristol Classical Press, 1986), pp. 1-20

'Lawrence's Autobiographies', *The Spirit of D. H. Lawrence*, ed. G. Salgado and G. K. Das (Macmillan, 1988), pp. 1-15

'The Restoration of *Women in Love*', *D. H. Lawrence in the Modern World*, ed. P. Preston & P. Hoare (Macmillan, 1989), pp. 7-26

Translations (with Cornelia Rumpf-Worthen) of D. H. Lawrence's German correspondence in *The Letters of D. H. Lawrence*, Volume V (1924-7), ed. J. T. Boulton and L. Vasey (Cambridge University Press, 1989)

Translations (with Cornelia Rumpf-Worthen) of D. H. Lawrence's German correspondence in *The Letters of D. H. Lawrence*, Volume VI (1927-28), ed. J. T. Boulton and M. H. Boulton with G. M. Lacy (Cambridge University Press, 1991)

'D. H. Lawrence: Problems with Multiple Texts', *The Theory and Practice of Text-Editing*, ed. I. Small and M. Walsh (Cambridge University Press, 1991), pp. 14-34

'A Lawrence Biographer in Nottinghamshire', in *D. H. Lawrence: The Centre and the Circles: Essays by John Worthen, James T. Boulton, Keith Sagar*, ed. P. Preston (D. H. Lawrence Centre, University of Nottingham, Occasional Paper No. 1, 1992), pp. 11-29

Translations (with Cornelia Rumpf-Worthen) of D. H. Lawrence's German correspondence in *The Letters of D. H. Lawrence*, Volume VII (1928-30), ed. J. T. Boulton and K. Sagar (Cambridge University Press, 1993)

'The Necessary Ignorance of the Biographer', in *The Art of Literary Biography*, ed. J. Batchelor (Oxford University Press, 1995), pp. 227-44

'Facts in Fiction: With a Short Argument about Authorial Intention', *Editing D. H. Lawrence: New Versions of a Modern Author*, ed. C. L. Ross and D. Jackson (University of Michigan Press, 1995 [1996]), pp. 40-63

'Drama and mimicry in Lawrence', *D. H. Lawrence and Comedy*, ed. P. Eggert and J. Worthen (Cambridge University Press, 1996), pp. 19-44

'D. H. Lawrence and the 'Expensive Edition Business', *Modernist Writers and the Market Place*, ed. I. Willison, W. Gould and W. Chernaik (Macmillan, 1996), pp. 105-23

'A Biography, by John Worthen', in *D. H. Lawrence: A Reference Companion*, ed. P. Poplawski (Greenwood Press, 1996), pp. 3-93

'D. H. Lawrence and Copyright', *Textual Monopolies: Literary*

Copyright and the Public Domain, ed. P. Parrinder and W. Chernaik (Office for Humanities Communication, 1997), pp. 83-93

'The Biographer and Perspective', *Writing the Lives of Writers*, ed. W. Gould and T. F. Staley (Macmillan, 1998), pp. 191-203

'Recovering *The Lost Girl*: Lost Heroines, Irrecoverable Texts, Irretrievable Landscapes', *D. H. Lawrence in Italy and England*, ed. G. Donaldson and M. Kalnins (Macmillan, 1999), pp. 211-27

Translations (with Cornelia Rumpf-Worthen) of D. H. Lawrence's German correspondence in *The Letters of D. H. Lawrence*, Volume VIII, ed. J. T. Boulton (Cambridge University Press, 2001)

'Introduction' to D. H. Lawrence, *The Widowing of Mrs. Holroyd* (Pine Street Books, 2002), pp. vii-xii

'Lawrence's Theater of the Southwest', *D. H. Lawrence: New Worlds*, ed. K. Cushman and E. G. Ingersoll (Fairleigh Dickinson University Press, 2003), pp. 243-57

'Introduction' to D. H. Lawrence, *The Fight for Barbara* (Oberon Modern Plays, 2003), pp. 5-7

'Lawrence, David Herbert (1885-1930)', *Oxford Dictionary of National Biography* (Oxford University Press, 2004)

'You Two Helped me Over Some Frontiers', *Windows to the Sun: D. H. Lawrence's "Thought-adventures"*, ed. E. G. Ingersoll and V. Hyde (Fairleigh Dickinson University Press, 2009)

C. Books and Pamphlets

D. H. Lawrence and the Idea of the Novel (Macmillan, 1979), pp. i-xiii, 1-198

D. H. Lawrence: A Life in Literature (Macmillan 1989), pp. i-xxvi, 1-196

D. H. Lawrence: The Early Years 1885-1912 (Cambridge University Press, 1991), pp. i-xxx, 1-626

D. H. Lawrence (Edward Arnold, 1991), pp. 1-136

D. H. Lawrence: The Early Years 1885-1912, revised paperback edn. (Cambridge University Press, 1992), pp. i-xxx, 1-626

Cold Hearts and Coronets: Lawrence, the Weekleys and the von Richthofens (D. H. Lawrence Centre, University of Nottingham, Occasional Paper No. 2, 1995), pp. 1-27

D. H. Lawrence and Comedy, ed. Paul Eggert and John Worthen (Cambridge University Press, 1996), pp. i-xiv, 1-216

The Gang: Coleridge, the Hutchinsons and the Wordsworths in 1802 (Yale University Press, 2001), pp. i-viii, 1-344

D. H. Lawrence: The Life of an Outsider (Allen Lane, Penguin Books, 2005), pp. i-xxvi, 1-518 [(Counterpoint Books, 2005 in USA)]

D. H. Lawrence's Sons and Lovers*: A Casebook*, ed. John Worthen and Andrew Harrison (Oxford University Press, 2005), pp. i-xii, 1-305

Robert Schumann: Life and Death of a Musician (Yale University Press, 2007), pp. i-xv, 1-496

T. S. Eliot: A Short Biography (Haus Books, 2009), pp. i-vi, 1-330

The Cambridge Introduction to S. T. Coleridge (Cambridge University Press, 2010), pp. i-xiv, 1-160.

D. Editions

D. H. Lawrence, *The Lost Girl*, ed. John Worthen (Cambridge University Press, 1981), pp. i-lvii, 1-426

D. H. Lawrence, *The Rainbow*, ed. John Worthen (Penguin Books, 1981), pp. 1-33, 41-574

D. H. Lawrence, *The Prussian Officer and Other Stories*, ed. John Worthen (Cambridge University Press, 1983), pp. i-li, 1-303

D. H. Lawrence, *Love Among the Haystacks and Other Stories*, ed. John Worthen (Cambridge University Press, 1987), pp. i-xlix, 1-289

D. H. Lawrence, *Women in Love*, ed. David Farmer, Lindeth Vasey and John Worthen (Cambridge University Press, 1987), pp. i-lxi, 1-633

D. H. Lawrence, *Lady Chatterley's Lover*, ed. Michael Squires: responsibility for the Explanatory Notes (pp. 339-72), the Dialect Glossary (pp. 373-4) and the Appendix (pp. 453-61) (Cambridge University Press, 1993)

D. H. Lawrence, *The First 'Women in Love'*, ed. John Worthen and Lindeth Vasey (Cambridge: Cambridge University Press, 1998), pp. i-lv, 1-532

D. H. Lawrence, *The Plays*, ed. Hans-Wilhelm Schwarze and John Worthen (Cambridge, 1999), pp. i-cxxvi, 1-824

D. H. Lawrence, *Studies in Classic American Literature*, ed. Ezra Greenspan, Lindeth Vasey and John Worthen (Cambridge, 2003), pp. i-lxxix, 1-632

D. H. Lawrence, *Introductions and Reviews*, ed. N. H. Reeve and John Worthen (Cambridge, 2005), pp. i-cviii, 1-616

E. Books forthcoming

The Life of William Wordsworth: A Critical Biography (Blackwell, 2013)

F. Exhibition curated

Lawrence in Notts: Creations and Re-creations (Weston Gallery, University of Nottingham, April – August 2005)

G. Selected studio theatre productions

1976 Samuel Beckett, *That Time* (University College Swansea Drama Studio)

1979 Edward Bond, *Bingo* (University College Swansea Drama Studio)

1980 Edward Bond, *The Sea* (University College Swansea Drama Studio and Patti Pavilion)

1981 William Shakespeare, *Hamlet* (first quarto) (University College Swansea Drama Studio and Swansea Festival Fringe)

1982 Edward Bond, *Early Morning* (University College Swansea Drama Studio)

1983 Edward Bond, *Summer* (University College Swansea Drama Studio)

1984 Samuel Beckett, *Rockaby* ((University College Swansea Union House)

1985 Howard Brenton, *Bloody Poetry* (University College Swansea Drama Studio)

1989 Samuel Beckett, *Krapp's Last Tape* (University College Swansea Taliesin Theatre)

In 1983 I prepared an acting edition of *Othello* used by the University College Swansea (Drama Section) tour of Italy in the spring of 1983: performances were given in Ferrara, Modena and Bologna. In 1986, with the approval of Edward Bond, I prepared a musical score for the British premiere of Bond's opera *The Cat*, to replace that originally written by Hans Werner Henze. The opera was first performed in the University College Swansea Taliesin Theatre in June 1986 by students of the Drama Section; the music was revised and the opera performed again in June 1989 at Portsmouth Sixth Form College.

Index

No index entries are supplied for 'D. H. Lawrence: A Single Life', pp. 100-16.

www.ingramcontent.com/pod-product-compliance
Lightning Source LLC
Chambersburg PA
CBHW021244060726
47590CB00005B/1889

* 9 7 8 1 9 0 5 5 1 0 3 3 7 *